Praise for *Who Do I Think I Am?*

"Anjelah is one of the greatest voices of our time. This book is what we all need."

—Amy Schumer

"How many years have we been quoting Anjelah's comedy in our household? Too many to count! I'm a HUGE fan professionally and personally. What's not to love about a woman who has a laugh-out-loud sense of humor and loves Jesus? SIGN ME UP!!"

—Candace Cameron Bure

"Anjelah represents our community and our stories that are important, hilarious, and relatable to everyone. She's awesome!"

—Fluffy (Gabriel Iglesias)

"Anjelah Johnson-Reyes's first book isn't just good, it's a blazing tour-de-force: so smart, dazzlingly funny, disarmingly wise, and deeply tender—you won't know what hit you. The same intuition she has when she performs in a room crackles in every word here, yet she brings a whole different level of electricity, artistry, and intimacy in print. Because *Who Do I Think I Am?*, like Anjelah herself, exists at multiple intersections, it defies easy categorization. Memoir? Spirituality? Comedy? Pure magic is what it is. Read this fierce, hilarious marvel of a book."

—Jonathan Martin, Author of *How to Survive a Shipwreck* and *The Road Away from God*

"The world is a better place because Anjelah works at her craft, brings a smile to our collective faces, and is continually (and consistently) herself. We all know she's hilarious and daring...but she shows us in *Who Do I Think I Am?* that she is also brave with vulnerability and humble with sincerity. She is not trying to prove anything, not trying to impress anyone, not trying to force a bestseller...and that makes reading this book an absolute delight. Bravo, my friend."

—Carlos Rodríguez, Founder and Director of The Happy Givers

"A book as funny, smart, and delightful as its author. I've had the good fortune of calling Anjelah my friend and watching her blossom through the years. This book will give you insight into what makes this woman so special. Enjoy!"

—Valerie Bertinelli

"The very first comedy show I ever saw in LA was at The Improv, and it was headlined by none other than Anjelah Johnson. Her brilliant set made me laugh so hard I had tears running down my face. I found her energy and her comedy so relatable, I became an instant fan. Years later, I am so grateful to call her a friend. Her book is hilarious and enlightening and inspiring…just like Anjelah. And for those of us who have spent our lives feeling like we're caught between two worlds or two cultures, I am so happy someone like us is sharing their story so we can all feel a little less alone."

—Melissa Fumero

"Anjelah's story will make you laugh, cry, and feel inspired. I was moved by the way she evolved in her faith without losing her moral foundation. Her courage and charisma jump out at you in this book. It's a definite must-read!!!"

—Brie Bella, WWE Superstar

"Anjelah had a huge impact on my career. She was the first headlining comic that took me on the road to open for her. I'm forever grateful for her. I loved reading her book and getting to read how she got where she is at now. Congrats, Anjelah!"

—Nate Bargatze, Stand-up Comedian

"Anjelah has been one of my biggest inspirations. Her story is familiar to mine. Growing up with big dreams in a place where you couldn't achieve them. Without a lick of dance training because she just had that certain something. She made it to Hollywood, travels all over the world doing stand-up, and makes the world laugh. The book is amazing and so is she!"

—KevOnStage

Three things to know about my girl, Anjelah: she loves Jesus, she has a hilariously saucy mouth, and she has a wildly adventurous mind and heart. What a joy to watch her soar to I've-met-Oprah-famous while still remaining authentically, audaciously Anjelah. That is who she is."

—Jen Hatmaker, Speaker, Podcast Host, and *New York Times* Bestselling Author of *Fierce, Free, and Full of Fire*

"Anjelah was making a name for herself before many of us had even started in comedy. Her perseverance and indomitable spirit are what make her not only a woman girls look up to but one of the purest and most genuine people I've met. I've learned a lot from her and I just love her so much."

—Iliza Shlesinger

"Inspiring, authentic, enlightening, and absolutely hilarious. *Who Do I Think I Am?* by my friend Anjelah Johnson-Reyes details her curious and humor-filled journey in a brilliantly impactful way. Prepare to have your own path emboldened, your limits challenged, and your growth stimulated, all while laughing out loud, literally, at every turn of the page."

—Touré Roberts, Author, Entrepreneur, Pastor of One LA

"Anjelah has chutzpah! This book is inspiring and relatable. For anyone who wants to know the secret of becoming successful while being true to who they are, *Who Do I Think I Am?* is the book for them. Anjelah is a force and this book will make you love her even more."

—Christina P., Comedian and Podcaster

"What an awesome read! I have toured with Anjelah for many years so I already knew many of these stories and the characters in them. *Who Do I Think I Am?* gave me insight into these situations and people that I never had. Some of these stories I EXPERIENCED and we still laugh about to this day (Las Vegas corporate show)! I really enjoyed getting the backstory of my friend's journey to success. If you love Anjelah like I do, you're going to love this book!"

—Mal Hall, Stand-up Comedian

"If you don't know Anjelah, you should! Her story is so relatable and real and beyond funny. Her timing, her material, her LIFE is all on the table and, man, it's hilarious. Full of contradictions, she can make any life story funny! Her comedy makes you think differently about our lives and her energy is infectious!"

—Eva Longoria

"Funny, moving, and inspiring."

—Loni Love, Comedian and Author

"My friend and fellow comic, Anjelah Johnson-Reyes, has been killing it on the stand-up stage for years, but there is so much more to her than just being funny. She's kind, generous, thoughtful, devout, and accepting. She's endured hardships and success throughout her life but has handled both with humility and grace, and, of course, humor. In her book, Anjelah shares her journey in such a way that is interesting and funny, but it makes you root for her even more. I really enjoyed getting to know her better through her vulnerability in the book, and like always, she had me cracking up so much that people around me thought I was choking. I even had to thwart an attempted Heimlich maneuver from a concerned citizen sitting next to me on a plane as I read it. I know it's not easy trying to succinctly tell your whole life story, but she knocked it out of the park."

—Fortune Feimster, Comedian

"Anjelah is a singular voice in comedy and storytelling. I feel seen and represented by her work and am so grateful for her talents."

—America Ferrera

Who Do I Think I Am?

STORIES OF CHOLA WISHES & CAVIAR DREAMS

ANJELAH JOHNSON-REYES

WORTHY

PUBLISHING

New York • Nashville

Author's Note: The book you have picked up is a really good one with lots of juicy stories. So juicy that I had to change some names and slight details. Also, keep in mind that all the juiciness of the stories is what I recount from my memory to the best of my ability. If you were there and you remember it a different way then you can write about it in your book.

Worthy Publishing
Hachette Book Group
1290 Avenue of the Americas, New York, NY 10104
worthypublishing.com
twitter.com/worthy

First Edition: March 2022

Worthy Publishing is a division of Hachette Book Group, Inc. The Worthy Publishing name and logo are trademarks of Hachette Book Group, Inc.

The publisher is not responsible for websites (or their content) that are not owned by the publisher.

The Hachette Speakers Bureau provides a wide range of authors for speaking events. To find out more, go to www.hachettespeakersbureau.com or call (866) 376-6591.

Library of Congress Cataloging-in-Publication Data

Names: Johnson, Anjelah, author.
Title: Who do I think I am? : stories of chola wishes and caviar dreams / Anjelah Johnson-Reyes.
Description: Nashville : Worthy, 2022.
Identifiers: LCCN 2021041421 | ISBN 9781546000433 (hardcover) | ISBN 9781546000457 (ebook)
Subjects: LCSH: Johnson, Anjelah. | Comedians--United States--Biography. | Actors--United States--Biography. | LCGFT: Autobiographies.
Classification: LCC PN2287.J576 A3 2021 | DDC 792.702/8092 [B]--dc23
LC record available at https://lccn.loc.gov/2021041421

ISBNs: 9781546000433 (hardcover), 9781546000457 (ebook)

Printed in the United States of America

LSC-C

Printing 1, 2021

To my younger self who had the audacity to go for a dream
that started as a fantasy and turned into reality.
Thank you for your bravery. I wouldn't be here without you.

CONTENTS

Who Do I Think I Am?

CHAPTER 1

Chola Wishes & Caviar Dreams

In third grade I got an assignment to write one of those "What Do You Want to Be When You Grow Up?" kind of reports. I decided to do mine on becoming a lawyer, which looking back, was very off-brand for me. I hadn't even seen an episode (or every episode multiple times) of *Law & Order: SVU*. But at the time, I guess I thought it was fancy and paid the bills.

To write about being a lawyer, I felt like I had to play the part. I lived next door to my elementary school and dug through the dumpster outside looking for trashy lawyer treasures thrown away alongside half-eaten bologna sandwiches. I scored some books, binders, broken calculators, and a big telephone with a ton of buttons. I was the Harriet the Spy of law. In my bedroom, I pushed my dresser up to the window, because big shots always had a view of the city, even though in my case, it was a view of the San Jose International Airport. I put the phone and my "law books" on the desk, sat down, and threw myself into my work. I furiously wrote memos with a red pen, because only adults had red pens. I rifled through important documents and answered a barrage of urgent phone calls, one after the other.

"I know, I know, I'm working on it!" I shouted into the receiver before slamming it down and whispering to no one, "Dammit, Cheryl."

I sighed dramatically and ran my hands through my hair, a universal sign of being extremely stressed out…at least that's what they did in the movies. My firm was so busy and successful, but I managed to make the time to turn the window into a drive-thru for legal advice and cheeseburgers—the two professions that meant the most to me, apparently. Between calls, I turned to the pane and said, "Hi, how can I help you today? And do you want fries with that lawsuit?"

Thanks to my in-depth research, I got an A on my paper. But in doing the assignment I discovered—hold all my calls, please—I actually did not want to be a lawyer. I wanted to pretend to be a lawyer. *I shall be an actress.*

From that moment on, my dream of being an actress started to grow. At first, I didn't say it out loud because I was ashamed. I lived in San Jose. What actresses had I ever heard of from San Jose? Screech from *Saved by the Bell* was born in my hometown, but that didn't matter, because I didn't even know about him until I just googled it. I didn't see actors around town either. It's not like I'd ever run into Meryl Streep at Casa Vicky Mexican restaurant. But I was gonna be a dramatic actress like Meryl. I practiced making myself cry without the use of Visine, chopped onions, or whatever the '90s equivalent of Sarah McLachlan's ASPCA commercials was.

I grew up in the heart of Silicon Valley during the tech boom. While I had no interest in becoming the next Steve Jobs, my dream to be an actress felt just as far-fetched—a fantasy, really. I might as well have said, "I want to be a princess!" The audacity. Who the heck did I think I was—this little Mexican American girl, who'd never acted in her life—to think that I, of all people, could make it in Hollywood? There was zero evidence I could. Back when I was a kid, there weren't many proud, educated, normal, hardworking Latino families on TV or in the movies to help point me in the right direction. There were no Latino Cosbys. No Cosbys-ez.

My favorite actress growing up was Sandra Bullock. She had darker features and long brown hair, like me. She didn't really look like a white girl, so in my mind, that was close enough for me to adopt her as my representation. After *Speed* came out on VHS, I watched it every day for months. I idolized her, or as the kids say today, I stanned her so hard. That's still a thing they say, right? Anyway, Sandy, if I may call her that, was beautiful and funny and charming. She could shoot somebody *and* make them laugh. When *Miss Congeniality* came out, that was it. I was like, "Oh my God, that's me. I want to do this. I can do this. I'm so good at being congenial."

On one hand, it seemed impossible and silly. On the other, I had this nagging feeling that wouldn't go away. I'd get mad at the movies because I wasn't in them. I was obsessed with anyone who looked like me who made it in Hollywood. Especially the cholas from any movie or TV show about gangs. To some people the movie *Training Day* was a film that showed corruption and violence, to me it was my dream come true! I remember watching *Blood In Blood Out*, and like most cholas/aspiring cholas, I swooned over Benjamin Bratt's dreamy Paco (that was his character's name; get your mind out of the gutter), but I was more focused on all the chola extras in the background. I was all, "Vatos locos forever" but I was also like, "Pfft, I could stand by that car!" I knew if somebody taught me how to get in a movie, I could do that. I just didn't know how to do it or where the car was parked to even stand near it. So I tucked the dream away in my heart.

I didn't try out for school plays, and I didn't realize I could sing until I got older. My sister, Veronica, sang the national anthem at local events, but I was way too shy for that stuff when I was younger. I was introverted and I was a homebody—so much so that I got special permission to run home from school during the lunch break. It was my ideal scenario—my grandma made me soup and we watched her Mexican game shows. They talked so fast in Spanish, and a bunch of beautiful girls would dance all over the place.

My mom signed me up for all kinds of activities, like tap and acrobatics, but I didn't last long. She put me in tae kwon do, and I never got past the white belt that came with the uniform. Follow-through was not my strongest trait.

The only activity that ever stuck was cheerleading, and even that had a shaky start. When I was eight, I joined the Santa Clara Lions, a local Pop Warner organization. My sister, Veronica, who is three years older than me, practiced across the field with her team while I would practice with my team, comprised of younger kids. The cheer we had to learn was super simple, like step clap to the left, step clap to the right, keep your arms stiff in a box, and then step clap some more. Yeah. Well. I couldn't step clap. The stiffness I nailed, though. I was totally off beat and had the coordination of a baby giraffe approximately one second after birth. I felt so dumb. I looked across the field and saw my sister watching me with such disgust. I vividly remember disappointing her because I couldn't get it right. (Don't worry, later on, she ends up being my biggest cheerleader in life!)

Somehow I made the squad (everyone did; that's part of the sign-up fee) and became a Thundercat. In my first year of cheerleading I was so shy and embarrassed, I stared at the ground the whole time and never smiled. By my second year, I broke out of my shell big time and became like the Gabi Butler of the Santa Clara Lions organization, without the blue eyes and zit cream endorsements, although I could have used some of the cream. I worked hard and became the flyer, the girl at the top of the pyramid. I went from hiding in the background to step clapping my way front and center.

I loved the competitiveness of cheerleading. I loved the ritual and pride of putting on our red, black, and white uniforms. Though, back in the day, somebody—probably the same guy who would later invent the thong—decided cheerleading tops should be itchy sweaters. I don't recommend doing athletic activities while wearing wool in the summer in California. Sweating profusely was worth it because my squads were hella good, and I got to be a part of making us hella good. We usually won first place at competitions (sometimes second place to stupid Oak Grove), and as I graduated from Thundercat to Panther to Wildcat (trust me, that's impressive), we made it all the way to nationals at Disney World in Florida (also impressive).

I was a cheerleader. That was my identity. I would follow behind my mom's grocery cart at Safeway practicing my cheers. I lived and breathed and grocery shopped cheerleading. And as every cheerleader knows, once a cheerleader, always a cheerleader—figuratively, anyway. These days, I'd need a chiropractor visit and a long nap if I were to try any pyramid situation.

I learned from a pretty early age that I did not like doing things I wasn't good at. Which is why this nagging desire to be an actress wouldn't go away. I really felt like if I tried it, I'd be good at it. Cheerleading officially made me a performer, but I still didn't dare tell anyone about my secret dream. When I was a teenager, I sat on the carpet in my bedroom in front of a long mirror and imagined I was acting and giving acceptance speeches for my critically acclaimed lead roles. I'd wave to Meryl in the audience, and she'd blow me a kiss with both hands, even though I won the award and she didn't, which is just so Meryl.

But I learned early on I had this tool inside of me…a sense of humor. And it didn't take me long to learn how to use it—in a good way, not an evil comic book villain way. I went through my old yearbook recently and all of the messages people wrote were about how "nice" and "funny" I was, which made me want to cry because it confirmed that being kind and funny has always been my thing—except for that one time in sixth grade I was mean to a girl named Natasha for no reason, and I still regret that. I was always quick-witted. It was like a game to me. I'd say a zinger and then someone would laugh. And that was a win for me. And then I'd go, *Oh, I got another one!* Some girls knew their good angle in a photo. I knew the jokes people responded best to. Charm was my gift, and it gave me confidence. I knew I wasn't the hottest girl in school (I was medium), but I also knew the hottest girl in school couldn't make everyone laugh. So, go me.

I learned what worked for me, then used it to my benefit. One of my first jobs was at a theme park, saying funny things on a microphone to guess people's weight, age, or birthday. I flirted with guys on the microphone as they walked by: "Excuse me, sir. Hop on this scale so I can guess your digits! If I'm wrong, I'll give you mine. Ayeooo!"

When I was fifteen, I finally felt confident enough to take a jab at being an award-winning actress. I heard a commercial on the radio for an open casting call, one of those ads like, "If you want to be in movies or be a model, come to the Holiday Inn Express on July 8!"

I didn't think it was creepy at all, which clearly shows my level of commitment. I found myself standing in a hotel ballroom in front of a handsome, yet slightly oily man who looked me up and down before marking YES on my registration card and sending me to the next audition round. You probably had to have three eyes and medical-grade BO to get a NO on your card, but in my mind, I had just gotten a three-picture deal at Paramount. I was so excited and naïve, I didn't realize they said yes to everyone in order to get more money.

One thousand dollars later, the next step was a trip down to a convention center in Palm Springs to parade myself in front of thirty "talent agencies." My mom and I drove down to the desert in our station wagon and got to stay in a hotel, which was so fancy. I was told to bring two photos of myself to show the agents, but all I had were some pictures a friend took of me for photography class that weren't even exposed correctly. The first day, we had to take a bunch of classes. In one, we were taught to walk like a model who was approximately eight feet tall and strutted down the runway with a sensual death stare. In a previous class we'd been told to "smile big and show big energy at all times," so I was very confused.

"Are we supposed to be serious or smile?" I whispered to my mom. "'Cuz they said to smile, but she's doing, like, sexy face."

They'd set up a microphone in the middle of the audience so we could ask questions.

"I don't know," my mom whispered back. "Why don't you ask?"

I got up, walked up to the microphone, and addressed the model.

"Like, you said that we're supposed to be smiling for the agents. But then when you did the example, you have, like, a real serious face. Like, which one do we do?"

With the nastiest look on her face she hissed, "I didn't say that," clearly forgetting that she, in fact, did say that. *Okay, girl.*

Shut down in front of the entire class, I slunk back to my seat, devastated I might have destroyed my dream of being an actress with one dumb question. Luckily, I had one more shot to make it. The organizers set up a big runway, with "talent agents" sitting all alongside it, though they could have been businessmen looking for the bar, who knows. I got to walk down it, like Gisele before she was Gisele, and show my headshots to all the agents as I walked by. Picture a flight attendant walking down the aisle holding out a tray of Biscoff and Stroopwafels, but all the passengers stare straight ahead or are sleeping. I basically was the flight attendant, and nobody wanted my cookies.

———————

I didn't get any inquiries or get signed by anybody. It was crushing, humiliating. Getting knocked down like that, I did have the thought,

Who do I think I am? At the same time, I still had that burning desire in me to be an actress. The flame had dimmed, but it wasn't extinguished. So I tried again a couple years later when I was seventeen, this time applying to a child acting school in San Francisco. I made a resume, even though I didn't even know how to make a resume. I used a bunch of crazy fonts, like Caviar Dreams and DejaVu Sans, and made it purple so it looked pretty.

I was accepted, but on the first day, I was informed that classes cost $1,700, which was $1,700 more than I had, so I quit. Not long after, I got a phone call from the school administrator.

"Are you still interested in joining our program?" the man asked me sweetly.

"No, I'm sorry, it's way too expensive for me," I answered sadly.

There was a pause.

"Honey," he suddenly sneered sassily, "you need us way more than we need you."

Click. And that was the end of that.

First of all, what did I even say to make him snap? Maybe he had been told no one too many times that day—like the people trying to get you to sign a petition to save the whales while you're walking into the grocery store. I was rejected again, but I refused to give up. I snail mailed my pretty purple resume to every talent agency on the planet and waited. And waited. In the meantime, I was barely passing high school because I just didn't care. The future I had in mind didn't require social studies or math or knowing how to fold notes in cute little shapes. The only reason I bothered to show up at all was cheerleading.

I did have one teacher in particular, Mrs. Zamora, who mentored me. She taught AP art, and even though I couldn't even draw a stick figure, she let me be her teacher's assistant because anyone could clean paintbrushes. I would make her laugh while I swept paper clippings. She sent me to other classrooms on secret performance missions. "Go over to Mr. Roark's class and sing something funny," she'd say. So I'd burst in and belt out the song "I Will Survive." In my yearbook, she wrote that she would see me on *Saturday Night Live* one day. Mrs. Zamora didn't just think of me as a class clown who was a nuisance. She truly believed I was a performer with real talent that would take me places.

But still, I didn't tell her or anyone about my dream of making it in showbiz. There was only one person I felt comfortable confessing my biggest secret to. Sandra was a friend of my cousin Michelle who I met before she moved to Hollywood. She moved totally on her own and was making it happen. She'd landed an NSYNC music video and a commercial for Ross. When I reluctantly admitted to her that I'd love to do what she was doing, she didn't laugh or brush me off. She said seriously, "If you ever move down to LA, I will help you. I will show you how to get started."

I was barely making it to school, so LA seemed more like a pipe dream than a possibility. By some miracle I graduated and got into junior college. For the next three years, though, I was aimless and didn't know what I was doing with my life. I enrolled in a drama class at JC, and it was one of the only things I looked forward to. Another student in the class had also ventured off to Hollywood, and like a vet back from 'Nam, regaled us amateurs with cautionary tales and sage advice.

"Don't be an extra," she warned.

But what about the cholas I saw in *Training Day*...

"Nobody respects the extras," she insisted. "You're the bottom of the totem pole. *Whatever you do, don't be an extra.*"

With no plans and no prospects, I did what every other twenty-year-old did in San Jose. I hung out with my girls and went clubbing. I was underage, but we were pros. We rolled up to the club in a group ten deep. My sister, who was legal, went past the bouncer first, then passed her ID back until it got to me at the end. By the time the bouncer saw ten hot Latina girls with long brown hair, he didn't know which way was up. Worked every time.

One of those nights, I ran into an old friend named Monique on the dance floor. Literally. I definitely heel toed right onto her toe. As we danced to "Get Ur Freak On," she leaned in and screamed in my ear over the music.

"Hey, guess what!"

"Yeah?!"

"I'm a cheerleader for the Oakland Raiders!"

"No way!"

She showed me her necklace, a silver pendant with the official Oakland Raiders logo on it. Only real Raiderettes got this special necklace, she told me proudly.

"That's amazing!" Monique was basically a celebrity.

"We have tryouts next week!"

"You're going on trial next week?!"

"*No*, we have *tryouts* next week! You should come try out!"

"Oh, that's not really my thing, but thank you! I'm good!"

I wasn't a shake your pom-poms and show cleavage kind of cheerleader. I was the kind who did very difficult stunts and wore sweaters. But when I got home, I couldn't stop thinking about Monique's offer to try out. It wasn't my style, and I wasn't a trained dancer, but what the heck else did I have going on in my life? I went to a school I didn't care about and out to clubs even though I didn't even drink. I didn't really want to be a Raiderette, but I did want to be an actress. I thought about Sandra's offer to help me if I ever made it to LA. *Maybe I could make it down there if I was a Raiderette first?* When that thought crossed my mind, for the first time, my dream didn't seem unattainable.

I was still unsure, so I prayed about it. I asked God, "What do I do with my life? I have no direction, but I have this opportunity to audition for the Oakland Raiderettes." Suddenly, I felt something unexplainable in my gut and my spirit and I came to a decision—I was going to try out for the Oakland Raiderettes. I was going to use this as my sign from God because it felt like a step in the entertainment direction. If I made the squad, I'd do it for one year, then I'd move to LA and pursue my dream of being an actress. If I didn't make the squad, LA was a no-go, and I'd take that as my sign to let the dream go and pursue something else I could be good at, like massage therapy or dog walking. I liked dogs. And walking was okay. I promised myself if I didn't make the squad, I would scratch the entertainment industry off the list forever.

Moving to LA would be the biggest leap of faith I ever took in my life. I'd never lived anywhere outside of my mom's house. I'd never paid rent or bought my own groceries. But I was going to use the Raiderettes tryout as a sign and go with whatever happened, good or bad.

The day of the tryout I drove to Oakland by myself. I brought several outfit changes, like I was the Latina member of Destiny's Child at the VMAs or something. Monique told me to wear tight clothing that showed off my body, so I wore sparkly shorts and a form-fitting crop top with rhinestones from Forever 21. When I walked into the Hilton conference center, I had flashbacks to the Palm Springs fiasco, where I felt so small and weak. This time, I felt like I had nothing to lose, and that gave me strength and power. There were seven hundred women milling around, vying for fifty Raiderettes' spots. My initial reaction was like *Oh, no*, but then I took one look at some of the outfits, and it changed to *Oh, honey, no...*" I eliminated at least two hundred girls right off the bat. I'm no Tan France, but a leather Catwoman costume should only be worn on Halloween or if you're trying out for *Cats*.

Just like in Palm Springs, the first part of the tryout was a cattle call. The judges literally looked us up and down, asked a couple of questions, and said yes or no on the spot. It was about personality and looks and nothing more. Along with three hundred other hopefuls, I got a yes and a callback.

On day 2, we had to learn a dance routine in a giant banquet hall. They had a choreographer up on a stage with a Britney Spears mic strapped to her head so she could count out the steps as she demonstrated complicated technical moves I'd never done before in my life. I had rhythm by now, but this was way above my pay grade. So I just sold it with attitude. Fake it till you make it, right? My face was twisting into all the poses my body couldn't hang with. I may not have spotted during my turns, but my hair flips were on point.

Suddenly, the choreographer paused the music, weaved her way through the crowd, and came right up to me. "Clearly you have no dance training," she said, "but you have something that cannot be taught." This was the most powerful backhanded compliment I ever received in my life.

After the audition, we all sat on the floor of the banquet hall anxiously awaiting our fate. When they called 193—my number—my first thought wasn't *Oh my God, I'm going to be cheerleader for the Oakland Raiders!* In that moment, I knew I was going to be an actress.

But first, I had to get through a season of football. At our old Pop Warner games, if I wasn't cheering, I was only interested in the snacks and hanging out with my friends. I'd never even been to a professional football game in my life, let alone been in one. Now, as an Oakland Raiderette, I had to look and play the part 100 percent, 24/7. We were more than dancers; we were representatives of the team on the field and off the field—we had to dress to impress even just walking from the locker room to our cars. For me, dressing to impress usually meant a cute lil' hat and not a sports bra. We were given a guidebook on how to act, walk, and dress, and we had mandatory weigh-ins to make sure we didn't spend more time with garlic fries than we did at the gym. We were given punishments for being tardy and took etiquette classes to learn which fork did what (start from the outside in) and how to put our napkins in our laps. Most important, anytime we took a sip of water, we had to wipe our lipstick off the glass—a problem I didn't realize was a problem.

At the time, every team in the NFL had a strict rule forbidding the fraternization of players and cheerleaders—except the Oakland Raiders. On our team, the official policy was a vague "it's frowned upon." But I was in my season of being a good Christian girl, and I didn't drink or carouse with football players. Non-football players... well, that was a different story. Stay tuned. So, while some of my fellow Raiderettes not-so-secretly partied with the players, in every sense of the word, I got a rep for being a bit of a Goody Two-shoes. I rarely got hit on by anyone and was relegated to the role of "funny little sister." I'd make everyone laugh doing funny accents and impressions of all the people I grew up with in San Jose or saw in movies. They particularly loved the impersonation I did of my manicurist. "Do the nail salon lady!" they'd beg. It was like I was back in Mrs. Zamora's class being asked to say and do funny things.

It's hard to explain how drastically my life changed in the year I was an Oakland Raiderette. I went from rarely leaving a few-mile radius around my house to jetting to Hawaii for a calendar photo shoot. I high-kicked my way onto a Jumbotron, made root beer floats at charity events, and signed pictures of myself at mall appearances. Even though I only got paid $80 per game (I know, I know), they did allow us to buy our calendars at cost, sell them at a higher price, and keep the profits.

I was interviewed for magazine stories even though I had no clue how to be a public figure. *Raider Nation* did a profile of me called "Anjelah Johnson: Accent on Personality and Sincerity." Apparently my impersonations were already newsworthy.

I picked the best year to be an Oakland Raiderette. Unbelievably, we went to the Super Bowl (unfortunately only down in San Diego, where I had been many times, and we got spanked by the Tampa Bay

Buccaneers), and I won "Rookie of the Year" on the Raiderettes. After the season ended, I deposited my $580 paycheck plus another $2,000 I made from calendar sales in my bank account, and the very next weekend, I headed to LA with $2,580 to my name.

I had my ducks in order. My mom gave me her emerald-green Toyota Camry station wagon and my cousin Joe Grande, a popular radio personality in LA, said I could live with him in Monrovia if I paid something called rent. I'll never forget driving down there and arriving in LA at dusk, seeing downtown's sparkling lights from the 210 freeway and getting butterflies—then driving right past it and thirty miles later being like, *Is Monrovia lost? Where the heck is this place?!*

So, I was a little farther away from Hollywood than I thought I'd be, but it didn't matter. I made it. The first thing I did when I got to LA was call up my friend Sandra. Like a boss, she kept her word. She helped me create a real resume, which was not purple. She helped me get professional headshots. She gave me cute hand-me-down clothes and shoes appropriate for auditions because I was poor and didn't have any money, and rent was steep in Hollywood-adjacent.

Best of all, she showed me how to sign up to be an extra.

A month after I arrived in Hollywood, I was ready for my first open call at Central Casting. "Now, when you get there," Sandra instructed, "you're going to see a line of people out the door waiting to sign up to be an extra. I don't want you to wait in that line. I want you to go up to the front window and ask for Sam. Before you go, I want you to stop at Ralphs and buy a tray of cookies. Bring that and a signed Raiderette headshot and give it to Sam and tell him you're new to LA and want to be an extra…"

"This sounds…real sleazy," I said as I envisioned the type of casting couches I for sure wanted to avoid.

"Just make sure they're chocolate chip, not Funfetti," Sandra said in all seriousness.

I assumed that Funfetti was some sort of Hollywood code cookie indicating that I'd be up for doing anything to land the part.

"I don't know why that's important, but you were in a Ross commercial, so I trust you," I said.

The first time I went to be an extra, I stopped at Ralphs and got some cookies. Then I headed to Central Casting armed with my bribe/delicious tray of baked goods and signed Raiderette photo. Sure enough, there was a line out the door. I walked past everyone, hiding my sleazy cookies behind my back, and went right up to the window. I knocked and said, "I'm here for Sam."

"Okay, he'll be right out."

I sat in a waiting room, and a few minutes later Sam came walking out of the back office wearing...an Oakland Raiders hat. "Hey, what's up?" he said.

"Hi, these cookies are for you. They aren't Funfetti, so don't get any ideas. And this is my headshot," I said (with a smirk, knowing he was about to flip out when he saw it was a Raiderette headshot). "I'd love to be an extra."

"No way!" he said beaming at the photo. "Give me your phone number and we'll get you signed up."

Sandra was the queen.

Two days later, Sam called me and asked if I wanted to be an extra.

"Um, yeah. Yeah, I do," I said trying to sound nonchalant while silently freaking out. Sam gave me all the info I needed and told me to report to Stage 24 at Warner Bros. Studio the next day.

It was the first day of the rest of my life in Hollywood. As I walked across the lot, I spotted the historic water tower featured in the Looney Tunes franchise and walked past the soundstages for *ER*, *Two and a Half Men*, *Everybody Loves Raymond*, *Gilmore Girls*, and *The West Wing*. It was magical, and I was overcome with emotion.

Here I was, this young Mexican girl, this little chola, who had the audacity to turn a fantasy, a dream, into something real. Tour trams whizzed by me, and I wondered if the people on them thought I was someone famous or important. It made me hold my head up even higher.

When I arrived at Stage 24, I saw the plaque on the wall and welled up. I was going to be an extra on season 9 of *Friends*, one of the most iconic shows in history.

I didn't want to look like a hot mess for my television debut, so I pulled myself together. I walked onto the set and saw Joey and Chandler's apartment and the Central Perk coffee shop, and my heart was so happy. The buzz of the bell ringing and people scurrying about doing very important things, the instantly familiar smell of the soundstage—wood and paint—it all hit me to my core. I never wanted to forget this feeling. I never wanted to be anywhere else. I could not believe this was my life. And to think I was almost a lawyer.

CHAPTER 2

I'm Mexican/Hella American

Let's go back to where it all started.

Since the day I was born, I've had kind of a split personality. Not in a serial killer way, think more Hannah Montana or Beyoncé/Sasha Fierce. I, too, had two alter egos at my disposal, who I could bring out at any time: Angela Nicole Johnson, all-American girl, and Anjelah Johnsonez, chola wannabe.

I've always felt caught between two worlds, being Mexican and American—although I've always been comfortable in both. I was born and raised in San Jose, California, by my parents, who were also born and raised in California. My mom, Susan, was a hairstylist, and my dad, Mitch, worked for a linen delivery service. I have a white last name (or black, depending on how you say it), and I don't speak Spanish—with the exception of appetizers, main dishes, and a handful of Selena lyrics. I'm Hispan-ish, if you will.

My mom, the daughter of Mexican Americans and the youngest of eight kids, never spoke a lick of Spanish. My grandma didn't want her children to get made fun of at school and wanted them to assimilate. So, after baby number four, she stopped teaching the kids, including little Susan, Spanish.

My dad, also the child of Mexican Americans, never spoke Spanish either. The story goes that my grandpa's cousin was reprimanded in school for speaking Spanish and locked in a closet. The teacher forgot about him and everybody went home for the day. His poor mother, wondering where her kid was, called the principal, the principal called the teacher, and the teacher realized she forgot him in the closet. Later that evening, they all went back to the school and he was still sitting in the closet by himself. I can only imagine how scared and traumatized this poor child was. So, from then on, my grandpa stopped speaking Spanish, his first language, and didn't teach his children.

What happened to my grandpa's cousin was straight-up racism. Racism es la puta. I guess I know a little more Spanish than I thought.

My parents named me Angela Nicole, which isn't exactly a spicy Latina name. Spicy would be like, you know, Jazmine Sanchez, Yvette Gonzalez, or really anything that ends in *ez*. While my older sister's name, Veronica, has a little zest, my little brothers, Mitchell and Kenneth, got more American names like me. My mom also dressed the boys like twins, even though they were fifteen months apart and the only thing they had in common was their height and their bowl haircuts.

My mom recently confessed that back in the day, "Mexican names did not sound beautiful to me. Conchita, nope nope. I thought, *Ohhh, Angela was such a pretty name, she will be beautiful.*"

"I will be honest and say I associated Hispanic names with poverty," she added. "Now I see them as beautiful and exotic."

The racism got to her, too, I guess. "So I was named after an insecurity?!" I cried.

"Don't get it twisted," she shot back. "I don't think many kids like the names their parents gave them. You think I like Susan? Are you kidding me, heck no!"

Despite the gentrification of our names and native tongue, in my family and in my house, we carried on some Latino traditions with pride.

Like, my grandma's special tamale recipe we made every Christmas. When she passed away, she must have taken that recipe to her grave, because we never made tamales again. Now we order them from the tamale lady down the street, but she's probably a grandma, so it still counts, I think.

There is, however, one classic Mexican thing about me: I have a massive family. Seriously, the number of cousins I have sounds made-up to some of my friends. Our family is so big, we literally have our own phone book. Every two years, we have a family reunion with five hundred people across multiple generations in attendance. It's so complex, there's a budget, and a board of directors–like committee with one representative from each family, like in *The Godfather* but with less chicken Parmesan and more carne asada quesadilla. There's a secretary who takes official minutes at meetings. Each family is assigned a color to design their own T-shirt, and we try to one-up each other with fancy designs. That's one friendly family competition; unfortunately, the biennial football game was permanently canceled after a fight broke out and someone ended up bleeding. Blood in blood out, fam.

My grandma hung out at our house a lot, watching us kids while my parents worked and watching her telenovela "stories," the ones with a lot of slapping and dramatic music. She spoke Spanish on the phone to her sisters and other relatives, and I waited impatiently to hear her signature phrase before she hung up, "Ande pues," because that meant she'd be free to make me bean, cheese, and lettuce tostadas or her delicious potato soup. Whichever. I loved both.

Being Mexican American meant I hit piñatas at birthday parties and had homemade tamales with rice and beans for Christmas, but I also ate ham and mashed potatoes and kosher pickles by the jar, which probably confused things even more. We made menudo for our family reunions but also had hot dogs and hamburgers. We did good ol' American traditional things like balloon toss, bingo, potato sack races, games of horseshoe, and gossiping about family members who weren't there. I mean, my family also went camping multiple times a year. Doesn't get more American than that.

One time when we went camping at Yosemite National Park, my cousin Michelle and I decided we were going to hike Half Dome. Now, I thought this was going to be a few hours max. Not because of my athletic ability, but because I apparently underestimate mountains. So, I figured my Nike tennis shoes would surely suffice for this nature walk. I took my schoolbooks out of my JanSport backpack and filled it up with about five bottled waters, a granola bar, and a handheld video camera. Turns out that hike was about 16 hours, and most hikers came prepared with CamelBaks, plenty of protein bars, hiking boots, first aid kits, and common sense. By the end of it, I was dehydrated and hungry, with blisters on my feet and a deflated ego. I was so mad at myself for getting into that situation. I wish someone would have told me what to expect so I could have politely replied with, "Oh that's cool, I'll wait here until you get back."

I grew up in a very diverse neighborhood with diverse cultural traditions that included Latinos, white people, approximately three Indians, one Black guy, and this weird lady who always kept her curtains closed. My Portuguese neighbors fried whole fish in their garage, and to this day, the stench of flounder is embedded in my nostrils. Every time I have fish and chips I think of them.

My mom worked as a hairstylist at a local salon owned by a woman named Meon. When we were home alone being latchkey kids, we called my mom at work for any reason ten times an hour. Meon would answer the phone with a pleasant tone:

"Meon Hair Design, may I help you?"

"May I please speak with Susan?" (At least we had manners.)

Meon's tone switched from professionally friendly to annoyed. "Susan, your kids again," she'd say. My mom was equally as annoyed.

"What, I'm working!"

"Mommmmm," I whined, "Veronica won't let me watch *Eureeka's Castle.*"

Click.

To her credit, Meon did not fire my mom. Thank God, because it wasn't like we were rich. We weren't *poor* poor, either, but I do remember us all huddling around the one heater panel in our house during the few cold California months or right after we got out of the shower. My aunt and uncle had money, and I remember how my aunt Celia sometimes found money in her jacket pockets or side pocket of her purse. I was shocked and awed that some people didn't have to account for every penny they had to survive. That was amazing to me and something I admired as a kid. I remember the first time I found money in an old jacket pocket as an adult. It meant a lot to me in that moment. I wasn't just happy that I found free money; I was happy that it was a simple sign that I was no longer at a place in my life where every penny was accounted for.

Our neighborhood was diverse and vibrant, but it wasn't 'hood. No lowriders rolling through or cars up on blocks in front yards. No cholos with tattoos hanging out on porches. I lived on a dead-end street, and every weekend our street was packed with cars of all the people who were coming to play soccer and basketball at the school next door. All the Mexican guys would roll up with Banda music rattling their speakers. It was like that was the neighborhood's announcement that the weekend had begun.

Our neighborhood was super safe and had a lot of senior citizens.

Which was fine when I was a little kid running around, but as I got older, I craved a little more excitement and danger. Now I wished for the lowriders and primered cars on blocks. The naughtiest I'd ever been up to this point was throwing oranges over the fence at Avô, the Portuguese grandpa next door, when he fried his stinky fish. I think he used the oranges as a garnish, so really I was just being an aggressively thoughtful sous chef.

When I was really young, I hadn't tapped into my Latino heritage. If I was around Mexican people who were speaking Spanish, I would stay quiet, just listen, and pretend to understand. As I headed into my preteen years, inspired by *Blood In Blood Out*, I desperately wanted to be more Latino than I felt I actually was. All-American Angela was old news. Now I wanted to wholly embrace my Mexicanness and speak Spanish fluently and be a chola, a tough girl from the wrong side of the tracks, with thin penciled-on eyebrows and a boyfriend with neck tattoos and maybe a couple of kids who would remind me that I wasn't their real mom. Dream big, you guys.

Unfortunately for me, I was just your run-of-the-mill prepubescent brown girl from the right side of the tracks in San Jose whose boyfriend was a *Tiger Beat* magazine poster of New Kids on the Block. Jordan Knight was my man, and I was his girl. In my mind. I romanticized what it would be like to live on the East Side, where all the Mexicans lived and worked. They had taquerias and panaderias on every corner. Meanwhile, in my part of town, we had one Chinese restaurant, a liquor store, and a bunch of airport hotels because I lived five minutes away from San Jose International Airport. In my part of town, we didn't have access to tacos and pan dulces. The best we could do was walk over to the liquor store and stock up on chile picante, Corn Nuts, and Charleston Chews.

Around the time of my cultural evolution and revolution, my mom made a fatal error—she allowed me to pluck my eyebrows. In my house, you couldn't just wear makeup or shave your legs because you felt like it. You had to ask permission in exactly the right way at exactly the right time and include a list of friends whose parents already allow them to do these things just in case you needed to pull the guilt trip card.

"Okay, just a little bit," she finally said, waving the white flag.

I ran into the bathroom, excited, and plucked away like a maniac, and girl, let me tell you, when I came out, my mom took one look at me and cried, "Oh *no no no no*." But with like at least seventeen more *no*s.

Too late. My inner chola was now front and center, and there was no going back. When I was allowed to wear makeup for the first time at a family function, my mom said I could wear auburn lip liner and ChapStick. That was her way of keeping it minimal. Little did she know she'd given me my chola starter kit. All I needed was a can of Aqua Net hairspray and I was on my way to Cholaville.

My sixth grade school ID was so innocent, no makeup. But the following year's school ID was like, who is this hottie and why does she look like she just shanked someone? As soon as I started wearing makeup, I got super interested in boys because I finally felt cute. I was a natural, master flirter, a trait inherited from my dad, a ladies' man who was very witty and always the life of the party. He was a delivery guy, and all the women on his route loved him and giggled at all of his jokes. Not all of his jokes aged well, though, as most of them are hit-or-miss dad jokes now, but A for effort.

When I broke out of my shell, my mom pointed out that I too flirted with all the boys, even the cashier at the grocery store. "I'm just being me," I said.

With a new personality, a newly painted face, and significantly less eyebrows, there was no stopping me. My sister, Veronica, who was my bestie, and I started going out, partying and cruising. We piled on makeup, using foundation and powder that were too pale for our faces, dark lip liner with ChapStick, and freshly plucked eyebrows.

We picked up our friends and ventured to the East Side, where everybody would go to cruise, get bomb Mexican food, or get into a gang fight. We would drive down Santa Clara Street all the way to Story and King Roads. Then we just turned around and drove all the way back. It was obviously a complete waste of gas, but when you're not old enough to get in the club, can't afford the cover charge, or didn't get on the guest list by calling in the radio station, then you settle for pitching in for gas money and cruising.

Cruising music depended on the mood or the car we were in. If we were in a lowrider, like an Impala, Cutlass, or any classic car, we listened to oldies. If we were in my sister's Honda or my friend Ana's Jeep, we probably listened to freestyle/hi-NRG music. Windows would be rolled all the way down. If it was a packed night and cars were bumper to bumper, we would sit on the windowsill and talk to all the guys who were either driving next to us or pulled over on the side of the street. We had pink business cards with our pager numbers and cute quotes like "Don't even Trip!"

Motorcycle clubs all parked at the 7-Eleven or this Mexican restaurant called El Grullense. Those guys would always have extra helmets in case any of us girls wanted to go for a ride. Sometimes we did, but don't tell my mom.

After we went cruising, we'd get back home in our safe neighborhood on the other side of town. No drive-bys, no drug deals—just families, Grandpa Avô, and working streetlights. And I resented it. I wanted to be tough and cool. I wanted to change the first three prefix numbers of my phone number from 452 to 279, like all my chola friends' phone numbers. Because if your phone number started with 279, then you were legit from the barrio.

I wanted to accept a collect call from prison like all of my chola friends who knew somebody who was locked up. They were always visiting prisons, but I didn't even know where the prison was located or what to talk about with someone who was doing hard time. Or even medium time. I'd ask my mom if we had any family members behind bars, hoping for a little street cred, and she'd just laugh and say, "No, but we have a lawyer and hairstylists."

In my elementary school, we didn't really have a bunch of cholo kids or parents. There was this one girl, though. We'll call her Tina Lopez. She was allowed to wear makeup and had eyebrows and feathered hair goals. She clearly had a rough upbringing, which made me think she was so cool. I thought anyone who had a tough vibe was cool.

I wanted to be tough and scary but not actually hurt anybody. Every summer my girls and I would go to Paramount's Great America, now California's Great America (we all had season passes, of course), and we would get into fake fights. Sometimes we would do that in the street when we were cruising. We'd pack fifteen of us into two minivans and roll down the street with the sliding doors open. (Again, don't tell my mom.) At a stoplight, we'd jump out and one of us would be like, "What's up? What are you looking at?" And another girl from the other car would be like, "What are *you* looking at?" And then we would throw our hair forward and throw hands without actually landing any punches, jump back in the car, and go get McDonald's—back when you could eat McDonald's for every meal and not worry about heart disease. It was all just for attention. Honestly, the only battle scar I ever got during this time came from the minivan door accidentally shutting on my hand and pinching the skin. I might have dressed like a chola, but I also still wore white cardigan sweaters and neon Band-Aids.

Now I'm going to tell you some things that might surprise or even disappoint some of you who know me as a good Christian girl or a comedian who doesn't say cuss words. First, I say cuss words now. That's not the part I was originally going to tell you, but I felt like since we were being honest with each other, I might as well put that out there. What I was going to say was I've done drugs. I'm not talking about ibuprofen, although I've dabbled in that too. I'm talking about the illegal/no longer illegal kind. The first time I smoked weed was with my cousin on a camping trip, and then I did it again later in a hotel bathroom on a sleepaway trip with my choir (joining choir was normal for cholas at my school). I stole a lighter at a gift shop so everybody would think I was a cool chola, but I was still pretty innocent until I became best friends with Monica, who was also in choir. She had a voice like an angel, but she was a real-life chola whose mom was super into drugs and had a drug dealer boyfriend, which made the super into drugs part very convenient.

I loved Monica. She was my role model, and I wanted to be her. She was beautiful. She was funny. I'd never laughed as hard with anyone else as I did with her. She introduced me to everything—boys, alcohol, and drugs we'd get from her mom's boyfriend. We hung out at their apartment downtown in the real 'hood, and the guy gave us crank. Oh God. We were *Breaking Bad*–ing and didn't even know it. We drank forties and did lines of crank in her bathroom and also in the bathroom of our junior high school in the middle of the school day. Where's a hall monitor when you need one?

I definitely was aware that this was probably not a good idea. Same with the time we met Monica's aunt and boyfriend at a sleazy motel, did crank all night, then walked around a nearby empty dirt field at three a.m. We could've been raped, kidnapped, or killed, or gotten very wet from a sprinkler system.

The morning after our bender my body and my hands cramped up like a praying mantis, and we thought I might be overdosing. Monica stood over me, and we begged God not to take me. We knew how to pray together because she went to church with me sometimes. We knew the words to say, we knew "in Jesus' name, Amen."

Slowly, the cramps started to go away, and I was able to move my limbs again. I didn't die. Later that day, we ended up meeting up with these boys in a park and making out. I didn't even like my guy; it was a take-one-for-the-team situation while Monica hooked up with the dude she liked. I remember my guy's mouth was so big over my mouth, and I thought, *This is such a gross situation. Like I almost died from too many drugs last night, and now my whole face is being swallowed by an ugly guy.* It felt like rock bottom. I hit my rock bottom at twelve.

Dying wasn't in God's plan for me, and neither was being a legit chola. Monica and I ended up on totally different paths. I got super into cheerleading and really excelled at it. I wanted that 'hood life, but I also liked being athletic and knowing I was really good at something. Monica took a different route before thankfully finally ending up at a healthy place in her life. After she got pregnant and spent some time in prison (I finally knew someone!), she ended up getting her life together and proving that it's not too late for anyone to make the necessary changes in order to live a happy and healthy life. I'm so proud of her and still consider her to be a dear friend.

I've gone through many different ideas of how God works. I've gone from saying "God is in control" to "I don't know that God is in control." I felt like there was this plan for my life and I couldn't veer far off even if I wanted to. As much as I wanted to be like Monica, and I really wanted to be like her, I couldn't, you know what I mean? Maybe God does have this divine plan over my life, but He's not up there pulling strings like a puppet master. Maybe it's more of a situation where I co-created this life with God because I made choices with the free will He gave me. I made these choices by listening to (or sometimes ignoring) God's small, still voice in my spirit. I'm still wrestling with that, to be honest. Because how did I end up a completely different person than my best friend?

I have no idea, but I do believe that God has a plan for me and you. It's up to us how close we want to stick to it.

I am so grateful that my mom never fully let me walk down the road to Cholaville. It's not an easy road. Most, if not all, of my childhood chola friends had kids in high school. Some went to prison. Some got heavy into drugs and alcohol. I tried my best. I got about halfway down the road and heard my mom's voice telling me not to make terrible decisions, and also dinner was ready. Or maybe it was God's voice, or maybe it was God speaking through my mom. Either way, I made a swift U-turn and came home.

But when I look back on my entry-level chola days, I understand part of where I was coming from. I wanted to be proud of my culture and my heritage, which is very multifaceted, but the chola aspect is what resonated most with me. Cholas are strong, proud women who know who they are and aren't afraid to show you—sometimes very close to your face. Or tell you—also close to your face. To be a chola you have to have a badass quality about you. You can't just dress the part or eyebrow pluck your way into being a chola. You have to *be* the part. I admire this kind of loud strength and have carried that admiration within me ever since my chola days.

How can you be more of something that you just inherently are? You can't. And you shouldn't try to. I've learned that you can be unapologetically proud of your culture, your heritage, and your heart, and you can celebrate everything about yourself without justification even if it looks different from others. For me, that's embracing being Mexican and American in my own way. Now, if anyone cared or dared to ask, "What are you?" I'd say proudly, "I'm Mexican/ Hella American/Bay Arean and a lot morean." I try my hardest not to compare myself or my journey to anyone else's (except for J.Lo, but everyone does that, right?). I trust that my path is specific for me, and I live fully in that. It's okay that I've ditched my brown lips for a soft pink. Today I'm surrounded by amazing family and friends who love me just as I am. I even connect with some of my old chola friends every now and then. We support each other and pray for each other. (Cholas go to church too—that's a whole other story! See chapter 4.)

Just so you know, I'm still evolving and learning about my background. I promise I will learn Spanish one day. I downloaded Rosetta Stone, but I'm still on the beginner levels. (You'd think a global pandemic and quarantine would be the time to do it, but nope!) But my motivation is no longer to prove myself. I just want to enjoy the gift of being able to connect to my culture and people on a deeper level. And also, so I can confidently say the absolute most important thing in Spanish: "Dónde está el baño?"

CHAPTER 3

The People Who Made Me Breakfast

I've mentioned how huge my family is, so now I'd like to introduce some of the most important people in my life. These people have all taken care of me in some way. Whether they took me to school, spanked me, or made me breakfast, they definetly made me who I am today. But listen, I want to include everyone I love; however, if I told you about each and every one of them, we'd all be here long enough to die from natural causes, so I will just get to a handful of them.

Let's start with my dad, because he's the biggest reason I am who I am today. I got his genes, and he gave me my royal inheritance (spoiler alert: it's rage). My dad was the first comedian I ever knew. I am my father's daughter. I am all the things he is. So, I just want to say right here, right now, Dad, I'm successful because of you. *Thank you.* I'm also in therapy. I'll just come out and say it: I went through some verbal and physical trauma in my childhood because of my dad. At the same time, I had a great childhood. One thing I want to make clear is that my dad is not an evil person or a one-dimensional villain.

He was a kid with his own childhood trauma who all of a sudden was a grown-up and then had some kids of his own.

My dad was always the life of the party, always cracking jokes and giving the best one-liners. He made us all laugh—his kids, his friends, the grocery store clerk, the ladies on his delivery route, the mailman, whoever. Any person in his path was a potential audience member and a potential participant in whatever joke he was about to improvise. He was quick, able to go rapid fire *zing-zing-zing-zing*, because if he was joke sparring with someone who was quick, too, my dad had to get the last word and the last laugh.

Everything was a game to Mitch Johnson, the most ultra-competitive person I've ever known. He was a star athlete, the leading scorer of his adult men's soccer team and lead-off hitter on his softball team. He was even my soccer and softball coach. But life was a game to be won off the field, too. My dad is the one who taught me how to be competitive. If we were just walking somewhere, out of nowhere he'd shout, "Okay, the first person to get to that tree wins!" And then we'd start running as fast as we could because it was a call to action. He never let me win, not one time.

My dad made up a lot of money games, like Who Wants to Be a Hundred Dollarnaire? He'd also set up three buckets—small, medium, and large—as well as a cup and a bowl. Just like at an amusement park, we took turns throwing a quarter into the targets, and if we made it, we'd get $1, $5, or $20, depending on which target we made it in.

———

Every Christmas, my dad poured out a sack of money—cash and coins—on the dining room table, so it looked like we were a drug dealer's house. But really it was his whole bank account just laid out, probably a solid $3,000. We had to guess how much money was on the table, without touching it, and if you came within $100, you got five bucks, within $50, ten bucks, and within $5, you got to keep the whole darn thing. Nobody ever won the grand prize, though. Nobody even came close, because he was tricky about it, like hiding coins under the bills and stacking hundreds so tightly you didn't realize there were four stuck together. It was as if we lived with the David Blaine of dads.

It's ironic that most of my dad's games revolved around money because he was frugal. Whatever amount of frugal you're thinking, think a little bit more than that. He was the mayor of Frugalville, which is a real place just south of Chesacheap Bay where he drove a Cheap Wrangler and ate Fruggie Pebbles for breakfast. To this day, whatever city he's in, he sends me pictures of the prices at gas stations—*$3.25? That's insane! Are they out of their minds?*

My dad wasn't just frugal, though; he was super resourceful and creative. He held on to an extra-large popcorn bag from every movie theater just so he'd be ready for a "free refill" next time. I wouldn't be surprised if he had a pocket in his jacket dedicated to various popcorn bags. To avoid paying team registration fees, he brought me to track meets the morning of and just signed me up, even though I had no training or uniform. He scoured grocery store parking lots for dropped receipts with coupons on them just to save three dollars off a large Round Table Pizza. For birthdays and holidays, he bought us grocery items and wrapped them in newspaper, like cereal and soda, so the whole house could share them. He wouldn't just wrap the "gifts" in newspaper and write our names on it; he'd get creative with the newspaper article itself. Like if he grabbed the sports section to wrap my RC Cola and the headline read "Angels beat the Sox!" he'd cross out parts of it and write in other words so it said "To my Angel, no it's not Sox."

He might not have been able to take all four kids to Disneyland—who could afford that even back then?—but we entertained ourselves for hours exploring his Exchange Linen delivery truck, which he parked outside our house sometimes. It smelled so rancid because it was filled with soiled bedsheets, moldy bath mats, and crusty napkins and tablecloths, but it was our own private germ-infested Space Mountain. I also vividly recall going to the landfill with my dad to drop off our garbage and search for treasures. That was a very specific smell that I'm 100 percent not interested in ever smelling again. I guess growing up I really enjoyed playing in very smelly places.

Superfun Dad splurged when it was extremely important, like for tickets to see WWF (now WWE) at the arena. He was always up for an adventure, if he could swing it financially, whether that was riding his Harley-Davidson with his boys to the Sturgis Motorcycle Rally in South Dakota or taking us on a road trip from the Bay to Arizona or Idaho. We stopped at all the ghost towns because we were all really into paranormal, haunted stuff, and as dad told tales about the dusty old buildings and dramatic shootouts, our imaginations ran wild. Anytime we saw an abandoned, rusted-out car on the side of the road, we pulled over to check it out. Of course, we'd seen horror movies, so we knew the risks, but we also knew that thirty-five years of rust probably meant the bad guy hadn't stuck around to get us. My dad inspected the car and spouted random facts, like, "Oh yeah, that's a '64 Camino, and see these bullet holes right here? That's from a Colt .38." I had no resources to verify any of his information, but why would I even need to? Clearly my dad was the smartest man on earth—from bullet holes to my third grade math problems. The man was a genius.

My dad was my original Google. He was so smart and could answer every question I ever had about any topic. He knew the make and model of every car and could also tell me what kind of bird just flew over our heads and why they had talons instead of claws. My dad was book smart (unless he was just making stuff up and relied on me not fact-checking him), and he was also street-smart. My dad's cleverness and magnetism could be used for both good and nefarious purposes. Even now, he's quite the player. My dad is very handsome and has a great smile and a twinkle in his eye. He's always had a way of making an entrance and owning the room, especially when he wore his classic '80s mesh half top and shorts. These days, he's traded in the man midriff for more of a Mexican cowboy "ranchero" vibe. He keeps his alligator cowboy boots in the original box they came in. He was the original sneaker head.

Since I was very young, I had always overheard women making comments about my dad and how charming and handsome he was. Nowadays, anytime I post a picture of my dad on social media, ladies (and some men, too) leave comments like "Oh, your dad can get it," or "Is he single?" I just shake my head and laugh. Part of me is grossed out and another part of me is really proud, like, "Go, Dad!" If you got the straights *and* the gays hollering, you know you still got it.

All the ladies loved my dad, including my mom's sister, Aunt Celia. In fact, my dad dated my aunt first before my mom, and he used to get in fistfights over Aunt Celia with my Uncle Tom, who Celia ended up marrying and having three kids with. After she chose Tom over my dad, my dad made a play for my mom, and nobody was happy about it. Aunt Celia even went to my mom's ex-boyfriend and asked him to get back together with my mom again "because I don't like that she's dating Mitch." Somehow, our family gatherings managed to not turn into a telenovela. Although when I was twelve my dad told us that we had a half brother we never knew about (cue dramatico music). So, maybe I should pitch this to Telemundo. I remember the first time meeting our brother, Ryan. It was so crazy because here was this grown-up version of my youngest brother Mitchell. Like, spitting image. There was no denying that he was related to us. And he spoke with a country accent because he was adopted in Georgia. We still make fun of his accent, which he still thinks he doesn't have.

Like most women, my mom was smitten with my dad's sparkling personality in the beginning, but she could never quite trust him. One time she was at his work party and, while in the bathroom, overheard another woman talking about how sexy my dad was and that they had "a vibe." It's not my place to go into the intimate details of my parents' marriage. But when I think of their relationship and how womanizing my dad was, I know I would never want to be in a relationship like that.

It took me a minute to figure out that my dad's charisma could also be a front for some major character flaws. Your dad is your hero and can do no wrong, until one day, some things don't add up. Of course, your dad can do third grade math and tell you about birds of prey, but then you get to an age where you realize he's for sure just guessing most of the answers, at best. When I realized that, it was like when I found out (earmuffs, children) Santa isn't real. When I first came to him for an answer about something and it was wrong, I put it in my mental Rolodex and thought, *That's not right*. And then it happened another time. And another. Then the shift followed not long after. My dad became less of a Superman and more of a human man.

I'm grateful for who my dad is and all the things he taught me. The problem was, as charming as my dad was, he was also very hot and cold, and very high and low. He was filled with rage, so you never knew which guy you were gonna get.

When my dad got home from work, we'd run out to greet him, and he'd take turns picking us up and swinging us in the air like a carousel. We were the all-American family until, whoops, one of us did something to set him off. Or maybe we didn't. Anything could trigger a violent meltdown or blinding rage. We had swinging wood saloon-like doors leading to our kitchen, and once, one of them swung back and hit his head. He got so mad he punched the doors off the hinges. That violent behavior wasn't directed toward us, but it was still scary, and I froze. I remember thinking, *Don't say words. Don't make him mad.*

I walked on eggshells to avoid my dad's wrath, but eventually his rage affected us kids directly. Just hearing the tone in his voice change from playful dad to shit's-about-to-get-real dad was enough to make your stomach drop and know something bad was coming. On my sixth birthday, my parents got me my first bike. My dad thought my birthday party would be the perfect time to play a joke on me in front of all of my family and friends. He had me close my eyes while they wheeled out a dirty, old, ugly boys' bike. When I opened my eyes, they all shouted, "Surprise!"

I couldn't hide my disappointment—I was barely six years old. Everyone started laughing at the joke, but it felt like they were laughing at me. I immediately started crying. My dad then wheeled out the real bike they got me that was pretty and girly and brand-new. But it was too late. The damage had been done. I couldn't even look at it because I was humiliated. My dad kept saying, "Open your eyes, look up," but through my tears I kept saying, "No!" My dad considered me rude and ungrateful, and sent me to my room. On my birthday. Looking back I get it. My dad was a jokester and he came up with his idea of the perfect prank to get the laugh, only he didn't realize he would hurt me in the process. When he coached me in sports, I could hear when his tone changed from "disappointed coach on the field" to "you're gonna get it when we get home." I vividly recall my teammates' parents telling my dad to calm down because "they're just kids!"

I have a lot of spanking stories that I could share, but there's no need to go into detail to understand that my dad had a temper and it got the best of him sometimes. Now listen, I completely understand spanking. I'll spank you right now if I have to. There is, however, a difference in spanking to discipline and spanking out of anger and rage. One is just that, a disciplinary action. The other is an excuse to hit someone because you're mad. My dad had a way with words that would keep my mom in her place and quiet. Still, she stood up to my dad the best she could, including one intense argument after she bathed me and spotted a large purple bruise on my back. She left me in the bathroom and closed the door, but I could still hear her shout at him, "Don't you ever touch my kids again!" Not long after, when I was about eight years old, my mom mustered up the courage and told my dad she wanted out of the marriage. She stood her ground, kicked him out of the house, and that was it.

My dad's rage did not ease up after their split. He was really bitter and hurt, and the first time we went to my dad's place after my parents' divorce for "his weekend," the police were called. I guess we kind of did turn into a telenovela. It was not pleasant between my parents for a long time. My dad made really mean jokes about my mom. He'd always been a jokester, but now his barbs could be angry and cruel.

My dad lost everything in the divorce. He took only a nightstand and some clothes. For the remainder of my childhood my dad bounced around and rented rooms from friends here and there. As long as he could feed himself and have a place to lay his head and take a shower, he seemed to be good. On future visits, we stayed with him at the Oasis Motel or a Motel 6, which was fun for us because Chuck E. Cheese was right across the parking lot and we snuck out and went there by ourselves while he napped. We Skee-Balled our way to a little bit of normalcy…and slap bracelets.

My dad took us camping a lot, and it's only in hindsight that I realized he did that out of necessity, not because it was a fun family activity. He had no home of his own or money, so for $25, we'd get a campsite, buy some Doritos, make sandwiches, and live in a tent for the weekend. My dad recently explained to me that our camping trips were, in fact, planned out of necessity, and he shared some of his feelings and experiences about the divorce. At that moment I realized I'd never looked at things from my dad's point of view. I'd always talked about my mom and how strong she was raising us on her own, but I never thought about how hard things were for my dad, how lonely he was and how he felt that everything was taken from him, including his house and family.

As fond as I was of those camping trips, there were darker memories I couldn't shake. And guess what, *ta-da*, I ended up in therapy on and off for years because, drum roll please, turns out I had that same uncontrollable inner rage that came out. Little did I know that the key to unlocking my royal inheritance, this gift that was bestowed upon me at birth, was a little thing called marriage, but we'll dive into that a bit later. For better or worse, I am my father's daughter. I get my personality from my dad, and my personality is what pays my bills, so I'm grateful to him for that. But I also inherited his anger, hot temper, pride, and love of alligator boots. Just kidding—sick.

In therapy I discussed my trauma and confronting my dad about it, but I wasn't ready. A few years ago, with all these feelings swirling around and top of mind, I did a podcast with my friend Jeannie Mai and sort of talked about my dad in a real way for the first time ever but immediately felt bad that I'd done it publicly without talking to him first. She encouraged me to talk to my dad, and I said, "Well, maybe if I see him in person." Two days later my dad texted me: "Hey, I'm driving to Arizona and I'm going to stop in LA. Do you have time to hang out?" And I was like, *Wow, well, I guess it's time. This is supposed to happen.*

For help I turned to my cousin Joe, the best therapist I've ever had so far. He urged me to write a letter to my dad about all the trauma he caused in my childhood and read it to him. Joe and I went through all the pros and cons of what could possibly happen if I actually was brave enough to go through with it:

Worst case scenario: My dad yells and says, "I never did that!" storms out, and leaves me there, and we fracture our relationship forever.

Best case scenario: He's extremely empathetic and apologizes and it starts a new path for our relationship.

Middle ground scenario: He's cool about it but is "sorry you feel that way."

With those outcomes in mind, I wrote my letter and left nothing out. I read it to my mom first, then my sister, because I needed to make sure I wasn't crazy and that these things actually happened. "No, yeah, that happened," they both confirmed.

I was so nervous before my dad arrived, wondering, *When do I do it?* In my mind, I envisioned my dad sitting at the kitchen coffee table by himself and that would be the perfect time to go and read him the letter. The first day he got there, we had dinner and watched TV. Nothing dramatic. The next morning, I woke up, came downstairs and there was my dad at the kitchen coffee table. Talk about manifesting. It was my sign from God. This was my time. So, I grabbed my journal and said, "Dad, I want to talk to you about something. I wrote this letter to you and I want to read it to you. Please don't respond. Let me just read all of this first and don't ask questions." As I started reading the letter my heart was beating so fast, but I was also really calm.

My dad responded to the letter with grace, love, and confusion. He didn't remember a lot of what I recounted, and I believe him. I don't think he was trying to get one over on me and pretend none of it ever happened. I believe he actually didn't remember these things because sometimes we as humans tend to compartmentalize and tuck away things that are scary, shameful, or painful to hidden places in our minds so we don't have to deal with them. Maybe we don't even know we're doing it; our body just goes into protection mode to keep us safe at all costs. Sometimes that means sticking a file labeled "I probably shouldn't have done that" in a sealed vault in the darkest corner of your brain room. I've done the work on myself to be able to look at my dad with compassion and understanding. My dad did his best with what he was taught in his own childhood and his own life experiences.

The letter was a breakthrough for us that neither of us knew we needed.

Now my dad and I have a great relationship, in the sense that he's my good friend who I can always count on to make me laugh. He still races me to the tree to prove he's faster and still got it. I may or may not let him win now. (I let him win; he's no spring chicken.) I don't go to him for marriage advice or anything like that, but if I ever want to hear a good story, learn some random "facts," or need to know the price of gas in Phoenix, he'd be the first one I'd call. I do love him deeply and he loves me—and the free popcorn in the greenroom at my shows.

So, that's my dad, but of course he wasn't my sole influence. My brothers Kennie and Mitchell are younger than me, but they helped shape my protective mentality. Sure, they would get on my nerves sometimes at home, but if anyone ever tried to mess with them, they had me to deal with. One time I got in a fistfight with a girl because I thought she was trying to give my brothers drugs. *Oh, I don't think so, missy.* Only Flintstones vitamins for my brothers.

There are a lot of women who influenced me on my dad's side (Johnsons) and mom's side (Castañedas), but for now I'll just tell you about the Castañeda side of my family tree—and let me tell you something: These women have very strong voices. They run the show, for sure. Even the ones who married in. Like, at Thanksgiving and Christmas, we all go to Aunt Celia's house—around fifty of us—and my uncle Rudy's wife, Aunt Susie, always stands up, taps the side of her glass, and proclaims boldly, "I just need to say something." Then everyone shushes each other, it gets really quiet, and Aunt Susie makes a powerful speech that makes everyone cry, including the men who like to cover it up with a manly clear of the throat.

I feel like my family is always looking for an excuse to cry. We go around the room and share what we were most grateful for the last year, all fifty of us, one at a time, one after the other. "I'm thankful for my job. I'm thankful for my health…" my cousin will start, then, like clockwork, her lip quivers and her voice cracks. "It was touch and go for a while." Whoever is sitting next to her then grabs her hand, and they share a warm glance and a supportive nod. "Thank heaven we're good now." More tears. This tradition takes about two hours, two boxes of tissues, and at least one intermission for a chips and salsa refill.

We may jokingly call ourselves the Cryañedas, but here's the serious truth about the women in my family: Even when we are weak, we are strong.

Look at my mom. At the same time she was dealing with divorcing my dad, she was raising four kids. After he was gone, she ran our family on bare minimum child support and a hairstylist budget, which meant sometimes she'd get appointments that day; sometimes she didn't. Sometimes she'd get walk-ins; sometimes she didn't. Sometimes she got a good tip; sometimes she didn't. It was hard not to have regular pay with four mouths to feed.

We didn't have a lot of money, but I never felt deprived—of love, attention, or material things. Not to mention the never-ending supply of free haircuts. We were her guinea pigs, so at one time or another I had the Annie perm, the Rachel, the Cranberry color, the Long Bang, the Short Bang, and of course the Chola, but I gave that one to myself. My mom is a very talented artist. She painted our faces like the Legion of Doom when we'd go to WWF matches with our dad. She did such a good job, they almost tagged me into the ring.

She wasn't the stereotype of the single Latina mom with the belt threatening to whoop our butts. That was my dad. My mom was very loving and nurturing, but she also set rules and boundaries. My mom was the levelheaded voice of reason and our moral compass.

After the split, my mom went out on dates exclusively with nerdy white guys—it's like they all got an email to their AOL accounts at the same time informing them that a pretty Latina lady was now on the market. I still feel bad about how much we made fun of their awkward dance moves, but have you seen middle-aged white guys dance? Actually, now that I think about it, they were the age I am now, but when you're young, mid to late thirties was middle-aged/senior citizen. She didn't go out a lot with her friends or spend a lot of money on herself. She wore the same pair of jeans with a hole in the crotch my whole childhood because if she got any extra money, she spent it on us. She made sure on my birthday, feast or famine, I got a fancy *Wizard of Oz*–themed cake because I was obsessed with that movie and Dorothy's ruby slippers. I had an *Oz* cake multiple years in a row, and I was Dorothy on Halloween so many times that the neighbors probably thought I just didn't have money for a new costume. The one time I decided to switch it up and go as Glinda the Good Witch, everyone was all, "Hey, are you from *Little House on the Prairie*?" Uh, first of all, rude. Second of all, what's that? The next year I went right back to being Dorothy.

I wish I would have appreciated my mom's self-sacrifice more when I was younger. I could be a little brat. One time she traded in her brown Astro minivan for a brand-new green Toyota Camry station wagon. When she brought it home, I was so mad. I whined, "Ewww, that's so ugly!" She was probably so proud she bought herself a new car, and I shit all over it. Figuratively. I wasn't *that* bratty.

What my mom accomplished was a miracle considering what she'd gone through, not only during the time she was married to my dad, but even before that. Once when I was an adult living in LA, we went out for dinner at a Chinese restaurant in Pasadena, and I asked her if she wanted to know the truth about all the bad things I'd done.

"Hold on, let me get a drink," she said, "and then we'll do it."

As we drank our cocktails, I told her everything, even about doing crank in the school bathroom and walking in an empty field in the middle of the night. "Oh my God, I didn't know!" she cried, but at the same time, she didn't clutch her pearls. "I was way worse than that," she admitted.

She told me stories I never knew, and I clutched *my* pearls. As a teenager, my mom was a hippie. I mean, c'mon, it was the San Francisco Bay Area in the '70s. She did a lot of different drugs and was with different guys and just didn't care. She didn't have a reverence for life and ended up in really dangerous situations. One time, when she was high on a drug she was told was just weed but turned out to be laced with something powerful, a jerk she was dating dumped her in a parking lot in the middle of nowhere and drove off. She had to walk miles alone in the dark to get home. I couldn't imagine how scared she was and how bad her feet hurt. I mean, was she even wearing sensible shoes? My mom recently admitted to me that when she was younger, she felt like she wasn't good at anything. So she decided that maybe if she got really good at sex she could be a high-end call girl. Not just a prostitute, a high-end one. Dream big, you guys.

By the time she was twenty, she had my older sister Veronica with my dad, whose rage and anger reared its ugly head as soon as they got married. "I had to grow up because I couldn't go home in my first month of marriage," she told me.

My mom had to become an old soul fast, but she stayed young at heart. And she looked super young—she still does. I loved that my mom was young and cool and pretty, and everybody always said so. They would say to me, "Daaaang, your mom is so young." I took that as a compliment. I was never embarrassed of her or made her drop me off far away at the movie theater. One time my mom's car was in the shop, so they gave her a convertible rental car. We were stoked! We convinced her to take us and our homegirls cruising downtown. We styled her hair like ours and had her dress like us and then hit the town. We thought we were so cool until one guy in a car next to us said, "That's their mom, aye!" I was like, "*Shut up*, we are cool!" We headed home after that.

Everyone called my mom "Mom." I always talk about how I envied my friends' lives, because I wanted to be in the 'hood. I know there was a part of my friends that wanted what I had, that sense of stability and joy that maybe they didn't get in their own homes. And protection. She caught a Peeping Tom staring in my sister's and my bedroom window once and chased the perp down the street with a baseball bat until he cried uncle, wailing, "What do you want from me?!" Another time, she left me sitting in the car while she ran into Walgreens, and a creep in an old truck pulled up next to me and started masturbating. I honked the horn and flickered the lights as a bat signal for my mom to save me. She ran out of the store immediately, yelled, "Aw, hell no!" at the perv, threw the green Camry into reverse, and we chased him down the freeway for fifteen minutes. He finally pulled over, threw his hands in the air, and screamed, "Leave me alone!"

My mom was mama bear to all the neighborhood kids, too. Everyone knew they were welcome at our house. My mom accepted and loved everybody—our neighborhood friends, gay friends, straight friends, smelly friends, everybody. My friends knew if they came over, she was going to feed them. They could sleep over any time—Saturday nights, after a Pop Warner football game, even on school nights. Coolest mom, right? They could come with us wherever we were going—yo, everybody pile in the ugly green station wagon, let's go! Even church. Some of my friends didn't even go to church, but they liked it if my mom took them.

Everybody knew they could count on Susie. She was the neighborhood mom, that's for sure. I didn't mind sharing my mom with everybody, but my siblings and I battled to sleep in her bed with her when she was newly single again. We called dibs, like how you call shotgun for the front seat of the car. It's possible my mom wanted to enjoy her bed to herself after sharing it with someone for so long, but she didn't let us know that. If I were her, I would have snored extra loud and been like, "Awww, you're leaving? K byyyeee."

That was the time I enjoyed most with her. That and going to church. My mom was raised Catholic, but she later became nondenominational Christian and believed her faith got her through the toughest times. "Even when I was in high school, thinking I was going to die sometimes with the things that I was doing, I'd always pray," she told me. "I knew there was a God out there and maybe He'd help me. Prayer got me through high school without getting pregnant, without becoming a drug addict, and without being somebody walking the streets."

I definitely grew more in my own faith because of my mom. After the divorce, she leaned on her spirituality more and we went to church more often. She even let me tag along to her adult Bible studies. As I grew in my faith and intuition, I shared these crazy dreams and visions I had with my mom. Like one time at one of her Bible studies we were praying at the end, and as I closed my eyes, I could see images in my mind's eye of some of the people in that Bible study and things that were going to happen in their lives. I felt God nudging me to tell them what I saw, but I was too afraid to, so I told my mom instead. Weeks later we found out my visions were correct, which really freaked me out. My mom told me that I had a gift, and she was excited because she had the same gift. Now I'm not saying we are psychics or prophetic; we both just have a strong intuition and hear from God through visions sometimes. I think all moms have that mother's intuition. Mine is just regular intuition.

Moms also have that uncanny ability to be our biggest champions, even when we maybe don't deserve it and are at our worst. I wish I could have been there more for my mom, but it wasn't until I was an adult that I started to see her as something other than my mom. In my mind back then, "Mom" was her personality. Then one day I realized, *Oh, she's more than a hair-curling chauffeur. She's also a daughter and a human being who has memories and has siblings who she looked up to or maybe was afraid of.* I forgot that my mom was just a kid herself when she started having kids, forcing her to grow up quickly.

My mom did such an admirable job raising four functioning adults, though I do recall a lot of help from the Costco box of wine in our refrigerator. Not to mention all the strong women in our family, who we jokingly call lathees, thanks to our friend Jeannette, who coined the term. It's our way of saying *ladies* in broken English with a thick accent. My personality was shaped by all of these badass lathees, who each inspired and influenced me in their own way.

Again, I want to mention all of my lathees, but remember that whole dying of natural causes thing? It would take forever, so I'll mention a few. The lathees in my family are always good for some sound advice and will be there for you, through thick and thin, no questions asked. Well, lots of questions asked, but at the end of the day they still ride with you. I spent a lot of time with my cousins and older sister Veronica, who is my best friend and also a huge influence on me. We shared a room until she moved out of the house. We're used to being in each other's space. When I fly home to visit her or she comes to visit me, we still share a bed. Seriously, my husband gets pushed to the guest room and Vero and my nephew Austin sleep with me. Austin is not just my nephew, he's my godson, which ultimately means that if anything were to happen to his parents, he would come live with me. But really it just means I have to get him extra presents on his birthday.

Growing up we fought a lot, as sisters do, but we also leaned on each other and had each other's backs. Wherever she went I went. She didn't have a choice. "Take your sister" was my mom's response anytime Veronica asked to go somewhere. "You're going for a bike ride? Take your sister," my mom would order. "To the movies? Take Anj," she'd insist. "To the bathroom? Sister."

When I was younger that was probably annoying for her, but as I got older and my brows got thinner, we enjoyed going places with each other. It was just an automatic thing that one of us came with the other. We shared clothes and makeup and then fought over said clothes and makeup.

"Is that my lip liner!?" She glared at me. "Well, you wore my polyesters last night!" Polyesters were our go-to going-out pants. They were basically black polyester leggings that went with whichever hoochie top we bought at the cheap store called Hi-Fashion. If we saved up enough money or mom got good tips that week we splurged at Judy's, 5-7-9, Miller's Outpost, or Contempo Casuals. We both were cheerleaders, and we both pretended to be cholas. We had lots of inside jokes, and we still do. Today she is probably the phone number most dialed on my phone. Every time I get in my car I call her. Even if I have nothing to say, it's just an automatic thing I do. Get in car, start engine, put on seat belt, and say out loud "Siri, call Veronica," to which Siri always plays dumb. "I don't have that name in your contacts. Did you mean Veronica Johnson?" she asks coyly. Don't get smart, Siri. You know that's who I meant.

I also played the little sister role to my cousins Shannon, Celena, and Michelle, who are Aunt Celia's daughters with my Uncle Tom, the Irish guy who got into fistfights with my dad. Us five girls were super close—like, if texting was a thing back then, we would all be on a thread.

If you think that the story I told you earlier about my dreams and visions shows that I had a gift you should meet my cousins Tish and Larissa. They could call you on the phone and read your mail that hasn't arrived yet, tell you what you had for lunch and predict if it would give you gas later. They were right more often than they weren't, so I would caution people: "Don't do anything bad or God will see it. And probably Tish and Larissa too." Even though I was relegated to the little sister role by my sister and all my cousins, Grandma Rachel, who lived at Aunt Celia's house after my grandpa died, secretly told me I was her favorite out of all my cousins. I didn't even like me the best out of all my cousins, so that took me by surprise. Maybe she said that to all of my cousins secretly—I can't be sure. All I know is that we had a very special relationship that really blossomed after my parents' divorce. My grandma started coming to our house a lot more to look after us while my mom was working.

My grandma was very generous. She'd give me a couple rolled-up dollar bills and tell me to go get myself a "sotha" at the local gas station. She could usually be found in her robe/apron, eating Popsicles or a snack of some sort while talking on the phone in Spanish to her relatives or lying on the bed on her stomach reading a book with a magnifying glass. Wherever she was, I was right next to her. While she read, I lay next to her quietly, playing with the skin on her free hand that didn't have elasticity anymore. My grandma didn't feel the need to entertain me, and I didn't need to be entertained. We had a soul connection that was deeper than words. Though sometimes we recited the Lord's Prayer together, which was stitched on a square, carpetlike fabric that hung on the wall over the bed:

"Our Father, who art in heaven," she'd start in her raspy asthmatic voice, and then I would join in: "hallowed be thy name. Thy kingdom come, thy will be done on earth as it is in heaven. Give us this day our daily bread, and forgive us our trespasses as we forgive those who trespass against us. Lead us not into temptation, but deliver us from evil, for thine is the kingdom, the power, and glory forever and ever. Amen."

She was more of a quiet observer than a big talker. She was the first person to ever tell me, "I could see you doing something like that, mija," as she soaked in her colorful, flashy Spanish programs on TV and cackled along with the fake laugh track. Which struck me as odd at the time, considering that while my cousins were always in school performances, my nickname was occasionally Eeyore, because I would feel sorry for myself, sigh, and say, "Nobody wants to play with me."

My cousin Michelle was in a singing group, a dance group, a smart kids group, all the groups, but Grandma saw something in me. (Okay, maybe she saw it in Michelle too, and they had their own secret convos, but this is about me right now.) I, for sure, believed I was the chosen grandchild. Until the day she died, my grandma still let me sit on her lap, and I was the only one who did that, even though everyone always told me to get off of her. "You're too big!" they shouted. "She's old! You're going to break her!" But that didn't matter to me. I still sat on Grandma while she sat in her favorite rocking chair. We really should have been concerned for the chair.

Sadly, my grandma passed away at the age of eighty-seven sitting in her favorite rocking chair, wearing a robe with Popsicle sticks stuffed in the pockets. I now like to wear robes, too, and if I find ChapStick or dirty tissues in a pocket randomly, I think of her fondly. For some reason, the smell of a warm wet washcloth also reminds me of her. It's such a vivid sense memory. I think it's because she used to wash my face with a washcloth when I got home from school. It doesn't happen every time I smell a washcloth; just every now and then the nostalgic smell will hit me. I like to think it's her way of saying hello and letting me know that she's still taking care of me.

My grandma saw me blossom from a shy Eeyore into a confident cheerleader who'd perform routines in the living room. Like that Raiderette choreographer who gave me the best backhanded compliment, Grandma Rachel saw that thing in me that couldn't be taught. It's bittersweet that she never got to see my success, but I know she knows. We had a spirit connection that definitely lived on after she died.

When my grandma passed away, my tia Mary stepped into that role and became my honorary grandma. She didn't volunteer, like, "You poor child, let me play grandma for you." I latched on to her and basically ordered, "You will play Grandma for me." I called her home "my house" when I was a kid so many times, Tia Mary's nick-name for me became MyHouse.

I invested in Tia Mary. I called and visited, and as I got older and was doing things to be proud of, I included her. I wanted her to be proud of me the way my grandma would have been. My grandma had twenty-five siblings, but Tia Mary is the one I connected to the most. When I say twenty-five, that's not a fake number to imply that there were a lot of kids. That's the actual number of Mexican siblings. Born in 1921, Tia Mary had a third grade education and worked in the fields picking vegetables in Utah and California. She married her teenage sweetheart, Mike, and he joined the Air Force. He taught her how to fix a flat tire so she could drive down to Southern California and visit him at the base. Tia Mary slept in her car outside the gate just so she could see him. She had no money for food, so his platoon buddies passed her apples through the chain-link fence. I feel like they could have at least grabbed a chicken sandwich or a granola bar for her or something, but beggars can't be choosers. I guess.

Tia Mary was so resourceful and tenacious. She got a job on the base doing laundry. Tia Mary was also one of the original Rosie the Riveters. She riveted the wings of the B-29 aircraft. I don't know the difference between a drill that screws in and a drill that screws out, but she was riveting things. She later worked at Levi Strauss and worked her way up from the factory floor to supervisor and finally to manager of the factory. She has a retirement letter from then presi-dent and CEO of Levi Strauss, Mr. Walter Haas, on her mantel, right next to a picture of me. She's as proud of me (and Levi Strauss, appar-ently) as I am of her, and she always gives me the best advice, like, "Mija, they say marriage is fifty-fifty, but that's a lie. It's seventy-thirty. We do most of the work."

To this day—she's 101 at last count—Tia Mary brings me up to every single vendor who comes to "my house"—mailman, cable guy, plumber. I've done movies and TV shows and headlined sold-out comedy shows all over the world. You know what she tells them? "Did you know my niece was a cheerleader for the Oakland Raiders?"

The women in my life are proud of me, and I am proud of them. I never knew just how strong my mom was back in the day. Unbelievably, she didn't think she was a great mom. She thought that she should have been there for us more, been more available, and made better choices. We're always our own toughest critic, right? "Whatever bad things you think in your head," I've told her many times, "I don't think any of those. I'm trying hard to think of a bad thing you did, and I can't think of one."

I didn't start talking about my mom honestly in my stand-up routine for a really long time. She seemed mildly offended to be left out, so I explained, "The reason why you don't have jokes is because you're not a hot mess. It's easy to make jokes about Dad because he's always doing something or saying something silly or ridiculous. Like how dinosaurs didn't exist because they aren't mentioned in the Bible. You're the most levelheaded person I know."

More recently, I've come up with material about how she leaves cryptic messages to me on Facebook. She randomly posts Scripture on my page that's like, "Though I walk through the valley of the shadow of death," and then everybody worries and leaves comments saying "Praying for you!" or "Let me know if you need anything!" Her posts are either cryptic or TMI—there's no in-between. She used to not understand how social media worked and that everyone could see the Internet, so she posted as if she was texting. "I made a good lasagna last night. It was *so* good, but it made me gassy. K, call me later." Now she's pretty good at it. She can do hashtags, and she comments on all my friends' posts. The other joke I do is that people say the phrase "I'm becoming my mother" and they're annoyed by it. I'm the opposite. I could only wish to be more like my mom, because she cares a little bit more than I do. She always has a fresh new haircut, wears accessories, and has long nails with different Cardi B designs on them every week. I think my mom is actually cooler than me. She was on TikTok before I was, and she knows all the newest TV shows. I guarantee you she's on season 3 of a show you haven't even heard about yet.

My mom is too humble to toot her own horn, so a few years ago we bought her a horn—attached to a brand-spanking-new car. I wanted to show my appreciation for all she'd done for me, and also apologize for sharting on her old green Toyota Camry station wagon (again, not a literal shart). We blindfolded her and surprised her at the dealership with a Lexus SUV. It had a red bow on it and everything. It still blows my mind that we were able to do such a special thing for her.

So if you see her around town, give her a honk and a wave. She'll either think you're tryna fight or she'll invite you over. (Mom, please don't invite strangers over.)

CHAPTER 4

I Love Jesus, but
I Will Punch a Ho

In the beginning, my family didn't go to church every Sunday. I didn't grow up religious, but for some reason I was the only child my parents made go through Catholic catechism. I guess they figured I would need the most help. If I remember correctly, I was really into eating the communion wafer, maybe because I was hungry? I'm guessing I didn't understand the symbolism of eating the body of Christ (I still have a hard time with that idea). Like, what part of the body are we working with here? Two-piece leg and thigh? Do we get sides with it?

My Catholic teachings were short-lived. My parents' divorce was—ahem—frowned upon by the Catholic church, so they left for greener mangers. They of course knew about Jesus, but they weren't properly introduced until they both were in a broken place, hurting and looking for help. Post-divorce is when they fully turned to and embraced Christianity. They finally agreed on something—just not together. My parents started going to two separate Christian churches every Sunday, at a minimum.

My dad used to party, carouse, and get in fights a lot, but then he gave his life to Jesus, "got saved," and changed his ways. He did a 180 and went the devout route. With my dad, it was all or nothing, almost in the same way an addict can't have a drink because if they take one sip, it's a one-way ticket to blackout city. To be a Christian, you can't sin. Well, you can, because the whole free will thing; you just shouldn't. Which is hard sometimes because some of the most popular sins are super fun. And all those things he used to do were sins.

Suddenly, we couldn't listen to the radio or "worldly music," meaning anything other than Christian music. When regular people say "worldly," that means you're well traveled. But to Christians, *worldly* equals sinner. On weekends with my dad, when we tooled around town in his little Nissan Sentra with tint bubbles all over the windows (he probably had a coupon for a cheap tint job), Tupac's "All Eyez on Me" was out, Chris Tomlin's "Amazing Grace" was in. My dad would pop in a cassette tape of Christian children's music, and I would listen to my favorite song about Samson and Delilah four hundred times in a row, smiling as I sang about how love is a lie and you can't trust anyone, especially the one you love most, because they will ultimately betray you and let people beat you up and make you go blind. You know, kid stuff.

My dad's favorite Christian bookstore was a frequent destination for an afternoon of fun. We perused all kinds of Christian paraphernalia—books, music, bumper stickers, and clothes. He splurged on T-shirts that altered famous brands to be super Christian, like the one where the Lexus logo became "Jesus" in their signature font, or the Harley-Davidson logo was changed to "Holy Risenson." My sister got a sweet vintage rock tee that looked like Guns N' Roses' *Appetite for*

Destruction but it said "Resurrection" and Jesus replaced Axl Rose's and Slash's skulls on a cross. My guess is neither Axl nor Slash signed off on that modification.

My dad picked a really small, really white, really vanilla church to go to because it was close to the house. It was a total snoozefest. Literally, half the congregation would be asleep by the time the tithe bucket was passed around, conveniently. Apparently having any fun at all anywhere was a sin now. Although one takeaway I got from that church was a song I still sing in the shower, a remake of "Louie Louie" that went, "A Pharaoh Pharaoh, oh baby, let my people go!"

My mom, on the other hand, was less strict, and with her we could listen to Tupac or Too Short, no problem. She joined a charismatic megachurch called the Jubilee Christian Center attended by three thousand people of every stripe of the rainbow—Black, Asian, Filipino, Mexican—and run by Pastors Dick and Carla Bernal. I loved them and their son (more on him later—stay tuned). The youth group pastors, Mike and Marie Cantwell, were my favorite, though. They had three angelic, athletic, handsome sons. The youngest, Benji, rode motorcycles, recorded his own Christian music, and loved the Lord. Everyone adored him.

Church with my mom was like a Holy Spirit extravaganza. They had an awesome band and worship team with Pastor Brian Waller as the worship leader. He was super charismatic and so fun to watch. He would lead the church to a state of joy that was almost tangible. They brought in traveling preachers like televangelist Benny Hinn. He was the best of the best, so we only got him once. At our services, people spoke in tongues, and our guest pastors, who had the spirit all the way in them, gave prophetic words to the congregation and laid healing hands on the sick. It was so exciting to witness a medical miracle. Like the time the pastor brought up a limping man who couldn't bend his knee and prayed that God would fix it. Suddenly the guy ran back and forth across the stage like a gazelle. Or when the preacher closed his eyes, proclaimed "Someone over here has a pain in their right ear!" and waved his arm vaguely to the right side of the church. Then a voice cried out, "I just felt my ear pop open! I couldn't hear out of this ear before today and now it's clear! Praise Jesus!"

My favorite was when the pastor would slay people in the Holy Spirit with his hand or blow on them and they'd "faint." I'd probably faint too if old-man coffee breath blew in my face. From the outside looking in I'm sure it looked so theatrical, but I don't think they actually planted people in the audience or gave them twenty bucks to fake it. (I would have done it for $15, though.) I'm sure a lot of these people really did feel the power of God. If I got called to the altar and got slayed, you better believe I fell back like a rag doll, resting in the spirit. I'm not gonna lie, sometimes I didn't feel it in my soul, but I still pretended and went with it because sometimes I didn't want to make a scene and other times the secret actress in me really enjoyed making a scene. Also if I didn't fall back and everybody else did I wouldn't want people to think it was because I was sinning on my off time. Everybody had their reasons.

At first, we went to church because my mom made us and we had no choice, but then we enjoyed going and wanted to go. It switched from "we have to be here" to "I can't wait to see my friends and that cute boy who looks like a cholo." And then I actually wanted to learn about it all. Most Sundays, I went to the youth group while my mom went to the regular main service. Sometimes I would stay in the main service with my mom, and I remember one sermon that really stuck with me. Pastor Dick was speaking about the importance of one's name. He mentioned that a lot of the names in the Bible had an *ah* at the end, as in Jonah, Isaiah, Elijah, and Sarah. He said the *ah* was the sound of God even in other religions, as in Yahweh, Allah, Buddha, and Krishna. So having the *ah* in your name meant that you were connected to God. That was my aha moment—the day I went from Angela to Anjelah. I changed the spelling of my name to show that I was connected to God. I figured since I was changing my spelling I might as well get real cute with it, so I switched out the *g* for a *j* because that would make the first three letters of my name my initials. ANJ for Anjelah Nicole Johnson.

As I got older, though, and went through my teenage mutant chola phase, I was torn between the two worlds. I did midweek Bible studies and services and went on a lot of camping trips with our youth pastors. I really enjoyed that church life, but at the same time, I was wildin out with my homegirl Monica, who was teaching me some other things, like how to do crank. I had an angel on one shoulder, saying "Hmm, you probably shouldn't be doing that," and a devil on the other shoulder showing me how to make out with boys. There was a part of me that would feel bad when I was doing bad things. Like I knew better but I also wanted to be cool, and I also just really enjoyed making out with boys. As long as they brushed their teeth and spritzed some Binaca, it didn't seem like the worst thing. My dad forbade makeup. I just made sure he didn't catch me wearing it. I hid Wet n Wild eyeliners like they were rolling papers. One time when I was a teen he drove past me while I was walking home. I had makeup on, so I jumped in the bushes so he wouldn't see me. He saw me. It was like a scene from a teen action movie. Imagine, there's our protagonist walking down this busy street with cars whizzing past her. She exudes maximum chola confidence. I mean, people step out of her way when they see her coming. A guy walking past her stares for a little too long, so she flinches at him and he scurries away. Then here comes our antagonist in his Exchange Linen delivery truck. He slows down to get a better look. She sees the truck and is ready to flinch at another dude for staring too long. Right as she makes eye contact, she realizes the dude isn't a dude—he's her dad! With catlike reflexes, she throws herself into a bush with her metaphorical tail between her legs. She's so fast, there's no way her dad saw her. In the movie, this part would have for sure been in slo-mo. So, maybe go back and read it again slowly. She lets a few minutes pass to make sure he has time to drive all the way out of the neighborhood, just in case. She pops her head out from her hiding place and what does she see? Her dad pulled over, leaned up against his truck with his arms crossed, waiting for her to get up out of the bushes.

You'd think I had a whoopin' coming, but no. That was the day my dad came to terms with the fact that his daughter wore makeup and was also not great at hiding.

I drifted away from Monica as the years went on and I fell for my very first boyfriend, Paul, a seventeen-year-old cholo from the East Side. He may not have graduated high school, but lucky for him that wasn't one of my requirements. Paul was a teenage dad with a son named…Baby Paul. He was my friend Becca's brother, and the first time I went to her house and saw him, I was like, "Heyyyy," and he was like, "Yo, what's up," and the next thing I knew we were making out on Becca's bed. Sorry, Becca.

Paul was a legit cholo, and that was so exciting and dangerous to me. To be honest, he wasn't exactly the stereotypical tough guy with tattoos all over his face who looked like he was about to commit a crime. He was a skinny, funny little Mexican dude who was blind in one eye. He was in a gang, and one time we were all hanging out and something went down, and just like in *Blood In Blood Out*, they all got up, jumped in their cars, and peeled out to go "handle business." I'm still not convinced the "business" wasn't going to grab burgers at Jack in the Box. I get why that would be an emergency, though.

Paul wasn't the violent type. In fact, he was very sweet. I wasn't ready to have sex, I knew it was a big deal, and I didn't just want to give it up. I was learning a lot in church about how as Christians we were supposed to wait until we were married to have sex. They also taught us to stay pure and not even get in situations where we were awakening our sexual desires until we were married. Other than "just don't do it," there wasn't much talk in purity culture about learning and embracing your body and those feelings in a positive way. Like, should we just ignore those feelings?

Here's a hypothetical of how it felt like that conversation would go: "Okay, so when he walks in wearing a baseball cap backward and smelling like he just took a shower, you want me to pretend that my lady parts are not vibrating?"

"Yep. And whatever you do, do *not* attempt to relieve said vibration with a boy…or a girl, but that's for a whole other reason."

I for sure felt strongly about not going all the way with a boy, but I would still walk the line of what was acceptable behavior. Those were strong vibrations. Also, my friends were getting pregnant in sixth and seventh grade, and in my gut, I knew that wasn't my path. To his credit, Paul never pressured me to do anything I wasn't ready for. I was playing stepmommy at the age of fifteen, and somehow that didn't feel weird at the time, and yet I knew if my dad found out about Paul and/or Baby Paul, I'd for sure be grounded or teenage spanked or have my lip liner taken away. One time I took Paul and Baby Paul to go camping with my mom and cousins. Although everyone liked Paul and was nice to him, the look on their faces the whole time was *What the hell is Anjelah doing?*

I had no clue. I was so close to the point of no return. I'd been doing drugs, I was dating a baby daddy gangbanger, and during my first year of high school, I felt so hopeless and sad. The recipe for depression was one part teen angst, three parts hormones, two parts spiritual confusion, and the rest of the parts unexplained emotions. I was one of the best cheerleaders on the varsity squad as a freshman, but I really hated school. I remember sitting on the football field feeling deeply depressed because I could not fathom going there for three more years. *Like, I have to do this every day until I'm 18? I can't do this. I don't want to do this.* So, I dropped out of high school and got permission to do independent studies at home. I also babysat a bunch of my little cousins because everyone in the family was like, "Well, Anjelah's home, let's use her for free!"

I hit the major teen angst chapter of my life and questioned everything. My parents introduced me to Jesus so I could have a relationship with Him and fully embrace Christianity, but it sometimes frustrated me. At first I loved it, but then when I did more than sing songs and get slain in the Holy Spirit—I mean I really paid attention to the teachings—it depressed me. It all felt so overwhelming, so I shut down and pretended to have a new medical condition that caused me to have to spend the entire church service roaming the halls and eating all the free cookies, which happened to be a lot more flavorful than Christ's body. When I stuck around the service, I noticed people were raising their hands and singing, "Father God," or sometimes they called God "Daddy." I didn't get it. I felt so disconnected. Daddy? Does God also search the grocery store parking lot for receipts with $3 coupons on the back?

There were times when I was super into it and other times where I felt like an outsider. I wasn't feeling it in my soul, and I thought, *What am I doing wrong? How come you feel it and I don't feel it?* As I absorbed information, I had existential crises. I asked myself the big scary questions, like *Who is God? What happens when we die?* I remember the day that I got the call that my youth group friend Benji had been killed in a motorcycle accident. It was a loss that paralyzed our community. There were no words that could comfort anyone who knew him. He was one of God's best creations, so how was this fair? How did this make sense? Anyone dying is sad, but Benji dying felt unreal. It was all hard to process.

I questioned scripture I didn't like; I mean, what was up with Job being okay with getting a whole new family? And I struggled to figure out the practicality of implementing all of this info in my daily life. Okay, yes, I should not say cuss words, not do crank, and probably not wear clothes with my chichis hanging out, got it, check. The fact that Jesus spoke in parables really annoyed me because I wanted Jesus to just be clear, black and white: *Here's the answer, I made your decision for you, now go do the right thing.* At the end of the day I just really wanted to know that I was doing it right and God was proud of me. At the time I didn't realize that there was beauty in the gray. I didn't understand that wrestling with the mysteries is where I would find God. It was daunting to think about, and I was frustrated that there were no definitive answers.

I was living a double life and was equally drawn to both. I was fully invested in the church world and still fully invested in my cruising, partying friends. Both felt good and both felt bad, but overall, I was totally miserable. Anytime something bad happened I felt like I was being punished or I was "reaping what I had sown." Like that time I made out with a boy and the next day I got appendicitis and had to go to the hospital and have emergency surgery. I was convinced it happened because I was out ho'ing it up the night before. I prayed to God to please take the pain away, and I promised I would never even flirt with another boy again. But the doctor who was examining me was super hot, so that was a predicament. I had just told God I wouldn't flirt with boys, and this doctor was clearly flirtworthy, but also he was examining all my private parts, so that's not the optimum time to flirt...or is it? He was a doctor, though, so at least God would approve—and probably my mom, too. After my surgery, I woke up a few ounces lighter without an appendix, hoping that Dr. Hot Pants scraped out some hormones while he was in there so I could keep my promise to God.

When I was fifteen, I went to Hume Lake Christian Youth summer camp with kids from churches all over California. Our pastors said this would be a week of getting to know Jesus more and playing competitive games against other churches. Say no more, pastor, you had me at *competitive.* My dad may not have taught me all the Bible scriptures, but he sure did prepare me to annihilate anyone who stood in my way on the obstacle course. I was so bummed to leave Paul and Baby Paul for a week but also kinda relieved to get away from my same old day-to-day.

The minute I hopped on the bus, something felt different about this adventure. My church was very diverse and ethnic, with Filipino, Black, and Mexican kids, and my church friends didn't feel like strangers. They were people that I had really enjoyed hanging out with and getting to know. They happened to love Jesus, and I immediately felt in my spirit *I can roll with you guys.*

By the time we got to Hume Lake, we'd already become a powerful, connected tribe. As we got off the bus, all wearing camo T-shirts with black war paint under our eyes, I felt the shocked and awed stares of our fellow campers from ten other churches. We were very fierce and very 'hood, and they were mostly conservative vanilla white kids from the suburbs.

We all attended morning worship together; ate breakfast, lunch, and dinner together; then, after supper, hit the chapel for another service together. In my cabin, before bed, I prayed with my new roommates. I vividly remember the night I truly felt the genuine love of God for the first time. The lights were out, and we were all lying in our beds, praying aloud with each other. Suddenly it felt like the Holy Spirit fell on us. We all started laughing and laughing, and getting louder and louder, and we couldn't stop. The spirit of laughter fell on us, and we couldn't control it. Our pastor's wife came in and ordered us to go to bed, but we could not stop laughing. We just kept going and going and going. We were high, but not on the drugs—on the Jesus.

Experiences like that—which transcended words and meaning—kept happening at the camp. I have so many amazing memories from really encountering God there. I had all these intense feelings, and I embraced them. I felt like *Whoa, this is joy. This is powerful. This is love. This is good.* I found my people, and it changed my life. The laughing, the competing, the bonding, the praying—it all opened my eyes. This was way bigger than partying. It was a deeper connection, the one I'd been searching for my whole life.

My epiphany led me to the realization that I had to make some big decisions. I had to change my ways, and I needed to break up with Paul and Baby Paul when I got home. Even though we weren't doing bad things (technically), I just knew he wasn't the one for me.

I got home from camp and immediately broke up with Paul, and from that moment, I was on my way. When I found my faith, I made a swift U-turn. I really started living my life focused on how a Christian would live. Not super religious like my dad, where I couldn't listen to Britney Spears. But I wasn't going to drink or do drugs anymore, and I definitely was going to save myself for marriage. As I got even more invested in church and learning about God, soon enough the teen angst disappeared and probably found some other victim roaming the halls of high school. I was now becoming a young adult with Jesus on my side helping me navigate the next season of my life. I had no idea what was in store for me and how incredible it would be, but I'm glad my guide had some help from God…Or he was God… Half God…K, I still didn't fully understand that part.

Little did I know how instrumental my new faith would be on the next part of my life's journey. I was basically a born-again virgin headed to one of the most sinful places on planet earth: Hollywood.

CHAPTER 5

The One Where I Almost Gave Up

When I announced I was moving to Hollywood, my dad told me it was a stupid idea, and my mom said, "I'll believe it when I see it." My sister, Veronica, was the only one who was like, "Yes, do it, go for it!" She told me she saw what I was capable of with the Raiderettes, and that she knew LA was the place where I'd blossom and my talents could be put to best use. A sister is like a great bra—totally supportive.

With my sister's blessing (only), I moved to LA at the tender age of twenty. I didn't step off a Greyhound bus and casually run into Steven Spielberg on the corner of Hollywood and Vine, only to be cast in his next blockbuster film alongside Tom Hanks and Meryl Streep. Remember, I drove my mom's old green Camry past downtown LA to Monrovia, where I moved into my cousin Joe's three-story condo. This wasn't part of the fantasy, living in a city where one of the top attractions on its tourism page was a Massage Envy. But it didn't matter. Living in Monrovia, I was just twenty-three miles and a three-hour commute in rush-hour traffic away from turning my secret childhood pipe dream into a real possibility.

Joe is my cousin, but he's not my blood cousin. He's the married in but not actually married baby daddy to my cousin Celena. At the time Joe was Enemy #1 to a certain faction of my family, but I was close to both of them, so I was Switzerland.

Joe and I formed a special bond. He was like a big brother/dad figure for me. He was a very big guy. His radio DJ names were Big Joe and Joe Grande for a reason. And I'm a tiny girl, but we ate the same amount of food. He made huge breakfasts—bacon, chorizo and eggs, potatoes, leftovers from the night before, and whatever else was in the fridge—and I ate everything he did. Joe was fond of cornering me in the garage, grabbing me in a bear hug so I couldn't escape, and suffocating me with swampy sewage farts all while laughing maniacally. I felt like I was dying at the hands/farts of a crazy man. That was his way of showing love, and I loved him right back, only my farts were cute.

Joe was a recovering addict and didn't drink, and I was a recovering teenager who didn't drink because I didn't actually like the taste of alcohol yet. Yes, I drank as a teenager, but I pretended to like it for the cool factor. Plus, I was still into being super Chrish and just trying to get it right. Joe and I were great sober companions, and he took me everywhere with him, including my first fancy premiere for a real Hollywood movie. I bumped into The Rock coming out of the bathroom, and we exchanged sexy glances. When I told Joe later, he said, "Oh yeah, he asked me about you."

"Shut up!" I said and pushed him. Was this my new life? Do I go to movie premieres and make flirty eyes with celebrities now?

"He did, I swear!" Joe insisted.

That was the only high I needed, and I rode that for about a year, telling anyone who asked (and anyone who didn't) that I eye banged The Rock.

Joe was a local celebrity and took me to his paid appearances at all the hottest nightclubs. His job was basically to take the DJ's mic and scream, "Yo! Who's having a good time tonight?" Then while the whole club went "Woooooo!" we popped tabs on our Rockstar Energy drinks, cheers'd each other, and downed them like truck drivers pulling an all-nighter. That was our idea of raging. Joe mingled and I danced until closing time, then on the way home at three a.m., we stopped at Alfredo's and went ham on their chicken tacos. To be clear there was no ham in the tacos, but if there was, we probably would have eaten it.

Sometimes we had company, because the ladies loved Joe Grande. I was always like, *Daaaaang, how do you snag the hottest chicks?* Joe wasn't ugly; he was just this gigantic Mexican dude who's not typically every hot girl's wildest dream. Do you want a guy with abs or a guy who can make you a bangin' breakfast and not judge you when you eat the whole thing? Women loved Joe because he was charming and had bright green eyes and lashes as long and lush as an Instagram influencer who just gave you her swipe up code for 10 percent off some detox tea.

Joe's harem of hunnies came over to the condo on the regular. I didn't care as long as they didn't use my Caress body wash. You can bring your own toiletries, ladies. (Caress body wash now reminds me of my dreamer self and of that season of my life when I was playful and a risk taker. I don't use it anymore, but every now and then if I smell it, it takes me right back to that condo.) Unlike Joe, during that time, I wasn't really dating that much yet, but I was known to be a serial cuddler or "cuddle whore," as Joe dubbed me, with whoever was down to drive to Monrovia. If you were ready for a night of hugging and leg pretzeling, I was your girl.

Joe's condo was *the* after-hours hotspot in the greater San Gabriel Valley. My bedroom window overlooked the front door, and sketchy people rang that darn bell at all hours. I'd go wake up a snoring Joe at four a.m., shake him, and whisper, "Somebody's at the front door!"

"They'll leave," he would mumble, then he would roll over and go back to sawing logs.

I rarely had my own visitors from LA, though one time a friend came to visit me, but she ended up sleeping in Joe's room, so I think she really came to visit him. The weekend turned into me sitting on the couch folding laundry and listening to George Lopez's stand-up albums on CD.

This was the first time I became a fan of stand-up comedy. Well, the second time. When I was younger I used to watch BET's *Comic View* with my sister, and we loved it. I just never really paid attention to the fact that this was a thing called "stand-up comedy." To me it was just a funny show we watched. Joe turned me on to George Lopez, and I listened to his CD frequently. I really resonated with George, because I could hear my own stories in his life. I loved his special *Why You Crying?* I always quoted him saying, "Right now, right now" and anything having to do with his grandmother. I loved his joke about how his grandmother timed her medicine according to her TV shows. George said, "One time somebody changed the channel on her, and she said, 'I couldn't breathe.'" Still makes me laugh out loud.

I missed my family so much back in San Jose, but I was learning how to be a grown-up. It was my first time living away from my mom and my first time paying rent.

Joe met a lot of famous friends through his job, including Noel "Noel G" Gugliemi, a character actor probably best known as Hector from the *Fast and the Furious* franchise. He was Hollywood's go-to cholo, and he's been in practically every SoCal gangster movie and TV show ever made, including both the movie and TV versions of *Training Day*. Little did I know when I watched *Training Day* back when I was young and thought, *I could do that*, that I'd end up meeting one of the lead cholos of the movie. It was an aspiring chola's dream come true. Noel also starred in *Fresh Off the Boat* and *Bruce Almighty* and a million other things. If there's a TV show or movie character named Hector, it's probably played by Noel G.

Noel offered to help me "update" my Hollywood resume. I had zero credits to my name, but I couldn't walk into auditions with a blank piece of paper. So I asked him, "How do you build a resume?"

"In order to get TV credits, you gotta have TV credits," Noel explained, as if this made any sense.

"What? How does that even work?" I asked naïvely.

"You lie," he said, like he was telling me what he had for breakfast that day (probably not as much as Joe and me).

Noel told me to copy his resume of actual projects that he really did, cross out his character name, and make up a girl's name instead. "I played Hector, so you just say you played Linda."

Easy enough. So that's what I did, and I'd like to come clean right now and confess that my whole career was built on deception. Linda was a liar, but a damn good one. Oh, I also added in a stage production of *A Streetcar Named Desire*. I'd never actually done the play, but I read one scene from it in my tiny acting class in junior college. You better believe I put that on my resume. My totally fake resume. Typically I don't condone lying, but these ones didn't feel like they were hurting anyone, so I still felt like I was a good Christian. Or at least a medium one.

Ultimately, my made-up dramatic turn as Stelllllaaaaaaaa was not the key to getting my foot in the door; it was my legit job as an Oakland Raiderette cheerleader. Just a month after I moved in with Joe was when the stars aligned and I landed that gig as an extra on *Friends*.

For two glorious, magical years, I worked on one of the most popular TV shows in history. At the time, it was the hottest show on NBC's Thursday night "Must See TV" lineup. The cast were the biggest stars on the planet, and I was friends with all of them. In my mind.

I'll never forget walking onto the set on my first day and seeing with my starstruck eyes the guys' apartment, the girls' apartment, and Central Perk. So surreal. I felt so grateful to actually be there, then I felt like I was actually gonna throw up because I had zero experience or training as an extra. Do extras even need training? Did I miss the instructions on how to be an extra because I got to cut the line thanks to my Raiderette headshot? I had absolutely no idea what I was doing. Just like when I was around a lot of Spanish-speaking people, I did more listening than talking. I watched this one girl get in trouble for trying to talk to Jennifer Aniston backstage. The assistant director appeared out of thin air like the wicked witch in *The Wizard of Oz* and shooed her away with his broomstick/clipboard. I didn't want to be that girl. I knew not to do that. I never saw that extra again.

I wasn't there to make friends anyway (except for Rachel, Monica, Phoebe, Joey, Ross, and Chandler, of course). I was there to learn and then to call everyone I've ever met to tell them I touched the Central Perk couch. I basically took free acting classes from Jennifer Aniston, Courteney Cox, Lisa Kudrow, David Schwimmer, Matt LeBlanc, and Matthew Perry—of course, they didn't know they were my teachers. They were busy starring in the show as I sat at a table in the background miming conversation with another extra or walking silently from the bathroom to Gunther's counter to order a latte. "When you hear Joey say, 'How you doin'?' that's your cue," the assistant director instructed.

If you made a peep during rehearsal, they stopped you really quickly. "We hear whispering!" a boom mic operator would yell out, annoyed. And they'd yank you offstage in a heartbeat if you were acting "the most" in the background. There was a very fine line between not sitting there like a statue and not taking attention away from the stars by gesticulating too wildly, throwing your head back for a fake laugh, or mouthing "Let's be besties" to Lisa Kudrow. "Calm down, ma'am, we don't need that," they scolded extras who just couldn't help being so extra. They were replaced, then never seen or heard from again.

Not me! I was the perfect extra. I became good friends with the second assistant director, Carlos. He was Latino (still is), I was Latino (still am), and we were both sarcastic (still are). He zinged me and I'd zing him right back. We made each other laugh, and he'd say, beaming, "You know what, I like you, I'm going to bring you back next week." Then I came back the next week, we zinged, and he'd go again, "Hey, guess what, I'm going to bring you back next week." And I kept coming back again and again and again, until the next thing I knew, I was one of the regular extras. That's when the cast started to recognize me and invited me on their smoke breaks. Well, some of them would be on a smoke break, I'd be walking by, and one of them would ask me a question, probably something like "Hey, what time is it?" and the next thing I knew I was in the middle of their conversation. I felt very important. It was as if I was the inspiration behind that episode where Rachel takes smoke breaks to try to get in good with her boss. Though that episode was in the fifth season of the show, a few years before I got there, so I guess it probably wasn't about me.

Ironically, keeping to myself is what garnered attention. Just being myself and minding my own beeswax is, I think, what made them feel safe to talk to me. The next thing I knew I was invited to the cast and crew Christmas party. A real Christmas miracle.

I rarely initiated conversations with the stars, but I can't say I never did. I remember once saying something first to Matt LeBlanc outside of the soundstage and then feeling dumb about it afterward. So, like a handmaid, I usually didn't speak unless spoken to. I'm not gonna lie, any contact with them was thrilling and a great party story. Lisa Kudrow took a bite of a teacake from the craft services table and said to me, "Mmm, these are good, right?!" Got good mileage out of that anecdote for at least a few years.

There was a hierarchy about who got to go first through the lunch line. Stars and producers went first, of course, then crew, lighting, etc., all the way down to the lowly production assistants and extras like me. One time Jennifer Aniston was late for lunch and just stood at the end of the line with the rest of us riffraff until the AD noticed the absolute horror of her pretending to be normal. "Nope, everybody move!" he commanded, as he swept her to the front of the line like a Secret Service agent. "We need you back on set ASAP!" She was so kind and gracious about it, which wasn't at all surprising considering she's a perfect human.

Chitchatting with Matt, sharing a pastry with Lisa, standing next to Jen in the era when she and Brad had the same tan and the same blond highlights—those things meant nothing to them throughout their day, but I clocked it.

During seasons 9 and 10, there might've been an episode or two that I wasn't in, but for the most part, I was there every week, hanging out in Central Perk with Joey, Phoebe, Rachel, Monica, Ross, and Chandler. Okay, maybe not *with*, but parallel to. In one episode, I even sat front and center on the famous couch miming a convo with another extra, while they all sat at a high top behind me. I guess they were going for a little bit of realism that week, like, c'mon, how could they manage to snag the only couch at a café in New York City every single time?

Pre-shoots were on Thursday and the taping was on Friday, in front of a live studio audience. That was always so fun and so energetic; the crowds were crazy hyped up. I was so pumped up too, because I got to watch these incredible comedic actors, who just happened to be the highest-paid actors on television, up close. I watched them work and process and memorize their lines and communicate with each other on screen and between scenes. I got to learn how fun it was to be on set and live your dream as an actress. I got to learn how hard it was as well, when tapings ran over six hours. When they messed up a line, how they'd recover. You could see when they got frustrated after a million takes that they still couldn't get their line. I did a lot of watching, learning, and noting how to do things. I paid attention to how they spoke and interacted with and were playful with the crew and the writers.

I got the best education an aspiring actress could hope for, and I also got my Screen Actors Guild union vouchers. Not an easy feat for a newbie, but thanks to Sam the casting director from central casting for putting me in the computer system as a SAG extra, I was eligible to get my SAG card and benefits after the first three episodes I worked. It was unreal. Other extras came up to me because they saw that I had the SAG vouchers, which looked different from non-union vouchers. "How did you join the union?" they asked, their eyes green with envy. I made something up because I didn't even understand how it worked myself. That's Linda for you.

In a way I felt like I'd already made it, even though I only earned about $115 per episode and stuffed my backpack full of craft services snacks to take home. Doing laundry at the condo, Joe really celebrated the fact that we were doing alright for ourselves. Once I got a dryer sheet and was about to put it in, when he walked up behind me, grabbed another one, and said, "What are you doing? One dryer sheet? No, no, no, no, no. You can use *two* dryer sheets now!"

My bromance with Joe was so instrumental in getting off to a good start in LA. Alas, soon it was time to move on and spread my wings. Not because of me—I would've stayed there forever. Unfortunately, within a year after I moved into the condo, Joe started dating a co-worker from the radio station and she moved in, too. She didn't hoover food like a garbage disposal, get our inside jokes, or appreciate that he dutch-ovened me and not her. Actually, she probably did appreciate that part. She also didn't find it amusing when he said,

"Hey, I smell weed," so we sniffed the air, but it was just one of Joe's silent but deadly farts he tricked us into inhaling.

One morning, I found a newspaper opened to the want ads at my spot at the breakfast table. Several apartments for rent listings were circled in red pen. "Hey, I don't know if you're interested," Joe's new lady friend said with a tight smile, "but I found some of these for you."

I could take a hint. It was fine, because I was mad at Joe anyway. We'd all gone out on a recent night and he introduced a bunch of us, including his niece, to Fernando Vargas, a famous Mexican boxer. The next morning, I overheard him on the phone say to his niece, "Fernando was asking about you." Wait, that sounded so familiar… then it all came rushing back to me. When he got off the phone, I confronted him.

"Did The Rock really ask about me!?"

Joe laughed so hard he cried. What a jerk.

I once shared this story in a TV interview and told the whole world how my cousin Joe tricked me into believing that The Rock asked about me. I tweeted the clip and tagged The Rock, to which he replied, "I'm pretty sure I asked about you." Joke's on you, Joe. I win!

I was going to miss Joe (but not his girlfriend, who later became his wife, but then they got divorced after one year and he circled apartments in red for her), but it was time to move closer to the action in Hollywood and to my friends Sandra, Maya, and Liz and my cousin Michelle. They'd all gone to Santa Clara University together and had been friends for a very long time. They were all making it happen, working as legit dancers and actors. I was barely twenty-one and broke, but I was just happy to hang out.

I'm so grateful my cousin introduced me to the 2620 crew. The address of Sandra's house, where they all lived, was 2620. I never officially moved in because it was already a full house, but I was a permanent fixture. It was our real-life Central Perk, but without the endless coffee and millions of dollars per episode.

Once again, like when I was on the Raiderettes—and my whole childhood, really—I was everyone's little sister, and they all took care of me. Sandra lent me clothes and shoes for auditions and let me have my mail sent to 2620 because Los Feliz was a way more acceptable address than Monrovia to snobby Hollywood types. Of all the girls in the house, I really bonded with Maya. People thought we looked like sisters, and she and I connected on the silliest things. I remember one day we went to see her new boyfriend Dave (who later became her husband) at his house, dressed up like cholas. We stood right in front of her not-so-chola Volkswagen Jetta in our toughest prison pose and waited for him to come outside. I think he laughed for four seconds then was like, "What are you guys doing here?" It was a great question, and the exact moment we realized the stunt bombed. We definitely thought we deserved more than four seconds of laughter. We were clearly mistaken.

It didn't matter to us if no one thought we were as hilarious as we did; we were always down for each other's stupid ideas. Like the time we drove out to a film location where Dave was shooting an independent movie. We were too tired to drive back home, so we shared a hotel room with him and like five other crew guys. It was me, Maya, Dave, and another dude squished in a bed head to toe like we were Charlie's grandparents in *Willy Wonka and the Chocolate Factory*. From then on we identified ourselves as IFCG, which stands for Independent Film Crew Groupies.

The ladies of 2620 were all young, single, and doing our thing. All the girls had dance agents, and through them I was able to sign with my very first dance agent. We worked hard and played hard. After we went out clubbing and dancing, I crashed on the couch or shared a bed with my cousin Michelle. I didn't want to miss the next morning's recap of the fun night.

We had a group of guy friends in Burbank who we referred to as the 1816 (it was a lot easier to say four numbers than seven people's names). They were all professional dancers, actors, and musicians and included future star Harry Shum Jr. We went to each other's houses for game nights and parties. We all became very close friends and were really just a bunch of twentysomethings chasing our dreams in Hollywood together. If one of us heard about an audition, we would share it with the crew. "Did you get called out for the Toyota commercial? They're looking for dancers; call your agent and tell them to get you in." We celebrated each other's victories and bookings. Anytime we saw one another in a commercial, in a music video, or on a billboard, we were all so proud. It's hard chasing a dream, but when you have a support system that celebrates your wins and picks you up after a loss, it makes it a bit easier to hang on and keep trying.

My faith was still a big part of my life, so I wasn't doing any truly crazy stuff during this season. All I was doing was looking cute, flirting, and dancing. Sometimes I exchanged numbers or made out with a boy, but it was never a *hookup* hookup. One of those times was actually at the 1816 house. Not with one of the 1816 boys, but with one of their friends who was there hanging out one night. His name was Steelo, and we had a good flirty vibe going, so much so that we ended up making out. My friend Harold saw us on the couch, and the next day he told me that he was disappointed in me because I was a good Christian girl, and he was sad to see me playing tonsil hockey with a dude. I was kind of embarrassed after that. I thought, "I can't have sex. That's bad. I can't drink or do drugs anymore. That's bad." It helped that my girls were super focused, so they drank but didn't get blackout wasted. They definitely didn't do drugs. They didn't care that I was a little prudish, especially because I was a highly coveted designated driver. I was basically Uber, but instead of getting paid, I got to sleep on my passengers' couch for free.

I think what they did care about is that I was always broke. Somebody always had to spot me when we went places. They were always going out to the hot spots, because they could afford to. They had real jobs and real money. I did not, but I wasn't going to *not* go. I couldn't live with that sort of FOMO. If we went for sushi, for example, and I couldn't afford a whole California roll, I'd just get miso soup or share whatever they were having and order a water with extra lemons so I could mix in a packet of sugar and DIY a mocktail. Thankfully, usually Sandra or someone else would say, "I got you." I also got really good at the "slow draw," a skill I inherited from my dad. He was the champion of taking forever to find his wallet. He patted down all his pockets, looked under the table, went to the bathroom, stalled, until finally his dining partner(s) reached for the check, and he'd go, "Are you sure?"

I didn't want to be a mooch my *whole* life, so I had to at least find my own place to live. I'd been praying about it every day since Joe's passive-aggressive boo asked me to leave. I wrote out the prayer in my journal to help manifest it more quickly. It said: *I want to live in Burbank. And I only want to pay $350/month. And I want to live with a family because I really miss my family.*

To supplement my *Friends* income, I got a job waitressing at Q's Billiard Club in Old Pasadena and immediately bonded with a sweet Hawaiian bartender named Kehau. I brought up my housing predicament and, miraculously, she mentioned her family had a room for rent in their house. In Burbank. For $350! I manifested this! Move over Deepak Chopra, I'll take it from here.

I knew I wanted to get plugged into a church as soon as I got to LA, so I started regularly attending services at the Oasis Church in Hollywood. Every Christian in showbiz went to this church—actors, directors, dancers—not only for its nondenominational and contemporary values and beliefs, but also because it was a place to meet people! I mean, any Christian who was looking to date another Christian would want to find them in a church, but imagine a church full of beautiful people trying to make it in Hollywood. Let's just say there may have been some backsliding going on in the congregation. Did I contribute to that atmosphere? You betcha!

I became a joiner. Every Sunday morning, I went to church at the Oasis. On Tuesdays, I went to Creative Arts Night and took advantage of the free acting, dancing, and singing classes. I became a greeter at the front door, which took me back to my job at the theme park, which was just to be charismatic and say hello to people. Finally, something on my resume I didn't have to lie about. I met so many amazing people at this church, including several new dancer friends, like Maria, Diona, and Penelope, who toured with Britney Spears and Paulina Rubio.

I later found out that Steelo was also kind of talking to Penelope. Steelo came clean and told her that he had made out with me. I didn't want her to think that I was some hussy stealing other people's men, so I called her and told her that I had no idea they were seeing each other, otherwise I would have stayed away for sure. My honesty and her vulnerability bonded us. After that, Penelope and I became good friends. Little did we know that it was the beginning of a lifelong friendship.

Through my new friends and dance agent, I booked real gigs that paid real money. The most I'd ever made in my life was $16/hour testing video games back in San Jose. True story and real job. Now I was being paid $250 to be a background dancer for the Russian lesbian pop duo t.A.T.u. at the MTV Movie Awards. I was one of a hundred schoolgirls who came prancing down the aisle through the audience wearing a plaid skirt, pigtails, and knee socks. Halfway through the performance, we took off our shirts and removed our skirts and twirled them around our heads. We were wearing wife beater tank tops and boy chonies, so we weren't nude or anything. For the grand finale, we had to kiss with our dance counterparts on the lips. I was uncomfortable with that part and so was my partner, so we ended in a hug and hid our faces.

My conservative Christian dad was not happy. He called me and didn't even try to hide his disappointment and disgust. "Hey, what are you doing out there?"

My dad also didn't appreciate my cameo in an Eminem/D12 music video, where I played a groupie double-fisting champagne flutes while a naked stripper slid down a pole behind me. He didn't realize how important it was to network with my fellow groupies. We were all, "What audition are you going on next?" but my dad was all, "What kind of decisions are you making?"

Maybe my new Hawaiian family wasn't thrilled with my new line of work, either, because not long after I got there, they asked me to leave. I'm really not sure what happened, but apparently I overstayed my welcome again. Maybe I drank too much of their acai out of the refrigerator without asking? At least I didn't dutch-oven anyone… that I'm aware of. All I know is that Kehau's parents were very good to me while I was there. They opened up their home and allowed me to get comfortable and be a part of their family.

One time I was fasting food and only drinking water, a common practice in the Christian faith. "Man shall not live by bread alone, but by every word that proceeds from the mouth of God" (Matthew 4:4). Well, Kehau's mom came running out to my car as I was about to drive to an audition and brought me a protein shake. She didn't want me to pass out while driving. Such a momma bear. I didn't drink it, because Matthew, but still, so thoughtful. They eventually informed me they'd be renting out my room to their niece, stat, and politely told me mahalo and goodbye, which translated to "kick rocks, Anjelah."

When *Friends* came to an end after season 10, I was so bummed. Yes, because I wouldn't be going to set anymore, but also because it was my favorite show and I, like every other twentysomething, thirtysomething, fortysomething, and probably all the way to ninety-something, never wanted it to end. We did a series finale watch party at the 2620, and I'm pretty sure we all cried as though we were mourning the loss of a best friend. We kind of were.

By this time, I had bounced around a little. I lived at Maria's house with Diona and Penelope. Eventually Penelope started doing so well in her career dancing for every music artist you can think of that she was able to buy her own condo in Glendale, and I moved in with her. This would be the second of many times to come where Penelope and I ended up living together. And from there, through a little bit of luck, a lot of divine intervention, and a ton of hustle, I started booking things like crazy. Sometimes when you're desperate, you have nothing to lose, and for me that fearlessness kick-started a truly prolific time in my career.

Maya, from the 2620 house, had an audition for a Sprint commercial. I wasn't invited but I showed up with her anyway because I fit the casting breakdown, too. This is called crashing an audition. It's tacky, but I didn't care. I wrote my name on the list, threw my headshot in the pile, and was shocked when they called me in without checking if I was actually supposed to be there. Well, that's the day I booked my first national commercial. Maya wasn't mad at me; she was happy for me. That's a true friend.

After that booking, I was a machine—Dreyer's Ice Cream and Snickers commercials; print ads for K-Swiss and Visa. I was on such a roll, I once walked into an audition and a competitor threw her hands in the air and said, "Forget it! Everybody go home! Anjelah's here."

I was killing it and working like a fiend. Carlos, the *Friends* second AD, took me to his next job on the UPN show *Love, Inc.*, starring Busy Philipps and Holly Robinson Peete, and promoted me into a new job, as the stand-in for Ion Overman. I got a fancy pass with my picture on it, I wore a sign that said Ion's name, I stood on her marks, and I said her lines right before they said "action!" Saying my own lines would have been better, but inch by inch I was getting closer to my goal.

The show taped on the Paramount lot, and on my drive to work I bumped praise and worship and gospel music as loud as my car would let me. I remember parking on the street outside the studio, and a lady standing in her front yard smiled and said, "You go, girl!" She clearly appreciated my commitment to Jesus and letting everyone within a one-mile radius know about it.

I felt so special. I had a real job in the real entertainment industry. Unfortunately, *Love, Inc.* was canceled after one season, but it had a lasting impact on me. Five very important things happened while I was on this job:

1. I learned how to walk in heels—and my teacher was none other than the prototype for the sultry Jessica Rabbit! She worked on the *Love, Inc.* crew, and if I remember correctly, her husband was one of the animators for Disney who helped create the iconic cartoon character for *Who Framed Roger Rabbit*. I mean, that's the story she told me. She could have been lying, but that is a very specific and creative lie to come up with. It was before the days of smartphones, so it's not like I could easily fact-check her. Also, I didn't care. I was just excited to finally learn how to not look like a camel when I walked in heels. I never knew how because I was a tomboy and I was bowlegged. I brought in a pair of heels, and on our lunch break, she practiced with me, up and down the set. I appreciated her deeply; however, I was not a success story for her because I still opt for tennis shoes any chance I get. Although I can at least wear heels now without ending up in the ER, so that's a win.

2. I bought my first brand-new car, a Nissan Altima, which was dropped off on the Paramount lot, like I was a big shot or

something. (I think Nissan probably wanted the free advertising to all the big stars, as if they'd see the car and be like, "Nissan Altima! I *need* one of those!") Thoughts and prayers for the green Toyota Camry station wagon, which broke down on the side of the 405 and was never seen or heard from again.

3. I started taking my first stand-up/joke-writing class at Oasis Church because it was free. After working on the show during the day, I would head over to the church for an evening class of setups and punchlines.

4. I got my first real TV credit! On the very last episode of the series, the cast rallied around me and asked the director to give me a small co-star role as a client of the dating agency. I walked into the office and Reagan Gomez-Preston's character asked me what I was going to wear on my big date, and I said, "A little black dress," and she said, "Well, you better wear this deodorant" and held up a super-popular deodorant that paid the TV show to mention it, but they're not paying me to mention it, so I shall leave you wondering. They got their product placement in, and I got my very first line ever on a TV show. It was official. I was headed for the Golden Globes. In my mind.

5. In sadder news, I witnessed my first E! True Hollywood (tragic) Story. Another stand-in, this really nice guy, reeked of booze every day. I was always amazed at how functional he was, because he definitely had a problem. One day, not long after the show was over, I saw him stumbling down Hollywood Boulevard. He was obviously homeless now, and it broke my heart.

I remember driving through Hollywood wondering who all these people who lived on the streets were and what their story was. Why were they here in Hollywood? Like, did they come here chasing a dream like me, get caught up, and now were on the streets? What happened? Did they not have a Joe, a Sandra, a Maria, a Penelope, or a friendly Hawaiian family to help?

I learned how fickle it all was. In showbiz, what goes up must come down…for everyone. Showbiz doesn't care who you are. For two years I rode the high of my beginner's luck only to see it all come crashing down. I went through some really humbling and humiliating moments.

When it came to my income, I learned that being in entertainment was feast or famine. I could be making serious bank, then be totally broke, then a $723 residual check for a commercial would magically appear in my mailbox.

I happened to be cash poor when I booked a role in a Kanye West pilot (way before he was a Kardashian), and I didn't have the $1,700 AFTRA union fee required to work on the show. I called everyone I knew crying hysterically, including my dad, who yelled at me for scaring him thinking I was in prison or dead, and was able to raise the money in the nick of time. But the day before we filmed, I got a call that my part had been cut. Classic move, Hollywood. I couldn't give the money back because I already used it to join the union, and now I had no paycheck to pay people back. Kanye owes my family and friends an explanation and a reimbursement.

Another time I auditioned for my first dramatic role on *The Shield*. I'm embarrassed to say I was still using my fake resume at this point. At the audition, the casting director read it as I stood in front of her.

"Wow, you were on *CSI*?"

"Yep, mm-hmm," I lied.

"That's funny," she said, "because I cast that show. I don't remember you."

Now, what would you do in this situation? Would you come clean and be like, "Ah, you got me! I was trying to see if you'd catch it!" Or would you just double down? Well, I doubled down.

"You don't remember me, girl? Oh my God, this is so you. You always do this! Okay. Remember I came in wearing a cute shirt and you were like, 'Where did you get that?' And I was like, 'Oh, Forever 21!'"

Clearly, she knew I was lying, but she let me audition anyway. Guess what, I booked it. I guess my reaction to getting busted was the real audition because she decided I was perfect to play the part of a homeless teenager. It had always been my dream gig to play a victim on *SVU*. This was close enough.

I had two lines, "You got a cigarette?" and "Nah, I'm no snitch." This was obviously going to be my chance to snag my first Golden Globe nod for guest supporting role, so I threw a big viewing party at Penelope's condo. All our friends were there. We had pizza, soda, and ice cream, so this party was raging Christian style.

My scene was the very last one in the episode because they save the best for last, that's how it works in Hollywood, I think? But an hour later, the last scene came and went, then as the credits got pushed into a tiny corner of the TV screen, the ten o'clock local newscasters popped up.

"Coming up tonight, a car chase turns deadly in Van Nuys…"

Wait—how are you going to hear my part if they're already talking? My award-winning acting had been eighty-sixed, relegated to the graveyard by cruel editors, who for sure had no idea they destroyed my hopes and dreams. But I knew, and so did all my friends and every stranger I told earlier that day at Target.

My friends were so supportive: "It's okay, that episode was dumb anyway." "I'm sure you were so good though." "Honestly I never watch this show, I don't think anyone does, so who cares!" You would think that would have been the most embarrassing part of the night, but I would say it was when everyone was leaving and I had to thank them for coming to my viewing party. "Bye guys, thanks for coming to view a TV show I wasn't in! I'll get it next time, am I right?!" Cue awkward laughter.

Then there's a slightly stalker moment that I'm not proud of. I was driving in Beverly Hills and I saw *Friends* creator Marta Kauffman walk into a 7-Eleven with her kid. I made a quick U-turn into the parking lot and ran inside, you know, in case she wanted to put me in something else, anything else, she was working on. "I have to say hi to her!" the dreamer in me insisted to myself.

I walked up and down the aisles, pretending like I wanted to buy something even though I didn't have any money to buy anything. She got in line to pay, and I came up behind her.

"Are you Marta Kauffman?"

"Yes?"

"Oh, hi. I was an extra on *Friends*!" I was very proud to be an extra on *Friends*.

She was a little weirded out and held her child a little closer. I didn't really know what to say after that, so I just walked out without buying anything like a creeper.

Suddenly, my turn as the it girl for commercials fizzled, and my career began to look like I was a has-been who hadn't even fully been yet. After *Love, Inc.* got canceled, Carlos didn't have a job either. He was my guy, the one who took me wherever he went. Now I didn't have a shoo-in anywhere. No stand-in gigs, nada. When my unemployment checks ran out, I went back to waitressing at any restaurant that would hire me.

Another friend from church owned a successful princess party company. She sent different Disney princesses to rich Hollywood kids' birthday parties. She hired me because I needed the cash, and which pretty lady do you think she let me be? Pocahontas? Jasmine? Wrong. She did not let me be a princess at all. I was a clown, and not the kind with the big honking red nose. I was one of those creepy porcelain dolls from the 1800s. I was that clown.

One time, I got my period and had the worst cramps and was nauseous. I could barely get out of bed, but you can't call in sick to a kid's birthday party, like *I'm sorry, Timmy, we're going to have to reschedule because the clown has cramps.* I mustered up the strength to show up but had white makeup running down my face the whole time because I was sweaty and crying. I was a sad clown and a child's worst nightmare. The kind of clown that scarred kids for life. Although, that's probably all clowns.

I also worked for a company that hired DJs and dancers for kids' birthday parties and bar/bat mitzvahs in these gated communities where there was a parking lot just for the house staff. A four-year-old's birthday party I worked at had a Pink's Hot Dogs truck and a dance floor, and it was my job to get all the shy kids up and having fun. I was really good at it, and it paid pretty well, too, like $200 per day and a free hot dog every now and then.

I was basically a go-go dancer for kids, which is similar to being a go-go dancer for adults, but replace the cocktails with juice boxes. It still wasn't enough money to afford my $900/month rent, but Penelope, bless her heart, said, "I got you." She was still raking it in as a professional touring dancer, so instead of donating her tithe to the Oasis Church, I became her charity. "My offering to God will be helping you out this month," she said to me on more than one occasion.

At this point, I got dropped by my dance agent and had no auditions and no income. There's a fine line between trusting your gut and being delusional. At that point, nothing in my life signaled *You're on the right track! Keep going!* It signaled *You gave it your best shot. Now go home and get yourself a Charleston Chew.*

CHAPTER 6

I'm Dating You Because I'm Hungry

A couple things stopped me from going back home to San Jose: I felt in my gut, in my spirit, that God was telling me, "Hold on. I know it doesn't look good, but you're not done yet." I also still had a roof over my head, thanks to Penelope and my sister, who sent me rent money and gift cards to the grocery store so I wouldn't be hungry. It's not like Veronica was rich or anything, so sending me that money was a sacrifice she chose to make. She believed in me, and when I was ready to give up, she wouldn't let me. Plus, the papas rellenas at Porto's Bakery in Burbank were too good to leave behind.

Still, money was tight and seemed to evaporate into thin air as soon as it landed in my bank account. Like the time I had to pay out of pocket for my car window to get replaced. You see, here's what had happened. I left my purse on the front seat of my car, like a dummy, and someone broke in while I was at the gym. Because of course they did. Not only did they steal my wallet, but they also made off with literally every accessory I owned, because the day before, I worked as an extra on a TV show and was asked to bring accessory options, so I brought my entire closet and then left everything in my car. Like a dummy.

A blossoming young ingenue can only survive on ramen and Cheerios for so long without breaking down and breaking out from all that sodium and sugar. My diet has since improved, but my pimples, not so much. I'm not ashamed to admit that I relied on the kindness of strangers for a healthy diet beyond soup and cereal. And when I say strangers, I mean men. I'd get asked on a date and think, *I don't really like you that much, but I am hungry. So, yes I will go to Chili's with you on Thursday…and Friday too if you're up for dessert. Not the sexy-time type of dessert—actual dessert. Molten chocolate cake à la mode, please.*

I went through this season where I felt like God was telling me to stop dating just because I was hungry. That I didn't really have respect for the act of dating, and I leaned on men to provide for me. God was trying to get through to me to say, "Hey, why don't you turn to me for that? Let me provide that security for you."

At first, I ignored this gut feeling.

One time at church, a cute guy made eyes at me during the service and I made eyes back, but like in a cartoon when they turn into swirling hypnotic circles while he turns into a pork chop. Neither of us was rich by any means; we were both struggling in LA trying to follow our dreams and make it happen. When he asked me out, he suggested that we attend another service together and grab a bite afterward. Perfect plan, very romantic, spiritual, and thoughtful. But the sermon ran really long and by the time it was over, all the good restaurants had shut down for the night. He was ready to just take me home, but I wasn't having it. I'm sorry, sir, but we had a verbal agreement, and that legally binding verbal contract clearly stated "church *and a meal.*"

So, I had him take me through a Taco Bell drive-thru. I could tell he was a little annoyed because he didn't even order food. He just got it for me and then dropped me off. Afterward, I felt a little gross from my actions…and from the three regular tacos, Nachos BellGrande, and cinnamon twists I shoveled into my mouth. I never saw him again, but that definitely wasn't my last date with Taco Bell, even though it should have been.

Another guy I met on the set of *Love, Inc.* invited me to go grab a bite at the Café, the legendary Paramount commissary. Buffet plus a possible sighting of Dr. Phil or the cast of *Girlfriends*? Yes, please! Unfortunately, after we got back to the set, he told people we went on a date. Oh no no, I'm not about kissing and telling, especially at work, and especially when there's no kissing, only sandwiching. So, I denied him. "That wasn't a date," I insisted, and I could tell he was devastated I shot him down. I felt kinda bad…but that was probably indigestion from wolfing down the Veronica Lake turkey club like an animal.

I don't mean to be cold and callous about my generous suitors. I probably should've stopped by Dr. Phil's set to dig deep into my psyche for the reasons behind my questionable behavior. Maybe I was more like my dad than I thought. My dad had a lot of lady friends but never called them his girlfriend. I had commitment issues, and I was selfish without realizing it. During this time of my life, my friends in the 2620 house dubbed me Taranjelah because all the boys got caught in my web. While Penelope and her boyfriend Steelo, also a dancer, were touring the world, Taranjelah was bored, lonely, and restless. So Taranjelah turned into a dating machine, the kind of machine that didn't have sex and cuddled a lot.

My assortment of boos was pretty random. I dated all kinds of guys, every stripe and color of the rainbow. Black, white, Latino, different kind of Latino, Asian, different kind of Asian, Indian, tall, short, fat, skinny. I didn't have a physical type. I don't know if this is something to be proud of. Having no discerning taste whatsoever could go either way. I'll let you decide.

I didn't have a type to the point where I thought I was going to end up marrying somebody super ugly because I cared so little about looks. (Spoiler alert: I didn't.) If I was gonna fall in love with a man, it would be for the right reasons, like their heart or their personality. I'd much rather be with a guy with a big nose or acne scars than a hot guy who was totally boring. If you had a neck goiter but were charming? You were golden. But also maybe get that checked out?

Cosmo may have had a list of "31 Things That Instantly Make Men Hot," but I could pare my ideal man down to five prerequisites:

1. Was willing to provide food and nonalcoholic beverages.
2. Was good at something. Could be playing an instrument, could be building a shelf, could be riding a unicycle.
3. Had to smell good. I loved when a guy smelled like he just took a shower and put on a really good deodorant—but did *not* drench himself in cologne. I used to wear Eternity for Men in junior high, and I didn't want to make out with someone who smelled like me when I was twelve. Plus, I have a very sensitive nose. I have a supernatural ability to smell when a guy's about to have bad breath. Like, maybe he doesn't have bad breath yet, but he's gonna in about three minutes. My nose is just that intuitive. When I lived with Penelope at her condo, I always thought things smelled bad. She'd be like, "Where's my milk?" And I'd say, "Oh, I threw it out, it smelled bad." She'd cry, "I just bought that!" New rule: I was not allowed to throw away groceries anymore.
4. Had to make me laugh.
5. Had to laugh at my jokes.

I'd gotten hit on by all types of guys. I loved a good compliment as much as the next gal, but there were a few things I noticed about the way guys would hit on me. Cue popular joke from my first hour special that I am fully aware is based on stereotypes: It was seemingly specific to their ethnicity. For example, some Black guys like to describe you when they flirt with you. Like, "Hey, blue shirt, how you doin'?" One time I went to a Prince concert at the Staples Center with Penelope, and we thought we were so cute all dressed up. I was even wearing heels. As I walked by a Black dude, he shouted out, "What up, bow leg!" That was not a compliment.

Some Mexican guys like to call you over like an animal, with the kind of noises and whistles a farmer makes to bring cows into a pen and chickens home to roost. "Chhhhh pssssssst pssssst psssssst!" Some Filipino guys simply point at you with their lips, and with white guys, you never actually see the white guy who's hitting on you because he usually sends over a friend to do it for him. The other white guy will approach and say, "Yeah, I got a buddy over there…"

If a guy didn't do those things, there was a pretty solid chance I would have dated him. I mean, I dated a lot of guys, but never seriously. I don't want to say that I didn't want to fall in love and get married—I definitely did—but I was never the kind of girl who dreamed about a knight in shining armor whisking me away to his castle. I didn't have my wedding day all planned out down to flower petal colors and the number of layers on the cake. I think one time when I was a kid, I put the sheer living room curtain over my head and pretended to walk down an aisle. It's possible I was pretending to be a creepy ghost girl to scare my brothers; I can't be sure. My dream, always, was to be an actress, not a wife. I just assumed the marriage and kids thing would happen one day. I didn't put much thought or effort into it.

Anjelah got ghosted a few times, but Taranjelah was a real heartbreaker. I would date a guy, and the newness was exciting. But then they'd get super into me fairly quickly, I'd lose interest, and it would fizzle.

Dr. Phil might blame my commitment issues on my dad and his

example of how to make "friends" but never give them a title, or perhaps a past trauma, when I was dumped by a guy who seemed to be the catch of my entire church. You see, after Paul/Baby Paul, I dated my megachurch pastor's son, Jesse. Pastors' kids, aka PKs, are like royalty or rock stars in the Chrish world. They are notorious for either being totally committed disciples of their parents or totally out of control. Rarely would you find a happy medium PK.

Jesse was charming, funny, and handsome and not your typical white guy—he had spice and could sing all the '90s R&B runs. Unlike my family, his had money. Even though they lived in Silver Creek Country Club, the wealthiest part of San Jose, they didn't judge me for being a girl from across the tracks. His parents sponsored me on a trip to Israel, where I got to see the Wailing Wall and the Dead Sea, and I was baptized in the Jordan River. It was an incredible trip that I never thought I would have the opportunity to go on. To be able to walk where Jesus walked felt surreal. His family really loved me, and my family really loved him. The only problem was that he still really loved his ex-girlfriend. He came by to let me know that he couldn't see me anymore because he was getting back with her. He was kind enough to drop off a purse I had left in his car. Only thing was that it wasn't my purse. Must have been his ex-/new girlfriend's purse. He messed up and I moved on. To being Taranjelah.

Taranjelah may have had commitment issues, but she always managed to be super Chrish. My friend Oscar used to come over for "intimate Bible reading nights," and we definitely had a vibe and a thing for each other, but we never even kissed. We only got busy with the Lord. If he stayed the night, he only did the cuddle walk of shame.

Now don't get the wrong idea—I wasn't exactly a nun either. I'd make out and get hot and heavy with a boy, and then feel so guilty the next day for bumping and grinding with my jeans on. Jean jamming was my jam. I was always safe though; my jeans were my condom. One time I went for a jog in my neighborhood and a good-looking guy pulled over to talk to me. He lived up the hill from me, and I recognized him from the grocery store, so we exchanged phone numbers. Later that day, I went to his house, we made out, and that was the last time I ever talked to him. I don't even remember his name.

If I didn't have a religious upbringing, I would have ho'd all the way out for sure. *For sure.* Once, at a party, I met a famous Latina actress I looked up to. I had heard that she grew up Christian like me. After a couple drinks, she took a deep drag of a cigarette and told me bluntly, "Before you get married, you absolutely have to have sex with other people." I remember being so turned off by it (and the cig). Why would I do that? How sad, like, *What happened to you? We used to be on the same page, and now you're telling me to have sex before marriage? With multiple people? Why would you even say that?* I was so disappointed.

I was very proud of my virginity; it wasn't easy to maintain, but it was super important to me as a Christian. I remember thinking that I wanted to please God and please my husband by saving myself for marriage. Anytime I would get hot and heavy with a guy, I would think, *As long as I didn't go all the way, I'm good.*

I think not having sex saved me from making bad/worse decisions, not to mention eased the heartbreak after the few times I got cheated on or dumped. My whole life, I'd been warned to not date a cop, because we had firsthand experiences in my family, but when a police officer asked for my number after I got held up at gunpoint at Roscoe's House of Chicken 'N Waffles, what was I gonna say, no? I was shook and vulnerable. He was taking witness statements and asked if I got a good look at the gun.

"I did!"

"Great, what kind was it?"

"I don't know, but I can draw it!"

He handed me a pen and a napkin. I drew a stick-figure gun that looked like it had been doodled by a child.

He thought I was funny and charming and obviously very gifted in making light of situations, although clearly not gifted in drawing, so after I Picasso-ed that gun drawing, he asked me to write my number down too. You really have to be a super trusting human being to date a cop because they get a lot of attention, and many of them get around (not all...settle down, defensive cop wifies). Girls love a man in uniform. Like, they flirt to get out of tickets, so imagine what they'll do for armed robbery. You don't even have to commit a crime to date a cop. They can walk into Subway to order a sandwich and walk out with five phone numbers.

Of course, I learned all of this the hard way. We stopped seeing each other after I discovered he programmed me into his phone as "Kevin." *Was I the side chick? I* was *the side chick!*

So, yeah, I made some mistakes, ignored red flags, and kept getting myself into toxic situations. I wasn't listening to the not-so-subtle messages I kept getting from God. He kept signaling, "Stop dating all these guys. I have bigger plans for you." Okay, God, you're right! I'm going to stop dating. Then the next day I would go out with another guy.

It was one disaster after another. I mean, I even dated a gay guy. I wasn't trying to flip anyone; I just did not have the gaydar gene and misread signals. I was way off. There was a handsome man who came to church with his mother and had a super-nice condo in Laguna Beach and super-nice cheekbones. We flirted and made plans for a sleepover at his place (cuddle whore, activate!), which was a big deal because nobody in LA ever wants to date someone beyond a thirty-minute radius if they can help it. If you live in Silverlake and your crush lives in Santa Monica, you're basically doomed. But I was willing to brave demon traffic on a Friday night at five p.m. to stay at this fabulous beach house—I mean, spend time with this fabulous guy.

When I got there, we were being super Chrish and decided to sleep in separate bedrooms. In the middle of the night, I got a little hot and bothered from the salty sea air and asked him to come lie with me for a bit, and I kissed him. I was the initiator. It was like a match trying to ignite a wet stick. I remember thinking, *I don't think this guy wants to make out with me.* Like, I'm not saying I'm an award-winning maker-outer, but he wasn't even interested in taking me for a spin. We called it a night, and he gave me a kiss on the forehead and went back to his room. I left with blue ovaries. Is that a thing? About a year later, I saw pics of him on Facebook fully out of the closet partying at a club in West Hollywood surrounded by men with handlebar mustaches. I felt kind of dumb. I should have known. I just thought he was trying to win a Christian of the Year award. Was I his test dummy to help him figure out his sexuality? Or did I totally misread that, and he just wanted someone to watch murder mysteries with, which, honestly, would have been right up my alley.

The bad decisions kept on coming, like dating a guy I met at Q's Billiard Club. He was funny; we connected; we were like, "Let's make out and do things." But then things fizzled romantically, so we decided to be best friends. He became my go-to guy and my fake boyfriend. If I needed something fixed, he came over with his tools. If he needed to go to a wedding, I was his arm candy. I wasn't just in it for the less-than-stellar wedding food; I liked spending time with him.

Anyone who's seen *When Harry Met Sally*, which obviously was everyone on the planet except for me at the time, knows what happened next. Men and women cannot be friends. Turns out our besties arrangement wasn't mutual. We went out to eat, and he vomited out all of the resentment he had built up toward me over the years of our friendship because he had feelings that weren't reciprocated. He kept track of all my sins and threw them in my face. "You say you want this, but then you go date this guy. You say you want that, then you go date that guy." After he dropped me off at home, I knew I'd never talk to him again. And I made a decision: No more guy best friends. He was the last one.

Deep down, I knew God was right. I wasn't meant to be dating right now. Not to mention the fact that at one point during this era, my dad, who grew up in LA, told me, "Don't date anyone born in 1971 to 1975" while I was in the greater metro area, because they could be my siblings. That's how much he got around in LA.

Despite warnings from above (and from out of nowhere that were a little TMI, Dad), I kept going out with boys. I had an epiphany where I sort of acknowledged it actually might be an issue in my life. Why couldn't I quit doing this? Serial dating had become what felt like an addiction. My heart was conflicted. At church on Sunday, I made a promise to God that I would seriously quit dating guys immediately.

Before the week was up, though, on Saturday night, I met a super-hot DJ, who happened to be Jewish, at one of the bar mitzvah parties I worked. I once went to a Christmas/Hanukkah party where the husband was Jewish and the wife was Christian. I thought, *How do they do this? How will you teach your children? Whose God? How do you pray if you both believe different things? Do you eat bacon on Sunday mornings or not?* I was very confused by this.

I put that confusion on the back burner for the DJ, who was super handsome with deep brown eyes. We got a vibe going, and when he asked me out, without hesitation, I was like, "Heck, yeah!"

The following morning, I sat in the front row of church. In the middle of my pastor's sermon, which was not even about dating, he suddenly stopped and said to no one in particular, "I feel like somebody here is dating unequally yoked. And God says you know better than that."

I nearly fell out of my chair.

In the Bible, 2 Corinthians 6:14 says, "Do not be unequally yoked together with unbelievers." In layman's terms, unequally yoked means you're not on the same page religiously. The pastor was talking to me. I was Christian and the DJ was Jewish. I went home and had an argument with God: *What the heck, God, this guy is so cute! He's one of your chosen people. And his mom probably makes really good matzo ball soup. Doesn't that mean something?* It was a dumb argument. I knew I was not supposed to date this guy, yoked or not. *Okay, fine, I'll go on this date with him to tell him that I can't date him.* That was my way around it.

The DJ planned the sweetest, most romantic date. This was no Taco Bell drive-thru. He took me to his favorite pizza place in this cute little neighborhood, then took me to a teahouse in a beautiful garden. In the car, he played his favorite song for me, "Pure Imagination," from *Willy Wonka and the Chocolate Factory*. We were having such a great time, I couldn't believe I had to end it before it even started.

I decided to try to work some missionary magic on him and reel him over to my team. I brought up church and God and Jesus and Christmas music to test him, but he immediately said, "Yeah, but Anjelah, I don't believe Jesus is God." It felt like an arrow through my heart. *Excuse me? What'd you say about my Jesus?* It was the nail in the hands and feet—I mean, coffin.

I took a deep breath. "I can't date you because you're Jewish and I'm Christian," I dramatically blurted out, explaining that it just wouldn't work. It was our first and last date. We had one little innocent goodbye kiss, like in an old-timey movie. Then I got in my car and cried the whole way home. RIP us.

I was super sad because I knew the jig was up. It was time for me to listen to and trust God. He'd been telling me over and over, "Listen, I'm trying to do something big for you here, so I need to be the only man in your life right now." I finally let go and let God be the only man in my life. We were monogamous.

After that moment, I stopped dating. I didn't have any agents, auditions, or opportunities coming my way, and I had zero plans. I turned the downtime into my chasing God time. I wanted to get closer to God, so I cultivated a relationship with Him on a whole other level. I journaled, read my Bible, sang my praise and worship songs, and prayed. People pray, sure. I prayed all day, for you, for me, for Him, for my future, my dreams, my goals, and my neighbor who definitely needed a divine intervention.

At first, I wasn't excited about reading and praying, but it was kind of like going to the gym. After a while something clicks, and you enjoy working out. That's what happened to me. I was working out my faith. All of a sudden, I craved what I called "my Jesus time." If I ever had to leave my house for some reason, I couldn't wait to get home, lock myself in my room, and pray for hours in my prayer closet. Yes, I literally went in my clothes closet to pray and cry and worship God.

Driving home one day, I was praying and talking to God and I felt giddy inside. I can't even describe it accurately. It was similar to the night at Youth Camp when we all couldn't stop laughing. I rolled down the windows and yelled as loud as I could, "Jesus, I have a crush on you!"

I didn't really want to date Jesus; it just felt like that was what was happening. Jesus had genuinely become the only man in my life and the only man that I wanted in my life. "Now," I told Him, "You said you wanted to do something big. What could that possibly be?"

CHAPTER 7

Shine Like a Diamond in the Sky

During my "gym workout of Jesus time," as I called it, I often had visions of myself in an actual school gymnasium, speaking to the students, who all knew and loved me as this very successful actress. I pictured the principal introducing me like MC Michael Buffer before a WWE match: "Here's Anjelahhhh Johnsonnnnnn!" The crowd would go wild in the bleachers, like, they couldn't believe *the* Anjelah Johnson was getting them out of geometry for an hour. Then, channeling Michelle Pfeiffer in *Dangerous Minds*, I'd blow their young minds with my inspiring journey from rice and beans to rice and beans in a nicer house.

I was fully aware that not everyone could spend days/weeks praying, manifesting, daydreaming, and occasionally napping in their closet like I had grown accustomed to doing. I had nothing else going on in my life, so there wasn't much else for me to do other than pray, worship, and journal. One day, as I stood by my window and talked to God, He cut me off because He had something important to say:

"What you have right now, all this time that you get to spend with me, is a luxury. There is a time coming very soon in your life when you're not going to have this luxury anymore, because you're going to be so busy doing the things that you love."

I felt God say that to me in my heart. Not out loud like in the movies, just a silent knowing. To which I replied, "For real for real?" And God was all, "Ya, girl, for realsies." Then I said, "But tell me what that means exactly, like, give me all the details." That was when he stopped replying…

God gave me His blessing and released me from any shame. "You're going to be working so much that you won't even have time to go in your prayer closet," He warned, but added, "Don't trick yourself into being like, 'Oh no, this doesn't feel right.' Don't give yourself a guilt trip. Don't get religious on me because this is a gift from *me*." When God tells you not to get religious, you put down your Bible, grab your purse, and get out of the closet.

Around the same time, I was taking acting classes at the Oasis Church's Creative Arts Night. One of the teachers, Lisa Alvarado, noticed I was naturally funny in an improv game and asked me, "Do you want to take my stand-up class on Tuesday nights?"

"Is it free?" I asked.

"Yes."

"I guess so?"

At this point I'd been to one stand-up show in my life, and it wasn't even at a comedy club; it was at a random restaurant. I was on one of my "I'm hungry so I'll date yous," and we got up to leave in the middle of a set (sorry, rude). On our way out, I heard the comic onstage try a funny accent, and it stopped me in my tracks. I turned around and watched the rest of his act from the back of the restaurant, doggie bag in hand. *Hmm, I think I could do that,* I said to myself. *My Vietnamese accent is way more accurate.*

Growing up, I felt very connected to that culture. My best friend Daniel, or D'Le as we all called him, was Vietnamese, and he always taught me things to say, like different greetings and simple stuff. I couldn't wait until January every year so I could say "Chúc Mừng Năm Mới" to all of my Vietnamese friends and all the employees at my favorite noodle place. A large number nine with extra sriracha was my (spicy) jam! D'Le's mom would cook pho for me. Well, she would cook it, and I would come over and have some. She liked me, but probably not enough to spend hours and hours cooking a pot of soup just for me. I think there was a part of me that thought I would end up with D'Le one day and this would be my family, and I would be living my wildest dreams of endless pho and Vietnamese lovin'. However, our friendship stayed just that: friendship.

We continued to go to each other's family functions and parties, and spent an equal amount of time going to church and hunting for haunted houses, which I understand are two very opposite events. It was so fun, though! We waited until the sun went down and got in his convertible Miata and put the top down. We wore layers of hoodies and jackets and brought blankets to keep us warm. We drove through the mountains, and when we found a supposed haunted road or haunted house, we would just stop the car and scare ourselves with the thought of a ghost or evil spirit being able to touch us because the top was down.

My mom took me for my first mani-pedi when I was twelve at a salon called Beautiful Nail, and the same wonderful woman, Tammy (that was her American name), did my nails every month for almost eight years. Unless she was busy, then I would head over to the East Side and go to Pro Nail Art, where John would do my nails. He called himself Don Juan John and always cracked jokes with me. If he was booked, then I was off to any other salon that would take me, and I'd have a new technician who I could impress with my limited knowledge of Vietnamese words. I have been to so many different nail salons in San Jose and met so many different nail techs, but Tammy was my favorite. "You're so pretty, you could be a model or a cheerleader," she always told me. The day I came into the salon carrying my Oakland Raiderette headshot to put on the wall, she beamed with pride. She called it.

I still had no desire to be a comedian, but the stand-up class was free, it was fun, and it was something to do. It turned out to be a great class. Lisa taught us everything from joke techniques, like the Rule of Three and Imagine If, to how to adjust the mic stand onstage. That you always shake hands with the host and, after your set, wait for the host to come back. Never leave the stage empty. We got homework assignments like "Write a joke about your name." I came back with a bit that you've probably seen at one of my shows or in my very first hour-long special. I'm Little Payasa Johnson, and I hope you don't like it.

One of the first jokes I wanted to write was a nail salon bit. I knew I could do the accent, plus it was a lived experience and something I assumed lots of people could relate to. My teacher said, "Nail salon jokes are so hacky. Everybody has a nail salon joke. I would steer clear." It was great advice from a pro who'd been on *The Search for the Funniest Mom in America* and *Last Comic Standing* about a topic that had been done to death. Like, airplane food, amiright? But I ignored her advice, and thank God I did. I was like, "You know what? I don't think anybody does it like me. So, I'm just going to do it anyway."

The bit was an homage to my relationship with every nail technician that I had ever met in all the salons I had been to in San Jose, whether it was Tammy or John or someone else, who always had a sly, somewhat passive-aggressive way of upselling me more services.

They were good at their job, and it turns out I was good at stand-up. I could tell I was the best one in the class, because at our graduation show on the *Queen Mary* docked in Long Beach, everybody else got to do five minutes, but Lisa let me do all twelve minutes of the material I'd written. "Just do your whole set," she told me.

Here's the thing, though. I was like, "Am I good? Or am I just better than all these people?" Clearly, I was the best here, but just because I was the best one in this class didn't mean I'd actually be good in the real world. Our graduation show didn't really help answer those questions since the entire audience was composed of everyone's family and friends and they were basically obligated to give a standing O. It was a warm, giving audience, not a drunk, heckling one. If I went out into the real world, was I about to have a rude awakening?

Lisa saw my potential and took me under her wing like a little baby bird. When she did ten minutes at restaurants, bars, and tiny comedy club rooms, she let me roll with her to see what it was like and introduced me to the bookers. "Anjelah's a comic too," she'd say. "She has five minutes if you have time." Every now and then they'd be like, "Yeah, all right, you want to go up? We'll put you up." And I'd go up and do my "Nail Salon" bit, because that was exactly five minutes.

I was so nervous at first, I didn't even hold the microphone. I stood in front of it with my hands on my hips like a football coach watching the game from the sideline. It was my safety pose. I guess I thought nobody could hurt me if I stood like that. If I dared take the mic off the stand, it got too real, and I couldn't deal. My heart would beat out of my chest, like *Oh my God, I'm doing a thing.* I was certain people could hear the nervous poops brewing.

The more I got up there, though, the more comfortable I became, and sooner than I thought, I was ready to fly solo. The gatekeepers started paying attention to my sets, and they'd say, "Oh, I also run Thursday night over at whatever bar. You want to come do my Thursday night?" Okay, sure! Then I got asked to do longer sets, which was great, but there was one teeny-tiny problem: I didn't have enough material.

In the early days of my stand-up career, I was trying to find my voice. I was no longer pretending to be a chola, but I was sometimes trying to be who I thought people wanted me to be. I'm Latina, so they wanted me to act Latina. I didn't yet have a grasp of my own point of view, and the shame I felt around not speaking Spanish as a kid was still too fresh for me. A lot of the shows I performed in at first were the Latino shows, like Refried Fridays. Most of the comics would use some Spanish in their sets or speak with an accent. I thought, *Oh. I can do that accent.* So I told stories about my parents, doing voices for them where they spoke in broken English. But the truth was, they were born in California, just like me. They didn't speak Spanish either. Honesty was key, but I was young, and I didn't know any better.

I asked my friends who did speak Spanish to give me words, like "What would my mom say to me?" One said, "Coño," and I was like cool, thanks. I used it in my act and then later found out it was slang mostly used by Puerto Ricans and Cubans, not Mexican/Hella Americans from San Jose. Oops, didn't do my research on that one. I changed it to "aye guey," the more appropriate regional slang that had multiple meanings, one of those being "dammit."

I was always nervous trying out new jokes, but I also had a built-in safety net with the "Nail Salon" bit. I knew it was a sure thing and everybody was going to like it. If the audience wasn't hot or wasn't buying my first minute—for example, the joke about my name, Little Payasa Johnson—the second I started that accent, forget it. The fact that it was so accurate is what got people, and they'd laugh instantly. "Nail Salon" was my cheat code. Sometimes I'd push myself and go, *I'm for sure not going to do it, because I don't want to cheat.* But if I needed a laugh and a confidence booster, I could automatically fall back on that. It always worked.

As I blossomed, I hit all the comedy rooms that were popular at the time—Buzz Café, Three of Clubs, Ice House, Chinese restaurants, dive bars—and went up wherever I was invited to hone my act, whether at a hole in the wall in Studio City or the legendary Improv on Melrose Avenue in Hollywood, the launching pad of famous comedians like Eddie Murphy, Ellen DeGeneres, Jerry Seinfeld, Dave Chappelle, and anyone who's anyone in live comedy.

Being a comedian was something I fought. I didn't really want to be a comic at that point. Ninety percent of the time, people invited me to their shows. I wasn't really reaching out, trying to get onstage. People would ask me if I was a comedian, and I would still say, "No, I'm an actress. I just do this for fun." I actually said that out loud to people, not realizing it could come off a type of way, like offensive or annoying or something. A lot of these comics had been writing for years, and were still working on their five-minute sets, trying to get stage time. And then I just waltzed in casually going, "Oh, you have room? Sure, I guess I'll go up. Here, hold my Shirley Temple."

I did take it seriously, though. I wasn't the type to just phone it in, so maybe I was just trying to protect myself. I had heard a lot of crazy stories about women trying to break into the male-dominated comedy scene, so I wasn't exactly sure what I was getting myself into. I learned some hard lessons for sure. The very first time I performed at the Improv on a Tuesday night, some guy offered to video my set for $35. Keep in mind, I was broke at the time, so $35 was an investment. But it was my first set at the world-famous Improv, so I felt like it was an important night to have documented. When I got the DVD (hey, at least it wasn't VHS), I was blown out by the lighting and you couldn't even see my face. I looked like a ghost girl who may or may not have been taking over the spirit of whoever was onstage. I was so bummed to lose out on $35 and a recording of my first Improv set, but I felt better thinking Ellen probably had a DVD (probably VHS, actually) inside one of her mansions, covered in dust, featuring a similar-looking ghost girl.

I went on the road, because that's what real comics do. My friend DJ Cooch invited me to be on his show in Yuma, Arizona, so I drove with him and a bunch of other male comics and shared a hotel room with the one gay comic, Thai Rivera—for safety and for funsies. It was my first real traveling road gig, and I was excited to be a part of the crew. I felt like I connected with the guys, and DJ Cooch was like my big brother protector. My first road gig was easy and fun; however, not all road gigs are created equal.

I did another gig in Miami in front of a very macho Latino crowd. This time I brought DJ Cooch to open for me. He was a veteran comic who knew what he was doing, plus he spoke Spanish and had the audience dying laughing. You'd think the audience would be ready to keep the laughs coming, but when I got onstage, it was as if someone had just killed their abuelas. All of them. They wouldn't even look into my eyes, let alone laugh at my jokes. Immediately the energy in the room plummeted. They weren't taking me seriously. This was the very first time I was supposed to do forty-five minutes but ended up only doing twenty-five and getting offstage because I plowed through all my material and didn't get any laughs, shaving twenty minutes off my set.

The manager of the club, Gideon, was watching me, and I was so embarrassed. He was very gracious, though, and said, "Give it another go. But for the next show, take your lipstick off, put your hair in a ponytail, and put your hoodie on." *I will look like a lesbian, but sure, let's go with that.* I'd try anything to win the audience over. Maybe there was something to this? Pittsburgh's *Tribune-Review* once wrote in a review that I "get dismissed by audience members who focus on her Baywatch body, big brown eyes and cover-girl smile."

The next show I went out there—no lipstick (I did wear mascara though; I'm not crazy), hair up in a pony, wearing a hoodie and tennis shoes—and it was night and day difference. Now when the men looked at me, they weren't looking at my midriff or any cleavage because that was covered up. I pulled my hair back, so I didn't have free-flowing pretty Sofía Vergara hair. I looked like a tomboy. I was not a sex object or a potential hookup to them. (I was never a potential hookup, but the first crowd maybe didn't get that memo.) They were finally listening to what I was saying instead of thinking *Pretty girls aren't funny. This isn't going to be good.* I was one of the boys, and they were way more receptive to me. I wasn't a threat to the women, either; I was one of their homegirls. For a really long time after that, my vibe onstage was your little tomboy buddy Anj.

This was all sort of subliminally sexist and way before the #MeToo movement. I have my own sordid tales to tell about the male-dominated and often sexualized comedy scene. I'll just tell one that sums it up in a nutshell: I was invited to perform at a private birthday party in Oxnard but would have to drive up there with another male comic I didn't know. I was uneasy about it, but, again, this is what real comics did and it paid $150, so I couldn't turn it down.

I drove over to the comic's apartment in Hollywood and snagged a coveted parking spot right in front of his place. We got in his car and headed to the gig. We had a very nice conversation the whole hour or so there, and all was fine. When we got to the party it was really fancy and catered, and a stage was set up for the comics in the backyard. I went up first and did well. My new friend went up after me, and I watched him from the back of the crowd, ready to support him.

Well…his whole set was about how he just wanted to jerk off to me the entire drive.

He was not funny and literally nobody was laughing. Instead of letting it go and moving on, he dug deeper and got more vulgar. It made the audience uncomfortable and completely humiliated me. I escaped into the house, which was off-limits, and hid in the kitchen. The man who owned the house found me and asked if I was okay. "That wasn't cool," he said.

"Yeah, thank you," I managed. "I'm fine. I'll just stay in here if that's okay."

The entire rest of the party, I had to think about how I had to drive back with this comic. There was no Uber back then, but even if there was, I would rather walk home than waste my entire paycheck on a ride home. With no other feasible option, I got back in his car and, the entire way back, leaned as far away from him as humanly possible, with my back to him, like a pissed-off teenager driving with her annoying mom. I made one call after another on my flip phone to anyone who would answer just so I didn't have to have a conversation with him. If I remember correctly, I talked to my sister, my mom, the receptionist at my dentist's office, and a Time Warner Cable robot for twenty minutes.

When we got back to his place, the comic tried to drive past my car to park, but I stated firmly, "Can you drop me off at my car?" Annoyed, he backed up to my car, and as I was getting out, he had the balls to say…wait for it…you won't believe this…

"Hey, so do you want to come up?"

I got out without saying a word, got in my car, and locked the doors. I pretended to make more calls in my car for a while so he couldn't take over my primo parking spot. *Burn.* We never crossed paths again. I forgot his name. I can't even picture his face. I blocked it all out.

It wasn't just the skeevy bros in comedy that made me meh about committing to this job as my true profession. I just wasn't passionate about it like I was about acting, until one major thing changed my mind: an unexpected big juicy paycheck! I got asked to perform at a Mormon Christmas party in Orange County, even though I wasn't Mormon. Didn't matter. They were looking for "clean" comedians, so I said sure, why not? When I showed up, it turned out to be a comedy competition. I tied for first place and won a cash prize of $600, the most money I'd ever made at one time in my life. That finally changed my perspective on stand-up as a profession and not just a hobby. I was like, *If I can make $600 in one night for ten minutes of work, hmm, maybe I* will *be a stand-up comedian.*

If you're like, "Dang, Anj, you were kinda shallow," I get it. The truth is, more often than not, that kind of money was really hard to come by doing stand-up. Most gigs paid peanuts—which, at certain times in my career, I would have accepted as payment. I was hungry. I might have even eaten the shells.

In January 2007, desperate for cash, I performed my twelve-minute set, which included the "Nail Salon" bit, at the Ice House Comedy Club in Pasadena for $25. There was a company there filming comics' short bits so Verizon Wireless customers could download them on their flip phones for 99¢. To get the twenty-five bucks, I had to sign a contract allowing them to not only use but also *own* that video. I basically signed my life away for gas money. To this day, that company owns the original footage of my "Nail Salon" bit.

But here's the crazy part: Around the same time I signed that contract, this new thing called YouTube was blowing up. That company was not really making money on the downloads—people stopped paying for content when they figured out they could get stuff for free online—and posted my "Nail Salon" video on their YouTube channel.

Literally overnight, and about four months after I took the stand-up class, "Nail Salon" became one of the first videos *ever* to go viral. It got something like 4 million views, which back then was unheard of. I went viral before going viral was a thing. Charlie hadn't even bit anyone's finger at that point and Justin Bieber still lived in Canada and had no tattoos.

The video started flying around the world like crazy. Millions and millions of people were seeing my bit. And I started getting calls and text messages from family members and friends who had seen it. My cousin Kristie, who at the time worked for a tech startup, got an email that had circulated around her company like wildfire, with the message "You have to see this! It's hilarious!" And it was little ol' me. She called me, amazed that it had been forwarded to her by several people. "Nobody even knows you're my cousin!"

My MySpace page (gone but not forgotten) was bombarded with thousands of messages:

"When are you coming to Australia?"

"When are you coming to the Philippines?"

"When are you coming to the Punchline in Atlanta?"

"When are you coming to get your cheerleading trophies?" That was my mom. She was ready for me to get the last of my childhood things so she could turn my room into an office.

"You went to Lincoln High School? My cousin went there!"

How did these people know where I grew up? I was so overwhelmed. I wasn't a real comedian—I only had twelve minutes of material I wrote in a free church class. But suddenly people knew of me across the planet. I didn't know how to be a celebrity. I didn't know I didn't have to reply to every single person who messaged me. I didn't know the etiquette or the boundaries. I spent four hours a day copying and pasting the reply, "Thank you so much for the support!"

Copy paste. Copy paste. Copy paste.

And then my first batch of trolls started replying to me, "Is this a robot? Because you already said this." My new fans were already so demanding of excellence.

"Oh, sorry," I replied. "I don't know how to be famous."

Once, I posted that I had a show in the back room of a bowling alley on a Friday night, which is actually way less shady than it sounds, and was shocked when several people actually showed up to see me live. "We drove in from Riverside!" they told me excitedly. That was like a three-hour drive, in demon traffic on a Friday night! For me? What?! Free bowling shoe rentals for everyone! Not on me, because I'm broke, but someone should really hook them up.

My new fans found me, but nobody in the entertainment world knew how to get in touch with me because I didn't have an agent. Suddenly, TV network executive assistants flooded my MySpace inbox, after enjoying the smooth sounds of Nelly Furtado on my profile page, of course. What? You know you remember your profile song. Their bosses wanted them to find the girl from the "Nail Salon" video. I ended up booking so many meetings—at CBS, CW, ABC, MTV, NBC, QRSTUV—that I had to go to Staples to buy a calendar. And a pen. I remember being at NBC like, *Here I am, this little Mexican girl from San Jose. What am I doing in this waiting room? Who do I think I am to dream so big? Wait, are those croissants free?*

I had no idea what was in store for me. I kept thinking, *Is this really happening? I really get to do this?* I landed higher-profile comedy gigs. I performed for the troops in Guantanamo Bay, Cuba, with the all-female Funny Hunnyz comedy troupe. I got a job hosting a show for a tiny network called Sí TV, and it was the first time I read off a teleprompter. I was taking meetings everywhere for pilot season, even though I didn't even know what pilot season was. Turns out, it has nothing to do with airplanes. I even met with the production company of my comedy idol, Ellen DeGeneres. She wasn't there that day, but I saw a giant poster of her in the waiting room, and that was good enough for me.

I was overwhelmed, but in a good way. I remember talking to my sister about it and saying, "This is either a little phase that I'm going through, or this is the beginning of the rest of my life." And that's exactly what it was. (I mean, so far, anyway.) It was the launching pad. This was it—what God had been preparing me for.

Four months after "Nail Salon" went viral, I got a new manager named Dave Rath, who repped some of the biggest names in the comedy business, including Patton Oswalt and Pete Holmes. Dave was like my work dad, the smartest guy in the world, who knew everything. I was a baby in the industry. I didn't know anything, and he taught me everything. He gave me advice on my career and my life, and I leaned on him for it all.

Dave introduced me to a stand-up agent, TJ Markwalter, who had his own little agency. I only had twelve minutes of material; I had no business having a stand-up agent. But they realized people were starting to pay real money to see me perform. So, they came up with a strategy of getting me headlining shows by putting up eight comics ahead of me to fill up the time. It was a tricky move, but by the time it was my turn, most of the audience just wanted to hear "Nail Salon" and go home. I would do my twelve minutes, which became fifteen minutes, then twenty-five, until I worked my way up to a forty-five-minute set.

Dave and TJ were sure I could step up to the challenge and took a risk on me, but it took me a minute to know my own worth and feel like I deserved it. I definitely suffered from a bad case of impostor syndrome back then. Who am I kidding? I have impostor syndrome today, and I'll probably have it tomorrow and next week, too. I'll most likely have a case of impostor syndrome forever. But just in small doses. Some days I feel like it was all a fluke, and other days I feel like a total pro and flip my hair with hella confidence.

But especially when I was starting out, I projected onto other people that they didn't like me because I was a one-joke wonder. I assumed everyone didn't respect me or think I deserved success. I didn't hang out at the Improv, Comedy Store, or Laugh Factory because I was insecure and I figured my peers didn't like me for blowing up so quickly. I didn't want them to figure out that I was a fluke or not funny or not talented.

At the same time, I did have confidence in myself. I tried to remind myself as often as possible that my hustle, my grind, looked a little different than theirs, and that was okay. Our journeys were apples and oranges. You run your race; I run mine. You do you; I do me. As much as I understood this, a part of me wasn't sure if I was capable of ever writing anything as good as the "Nail Salon" bit ever again. And it did a number on my brain.

I was invited to all sorts of high-profile meetings but showed up empty-handed. I had nothing new to brainstorm about because I was scared "Nail Salon" was the peak of my funny, and I didn't want to embarrass myself. A very famous director, Robert Rodriguez, saw "Nail Salon" and invited me to his private studio in Austin, Texas, when I was in town for a hosting gig. I mean he was major—he made movies like *From Dusk Till Dawn*, *Sin City*, and *Spy Kids*—and he sent a fancy car and driver to pick me up.

So, I arrive at his studio and he sits me down, and I'm fully unprepared for this meeting. I was like a deer in headlights and didn't have one single idea to pitch him. We talked about my "Nail Salon" video and how it popped me off, but I admitted I didn't know what to do next.

Robert didn't act like I was a loser or wasting his time (at least to my face). He was so kind about it. He told me a story about his friend who wrote and directed a movie that did really well. That he was in that same place—like, what am I going to do to beat that? He got stuck creatively. And he was afraid to create because he didn't think he could top himself. But he just kept creating and creating and then one day, poof, he made *Pulp Fiction*. (There was probably more to it than "poof," but you get it.) So, um, yeah, he was comparing my dilemma to that of Quentin Tarantino, one of the greatest filmmakers of all time, who didn't know what to do after *Reservoir Dogs*.

Anyway, the moral of that story is that I had this unbelievable blessing of an opportunity to be mentored for an hour by Robert Rodriguez. And looking back, I could kick myself for not having ideas to pitch or even keeping in touch with him so I could start a relationship and be in movies like *Machete* or *Spy Kids 2*. But I did not. I talked to him that one time and that was it. But he was so nice and so right. I had to keep creating, be vulnerable, and put myself out there.

My agents and manager landed me an audition for *MADtv*. I had to bring three celebrity impressions and three original characters to show the casting directors. Now, I had never taken a sketch comedy class at a prestigious comedy school like Groundlings or Upright

Citizens Brigade or Second City. I didn't have a Stuart or a Miss Swan in my arsenal. The only character I'd ever attempted to play was chola Anjelah, and well, she was always in my back pocket ready to come out if need be.

I wasn't about to go to this audition unprepared. I scoured YouTube for celebrities I could imitate, and I landed on Jennifer Lopez. I noticed during red-carpet interviews that she had a high-pitched laugh and a very specific wave that looked like a talking hand puppet. There was one interview where the guy told her it was for a news station in Philadelphia, so she looked into the camera, did the hand puppet, and squealed, "Hi, Philly!"

So that's what I did in my audition.

"Hi, Philly!" Hand puppet wave. High-pitched giggle.

I just kept copying it over and over, no matter what question the casting directors threw at me.

"Who are you wearing tonight?"

"Hi, Philly!" Hand puppet wave. High-pitched giggle.

"Where's Ben tonight?"

"Hi, Philly!" Hand puppet wave. High-pitched giggle.

They absolutely loved it. Now, could I sustain a full sketch pretending to be Jennifer Lopez? Probably not. But they didn't know that. They thought that I just made a comedic choice to make J.Lo stuck on this one answer for every question. I also did Roselyn Sánchez on *Without a Trace* (tilted my head up, spoke with an accent, stared down my nose) and Paula Abdul's signature drunk (or at least she pretended to be) clap on *American Idol*. For my original characters, I took a joke I wrote about my grandpa saying, "Did you google it to me?" and instead acted it out as my grandma. I also did an original character I called Bon Qui Qui, who at the time was my "sister" and wanted to be a rapper.

I went into the audition 1,000 percent prepared but also totally fearless, because I thought I had a better shot of winning *American*

Idol than booking *MADtv*. But maybe not if Paula Abdul knew about my drunk impression. When I got a callback, it got real, really fast. I cared. A lot. I remember sitting outside the studio in my Nissan Altima, listening to Jennifer Lopez's song "Que Hiciste" at earsplitting levels to hype myself up. I had no idea what the words meant because it was in Spanish. I didn't know or care that it was a breakup song about cheating. I sang it anyway with all my heart. I empowered myself, felt those vibrations, walked into the audition, and booked the show. *Hi, Philly, ande pues!*

The best part about this story is that I had learned from my biggest mistake. When I signed my *MADtv* contract, any characters that I came in with, that I had already developed before the show, were mine. That meant Bon Qui Qui.

On my first day of work at *MADtv*, the longest-running show on Fox other than *The Simpsons*, I had to go to the writing offices in a tiny studio off Gower in Hollywood. I got goose bumps when I pulled my Nissan Altima into a designated parking spot with my name on it.

The writers' room was like a big bullpen, and then there were offshoot offices where they'd all break off and write sketches with each other or with cast members like Michael McDonald, Nicole Parker, and Bobby Lee all day.

There was a writer's strike looming that year, so everybody was pumping out scripts as fast as they could. I was brand-new and totally unknown, so the staff writers had to get to know me before they understood what to write for me. I remember the first question I was asked was "Hey, can you do Tila Tequila?" Great, they were already asking me to drink on the job.

Since I was the rookie, nobody really wrote sketches starring me, or if I was cast in a sketch, I had zero or maybe one line at the most. I was Detective #2 or the Native American girl—not that there's anything wrong with either of those roles. I'm sure they were lovely people, just not what I was shooting for, career wise. I figured out quickly that if I wanted to get quality airtime, I was gonna have to write my own ticket. That's when I created the sketch "King Burger," starring a sassy fast-food worker named Bon Qui Qui who calls security on pesky customers with complicated orders and has aspirations to be a star rapper.

I cast Michael McDonald as the manager, Mr. Williams, and Bobby Lee and Arden Myrin as the customers. I had Jordan Peele in mind to play Bon Qui Qui's crush Dawan, who just finished house arrest, but Jordan was already reading too many sketches that day, so I chose Keegan-Michael Key instead, who ended up being the perfect Dawan.

Bon Qui Qui was based on two real people. The first was a drive-thru employee I met when I was a teenager in Memphis, Tennessee, who was blunt and rude and totally in her own world. I'd never experienced customer service that bad before. But most of all, Bon Qui Qui was the embodiment of my brother Kennie, who happens to be gay and fabulous with no filter. At the time, he was not sober, so he was very wild and would pop off at the mouth, saying the craziest stuff. He was funny but always getting in fights at the bar/club/store/school/work/street/earth. He was also a trendsetter (he still is). He would come up with new catchphrases or a new way to laugh, and then all of his friends would do it, too. Whatever he did always caught on. Like, when you see a runway model wearing a shirt made out of a paper bag, and the next day everyone gets themselves a paper bag shirt. That's Kennie. The paper bag shirt designer.

I took that quality from him and put it into Bon Qui Qui, like how she had a different way of pronouncing "Security!" as "Saccurrity!" She had catch phrases, like "I will cut you," and said the things you think but don't say out loud. In the beginning of the sketch, she's on her phone and a girl's trying to put in her order, and Bon Qui Qui's like, "You see me in the middle of a conversation? Don't interrupt, ru[de]."

Once everyone was done writing their sketches, they went into a big binder that was read at a big table in front of the fancy executives and producers. When my sketch was read by my cast members, everybody laughed, and they picked it to be filmed in an episode. I was like, *Wut? Me?* I grew up a fan of Stuart, and here he was a cast member in my sketch.

The day we filmed, I sat in the hair and makeup chair and they asked me, "Okay, what's your vision for this character?" We tried different things with Bon Qui Qui's wig and gave her really long nails. And then we filmed it. It was huge. It was a great example of what Robert Rodriguez said to me. You show up, create something that brings you joy, and trust yourself. Trust who you are and the creative juices in you, put it out, and, yes, maybe it fails. But you get back up and don't let that scare you. You try again. Failure is part of the process.

I once wrote this quote to myself: "In order to stare failure in the face and say, 'you can't have me,' you have to get close enough for it to hear you." We need to experience heartbreaks because they build something in us. With no loss, there's no appreciation for the win. You need it all. If you don't experience the dark, how do you know what light is?

I was on four episodes of *MADtv* before the writer's strike shut down production. By the time the show came back, I and the two other newest cast members were let go. Would that be considered a failure? Bon Qui Qui was the only full sketch I ever starred in on the show. But the clout, the street cred, of being a cast member would get my foot in so many doors and lead to so many opportunities. And guess what else? At the *MADtv* twentieth-anniversary reunion show in 2016, Bon Qui Qui was voted "Fan Favorite Character" over Stuart, Miss Swan, Dot, Lorraine, and Kenny Rogers. Personally, I would have voted for Stuart.

This was the year that changed my life. The title of this chapter,

"Shine Like a Diamond in the Sky," is a reference to a line from my most famous character in my most famous bit, "Nail Salon." After I decided to stay in Hollywood, *in one year*, I went from having nothing to online stardom to booking *MADtv*. And it came after God told me, "I'm trying to do something big in your life. Focus on me. Block out all the other things, 'cause I got something in the works." I put God first, and I also trusted that God would allow me to have the desires of my heart.

In such a short time, I learned to pick and choose my battles, gigs, and opportunities. I learned not to be thirsty for everything. After "Nail Salon," I was afraid that I would not have anything of excellence to offer the world. When Bon Qui Qui debuted, I had another flood of people hitting me up and becoming dedicated fans. I came out with one banger, then I came out with another banger. Both are now a part of pop culture. If you're in a new city and you google "Nail Salon" because you want to go get your nails done, my You-Tube video will pop up, guaranteed. That company that filmed me at the Ice House that day makes money off you watching it instead of me, but that's aight. I've been able to use that video to build a lifelong stand-up career.

The nail salon video contract debacle taught me a valuable lesson that is priceless and has come up time and again in my career. Because I screwed up that contract, I knew not to do it again with Bon Qui Qui. There was a moment when Bon Qui Qui was so popular, she got a movie offer with a major production company. I was still a newbie at the time, and the producers thought I'd be naïve and desperate enough to accept a deal where I'd only make an actor's day rate, about $800 per day, and would not have creative input in the movie or get any producing or writing credits. I walked away. I turned down a Bon Qui Qui movie. Bon Qui Qui would have called "saccurrity!" and wanted to cut me, but I know it was the right decision.

As cliché as it sounds, everything happens for a reason. I think maybe God was protecting me. In the end, I owned her character, her music, and her merchandise and was able to get her a record deal and two musical tours with backup dancers and a stage production that matched any other pop star's show. Bon Qui Qui was so big and successful—her record contract literally says her name—and that's what people wanted from me all the time. I had so much fun with her, but I knew I could do bigger and better things if I just trusted myself, so I retired her.

"Bon Qui Qui," I told her, "I love you and I thank you. But it's Anjelah's turn now."

CHAPTER 8

Chin-Checked by Prince, Ordained by Oprah

One of my favorite things about being in showbiz and being what I call "medium famous" are the surreal moments I can't wait to tell someone else's grandkids.

Right after I bounced from *MADtv*, I booked my very first real role on an untitled TBS comedy pilot starring Valerie Bertinelli, about a single mom raising two teens while running a lumber business. I was cast as her co-worker Marla, described in the sides as a "ditzy cashier." For the audition, I brought my inner chola Anjelah out and added a hippie/stoner twist. To my surprise, I killed it, and I got the job. It felt so good, like I really earned it.

The day we shot promo photos, they did one with the whole cast, one with Valerie alone, and, to my utter shock, one with just Valerie and me. In my mind, I was only an extra as I had been so many times before, so when they said they needed me for the shot, I literally pointed to myself and then turned around to see if they were talking to someone behind me. It was that awkward move from TV shows, except live in person and in front of a major TV star. Needless to say, I was so hyped up but hid my excitement behind a professional poker face. Inside I was freaking out, like, *OMG, I'm seeing what you're putting down and* I am picking it up. *You think Marla is going to pop off as a fan favorite character!*

Well, Marla didn't pop off because the pilot didn't get picked up. It never even got a name other than "Untitled" (that I'm aware of). Never a good sign. It was such a bummer because I had great chemistry with Valerie, and still do. Valerie is very special; she's as warm and wonderful as she seems. She's always been a cheerleader of mine and a supporter of my comedy career. She's come to my shows many times, and even invited me on her Food Network cooking show. She's still my really good friend today.

Having super-famous friends is like having regular nonfamous friends, only fancier, and there's a bit of a learning curve to it. One time, she invited me to her Super Bowl party at her beach house in Malibu, and my immediate Mexican response was "What can I bring?"

"No, don't bring anything," Valerie said. "Just show up!"

I was like, "Okay, cool..." But Mexicans don't just show up to a party. We contribute. I decided to make my own salsa, Tia Mary's special spicy recipe. The day of the party, I stopped by Vallarta, a Mexican supermarket, and grabbed a big bag of their homemade chips, which are oily and disgusting but so good and authentic. I showed up to her house carrying my mismatched Tupperware of salsa and a giant bag of tortilla chips, because that's how we Super Bowl.

But as soon as I walked through Valerie's front door, I froze. Uh-oh. This was a full-on fancy catered spread, with a professional chef standing there in his tall white poofy hat. I was so embarrassed. Someone—a butler, the first footman, the stable boy, I don't know fancy words—took my Tupperware away, somewhere magical, then reappeared with my chips and salsa in decorative crystal bowls and placed them on the white-tableclothed buffet between the chilled Alaskan king crab legs and the beef tenderloin carving station. Way fancier than I had anticipated.

There are many perks to getting your foot in the door in Hollywood, such as being offered prime meats and seafood at parties like it's no big deal. It's also true that celebrities get preferential treatment that they don't deserve. I sometimes feel uncomfortable calling myself a celebrity, so I will just refer to celebs as they/them. They get the best table at the restaurant—even if they're not elite or A-list, because even being just kind of a celebrity still carries weight. "Oh, you were on *MADtv*? Right this way!" You might even get a free dessert, or sometimes all of the desserts, on the menu, for free. *I know.* Not fair, but impossible to pass up, especially as someone who was never allowed to order off the dessert menu as a kid. We had leftover Halloween candy at home year-round that was free.

Celebrity (as a noun) is so weird. When I was a Pop Warner cheerleader, there was this Latina girl from the Bay Area who was a friend of a girl on my squad and had one song on the radio, and it blew up. At a cheer competition, I walked around with her and people swarmed and bombarded her with autograph requests.

"What's it like to sign an autograph?" I asked so curious.

"It's whatever," she said dismissively.

She was clearly really good at being famous already. Even though my dream wasn't to be famous, I promised myself if I ever got really famous, I'd never take it for granted that people wanted me to sign my name on DVDs of my most famous movies or even weird body parts. When I became a Raiderette, my first introduction to being a celebrity was learning how to take a photo and do an autograph. Our handlers insisted we make our signature different than the one that we wrote normally, like on the back of a check, because, ya know, identity theft. I came up with making a halo over the last letter in Anjelah.

Flash forward fifteen years and many hand cramps later, I finally got why the teen pop star was so blasé about signing autographs. Don't get me wrong, I'm very happy to do it, but now I'm all about speed and efficiency—I've got mine down to a big capital A then a squiggly line. I was one minute ago years old when I realized my autograph is a sperm.

When you're famous or work with famous people, you get to meet different celebrity stylists. As the daughter/sister/niece of a hairstylist, I know that perfectly coiffed hair is not an option—it's a priority. It's not like a "the cobbler's children have no shoes" situation. I'm not about to bring shame on my family with nasty extensions or split ends. Since my mom lived in San Jose, I had to pay for haircuts once I got to Hollywood. I met celebrity hairstylist Robert Ramos, who has shorn the locks and created signature looks for stars including Kelly Clarkson, Bette Midler, Jessica Alba, and pretty much anyone in Hollywood with good hair. Becky too.

Bette Midler sat next to me under the hairdryers once after having her divine curls zhuzhed up. She gave me honest advice: "Never read your reviews. It's not worth it. You don't need to know." Bette invited my mom and me to her fabulous show in Las Vegas, and we got to go backstage and take a photograph with her. Bette-er yet, when I did a show in Vegas, Bette actually showed up to it. I thought she'd listen to my set and sneak out, but she stayed for the whole show, which was a stellar lineup of fellow comics Gabriel Iglesias and Pablo Francisco. Then she came backstage and took pictures with everyone, including my dad, who I believe may have been speechless for the first time in his life.

I remember feeling like a boss because I got Bette Midler to come to our show. Selling out a show itself felt validating that I was doing well. But having a celebrity fan was a different type of validation because it meant a peer was cosigning your work. Another time, the hilarious and legendary comic Brian Regan walked over from his show at the big theater across the street to the little theater I was performing at to say hi in between my first and second shows. I was so honored because he was one of my biggest comedy inspirations. He was the first person I saw do real live stand-up at a real comedy club. Brian is a hilarious comic who works clean, meaning he stays away from cursing and taboo subject matters. He really just shares relatable funny stories and was very influential on me.

There's that saying "Don't meet your idols." I haven't really had that experience. I would say instead, "Don't meet your celebrity crushes, because they definitely don't want to date you." Like I met Josh Duhamel at an event once pre-Fergie, and I already had us married with three dogs before he said, "Nice to meet you, too." That's actually all he said to me, so that marriage didn't end well. I had a huge crush on Wilmer Valderrama, and I was convinced I was going to date him. Then I met him at an event with my cousin Joe. We took a picture, and I was being all flirty. Wilmer knew how to do the flirty vibe back. He played along, and I thought in my deluded little head, *I'm pretty sure I can make this happen.* Um, I didn't make it happen. But he's a homie now, and he's never once thrown my thirst back in my face. A true gentleman.

As I believe I've mentioned, when it came to dating, I could be a little hungry and a little thirsty. In my early days in Hollywood, I saw a headshot of a hot actor, one you might have heard of and possibly lusted after yourself, on the wall of a Latino heritage store in a mall in East LA and blurted out uncontrollably, "Who is that?" Picture a cartoon character with heart eyes, steam coming out of the top of her head, and her tongue unfurling to the ground. That was me.

A month later I went to a movie screening and that very same hot guy walked past me in the foyer. We both did the look-back-at-each-other thing at the same time, so we turned around, walked up to each other, and introduced ourselves. That was the end of it, though. We didn't buy popcorn and sit together and hold hands. We went our separate ways, but I couldn't get over it. The entire movie I thought about him. I couldn't believe I met the same hot actor I saw in that mall photo. Such a small world!

I moved on with my life because I had no other choice. A week later, I drove to LAX to pick someone up (must have been someone special to get a ride home from the airport, because in LA that can be an all-day affair). I pulled over in a no-parking zone to wait for my friend, and who do I see standing over at the curb with a suitcase? Yes, the hot mall/movie theater guy! He must have just landed and was waiting for a ride. *Wow, this is the third time. This is kismet!* I thought. *I have to go exchange information with him!*

I put my car in park and ran over to him.

"Hey, I don't know if you remember my name…"

"Yeah, hey, how are you?" he said, his beautiful eyes lighting up.

We gave each other a hug, and it was like a romantic scene in a Hallmark movie.

"This is so weird and random," I said breathlessly, because there was a lot of bus exhaust. "I'm picking somebody up and I just saw you again and I just had to come over and talk to you. Here." I gave him my actor "business card," which had my headshot and agent's phone number, plus that I was in the SAG-AFTRA union. Very important, in case he didn't date non-union. "Let's stay in touch."

"I'll give you a call," he promised, then looking over my shoulder added, "Um, I think you're getting a ticket." Dammit.

I flipped around and saw a policeman hovering over my car because I left it in a crosswalk to run after this hot actor, as if he was going to see me and slo-mo run into my arms like every rom-com ever.

Sadly, a few make-outs and a $150 fine later, the hot actor and I fizzled out. My friends nicknamed him "Man-whore," because he was just a very good-looking famous guy who was a charming *player*. He never wanted to meet me in public anywhere; I could only go to his house in the evening, and as we all know by now—say it with me loud and proud—I wasn't an "all the way" kind of girl. But we're cool now, and he is actually a good friend of mine today. I don't know if our spouses even know that we made out a couple times before them, so I may have some explaining to do.

Playing it cool around celebs was not always my strong suit. When I was brand-new to Hollywood, people warned me, "Everybody in LA says they're a producer. Don't believe them. Don't give them your number." Okay, cool, got it. Then a girlfriend who was in a music video for the artist Frankie J invited me to hang backstage with her during one of his concerts. We were in the greenroom when this random guy came up to me and said, "I'm a producer. Are you a dancer?"

"Yeah, we're both dancers," I said, all proud. I had been both a Raiderette and a go-go dancer, so I qualified. When I say I was a go-go dancer, I don't mean that I was naked or even half naked dancing sexy in a cage over the nightclub dance floor. I was usually wearing jeans and a dope pair of sneakers, dancing as if I was about to be in the movie *Step Up* with Channing Tatum. But the cage over the dance floor part was real.

"I'm producing this party next week, and I need some dancers. Would you guys want to work this party and dance?"

"Yeah, we can do that," I answered, ignoring every single warning and cautionary tale I'd ever been told in my life. I mean, I had never heard the word *stripper*, so I gave him my number.

A week later, the "producer" called me and said, "I need six dancers for this party. Can you bring six of your dancer friends?"

"Yeah, I can do that *real* easy." Now I was bragging.

He gave me an address and told me we'd all be taking a bus from there to the location. Which could have been the Boobie Bungalow or a private airport to fly us to the Brazilian jungle to have our organs stolen. Didn't matter.

"I got you," I said.

"By the way," he said, "it's for Michael Jackson's birthday party. It's at his Neverland Ranch."

Let that be a lesson to all of you. *Always* give your phone number to anyone who says they're a producer. You can't win the lottery if you don't play! Anyway, instead of calling the five hottest girls I knew, I called my closest friends, even if they couldn't dance or they were guys. Technically, he never said it had to be girls. I called my friend Harry and shrieked, "You wanna go to *Michael Jackson's* house this weekend?!"

The day of, my five closest friends and I took a charter bus to the famous Neverland Ranch, a couple hours outside of LA. It was unreal. We weren't allowed to take pictures, so I made a mental note to remember every single detail. We drove in the gate and were dropped off at a little train depot. We took an old-timey locomotive named *Katherine*, in honor of his mother, around his ginormous house to his private amusement park. A lot of the rides were shut down—the merry-go-round, Zipper, bumper cars, pirate ship, Ferris wheel—and I realized we were sort of late to the party. We walked into a banquet room and saw go-go dancers already dancing on their platforms.

"I guess somebody else hired dancers too," the producer shrugged.

"What do we do now?" I asked.

"Enjoy the party, I guess."

"Done."

We officially punched out and were ready to party. We acted like kids in a candy shop, running around Michael Jackson's ranch, which had actual candy shops on the property. I stuffed my face with free giant candy bars and popcorn and kept my eye out for Elizabeth Taylor and Bubbles the chimpanzee, you know, just in case.

We were definitely the B-squad. There must have been a party for A-listers earlier, and there were rumors that Lil Jon and Ashanti had made an appearance before we got there, but whatever. We didn't care because we were there now, having the time of our lives, and we were prepared not to stop 'til we got enough.

We went back into a tent where a DJ was playing music and people were dancing. All of a sudden, I saw people huddled around a doorway near a big security guard. I went up to him and whispered, "Hey, what's happening over here?" I thought he didn't hear me because he was so tall and I was whispering into his belly button.

"Stand by me," he whispered back, then winked. He probably didn't wink, but it felt like he should have. I was standing back and standing by. I whispered to my friend Angie Vee, "Hey, come stand by me." I didn't know what was about to happen, but I knew something was about to happen and we should all be standing by each other whispering.

"Ladies and gentlemen!" the DJ announced. "Please welcome the birthday boy himself…*Michael Jackson!*"

Then, the birthday boy himself, *Michael Jackson*, walked out the door right in front of me. Like so close I could smell his hair or accidentally on purpose touch his gloved hand. I didn't do either, but I could have. When I tell you I became one of those girls they show in concert documentaries screaming and crying hysterically for Michael Jackson, believe me. I was screaming like a maniac, and I had actual tears streaming down my face. Angie and I kept looking at each other saying, "Why are we crying?!" We had completely lost control of our bodily functions, but it was Michael F-in Jackson.

MJ came out, twirled around, and let everyone take a looky-loo like he was prize-winning steer, then disappeared back into his house never to be seen again. That was the end of the night. We got back on the little train and back on the charter bus, and I slept the whole way back like a baby who had to be carried into the house by her daddy after riding all the roller coasters at Six Flags.

As time went on, I learned how to control my hysteria in front of fancy people. Then there was the time I was the plus-one of a plus-one at an A-list, star-studded after-Oscars party at Prince's house. Or the Artist Formerly Known as Prince. Or maybe he went by the symbol at that point. I can't remember. I mean Brad and Angie and Leo were there. I was playing pool (probably more like hitting random balls with the stick and hoping for the best) with my friend and B-boy extraordinaire Do-Knock when Prince walked in the room with his friend and picked up a pool stick. I thought, *OMG, this is a story I'm gonna tell for the rest of my life! I'm about to play pool with Prince.* Do-Knock said, "What's up, man. Wanna play?" Prince goes, "Yeah, with him," then pointed to his own friend. So, we put our pool sticks down and left. Ever heard of calling "next," Prince? Just kidding. RIP, Prince. You were the best to ever do it, and I would gladly get kicked off a pool table by you again if I could.

At the same party, Do-Knock and I were dancing on the dance floor, and everybody was clearly impressed with his B-boy moves. We took a break and walked over to grab a drink. Just then a very famous R&B singer (I won't say his name, but it rhymes with Smusher) motioned to me to come over and dance with him, but I turned him down. Who do I think I am?! My own psychological evaluation was that he was just trying to one-up Do-Knock, a professional dancer, who the singer assumed was my boyfriend. Like, maybe he was jelly of Do-Knock. What if I was his girlfriend though? How disrespectful was that to ask me to dance? Rude. Do I regret rejecting him? No. (Yes.)

Once I became higher profile (which took me from no profile to medium profile), I rarely got starstruck anymore because you kind of see the sausage getting made and you realize people are people—it's clichéd, but true. I wasn't really the type to show up to a party just to be seen. I remember one friend was stunned when I turned down an invite to Lindsay Lohan's record release party during the heyday when all the young starlets were besties with all the other young starlets, and they'd do bestie things like ride around in cars together and pretend like they didn't notice the six hundred paparazzi standing outside the window. It was always a cool bonus to get invited to the hottest clubs to party with the latest it girls, but it was never my driving force. I'd rather stay home and watch *Law & Order: SVU.*

At the same time, sometimes it's fun to meet a famous person that you've seen on TV. When I shot the movie *Enough Said* with *The Sopranos* legend James Gandolfini, I was so in awe of him as an actor, I could barely speak around him. He called me on it: "You're a quiet one, aren't you?"

"Actually, I'm not, but I am around you for some reason."

"Why?" he said kindly. And I had no answer other than a giddy smile. Then he called me "mama" the rest of the shoot, and it was hugs all around. At one point he came to my trailer, knocked on the door, and said, "I hate to bother you. Do you think my son could take a picture with you? He's a really big fan." Jim's son (only his friends called him Jim) was a fan of mine?! I'm still floored when famous people or famous people's offspring say they are a fan of mine.

Contrary to popular belief, all famous people don't know each other. The media would make you think so, though. I posted my funny story about being chin-checked by Prince, but after he died, a magazine came out with an article called something like "Five Latinas Connected to Prince." It was Mayte Garcia, his wife; Sheila E, his drummer and former lover; Carmen Electra; Bria Valente—like, real connections—and…me. I never even had a conversation with him; he just told me to get off the pool table. They also spelled my name wrong, btw. But I still felt cool to be in an article that wasn't scandalous.

My "relationship" with Prince was a major stretch. And by stretch, I mean a full-blown lie. There were also two major lies on Wikipedia about me. You know how anyone can write anything on there? The first one was that I had a foot fetish. I mean, I think feet are important, but that's the extent of my relationship with them. The second was that I was in a lesbian relationship with Piper Perabo, star of *Coyote Ugly* and *Penny Dreadful*. Maybe someone saw me perform with my hair in a ponytail and made an educated guess. I've never met Piper in my life, but according to this juicy gossip item, we were seen coming out of a club together, which is possible since people do regularly leave clubs, sometimes simultaneously. It was fine, though; Piper seems like she'd be a good pretend girlfriend. She's so pretty and probably super fun to hang out with. At least my name was spelled right that time.

Just because you're famous doesn't mean you don't get humbled. For my very first big red-carpet event, appearing as a *MADtv* cast member in front of the Television Critics Association, my limo driver was on his way to pick me up, got lost, and ended up in North Holly-wood, an hour away. In a last-minute audible to get me to the event on time, my manager's assistant had to drop me off. Her car hadn't been washed in three years and was covered in bird poop. Like you would have thought she was an eccentric artist type who picked white polka-dot paint, that's how much poo we're talking. When we pulled up to the Santa Monica Pier, in between big, beautiful black Esca-lades with tinted windows, I was photographed stepping out of a literal poopmobile. I think they actually didn't get any photos of me stepping out because they assumed the driver took a wrong turn into a private event, so I just slipped by, thank God.

Another time I was invited last minute to a red-carpet event in Dallas and I asked my friend to pretend to be my publicist because I didn't want to show up alone and look unprofessional.

"Okay, what do I do?" she asked.

"When we get there, there will be photographers and journalists and you just say to whoever's first in line, 'I have Anjelah Johnson here,' then spell my name so they know how to write it correctly." We rehearsed it a bunch of times.

When we got to the event, it wasn't even a red carpet. It was a lame nightclub event that advertised it as a "red-carpet event" so people thought it was fancy. They just had a step-and-repeat backdrop for anyone who wanted to take a selfie. There were no journalists and/or photographers. Turns out I wasn't invited to a big fancy event because I'm big and fancy; I was just on the guest list with some radio contest winners. We did all that role play for nothing, and the event didn't even have any snacks.

Even if there were journalists and photographers, there was always the chance they had no clue who I was back then...or even now. At a charity event, my friend America Ferrera walked the red carpet right before me, and the flashbulbs were all *POP-POP-POP-POP! POP-POP-POP-POP!* "America! Look over here! America! Great angle!" Then I went right after her and the flashes went *pooft*. Crickets. *Pooft.* Crickets. My brother Mitchell, aka Sonny, who I often employed as my "saccuritty!," ran behind the paparazzi, took out his phone, and shouted, "Anjelah! Look over here! Anjelah!" He was the only one calling my name. Bro's before pho's! (As in photographers...no? Okay, fine, but my brother did come through for me on that one.)

So, it's understandable that my impostor syndrome loomed large when I was informed by my team that I was being considered as the stand-up entertainment for...wait for it...Oprah's Girls' Getaway Cruise with Gayle King a few years ago. I'd spend three days and nights boating to the Bahamas with arguably the biggest superstar in the history of the world. Next to Jesus Christ, obvs.

Oprah and Gayle weren't just going to hire anybody to come sail-O-way with them. (Get it? Sail. O. Way. I can't take credit for that slogan; the genius marketers at *O Magazine* made that up.) They watched videos of me and a bunch of other comedians and, to my shock, picked me to perform, sing late-night karaoke with them, stuff ourselves silly at the tropical BBQ buffet, and become O and G's third best friend. At least that's what I pictured in my head.

I was so excited but also terrified. I kept thinking they'd be disappointed they chose me, and that nobody on the cruise would like me because they paid a lot of money to see Oprah Winfrey, not Anjelah Johnson. Which is so stupid, but it's what many artists play over and over in their minds. Maybe not every artist. I'll just speak for myself. Even though I have more than enough proof that I am talented and gifted and people like me, that negativity still creeps into my brain.

So, I was already a little freaked out, then the night before we embarked, I sat in my hotel room talking on the phone to a friend who knew another friend whose wife was really close to Oprah. To my delight and amazement, I was only three degrees of separation away from the second-most famous person in history.

I was nervous about the possibility of talking to Oprah. I knew I would have exactly one chance, during a private dinner and meet-and-greet with her and Gayle. "She meets a million people every day," my friend reminded me, and according to her friend, "She knows when she likes someone and when she doesn't. You gotta nail it because she knows right away." Here was the most important part: If Oprah likes you, she will say three magic words to you: "You've got it."

Great, no pressure. I didn't want to blow my small window of opportunity to impress her and stand out from the rest of the riffraff, so I did a Google deep dive on all things Oprah. I found a documentary about her school in Africa, and sure enough, there was a part where she said it herself—if she met someone and connected with them, she'd tell the person, "You've got it."

This was a real thing. This was serious. It couldn't be like my Michael Jackson buffoonery. There's no crying when you meet Oprah. There's actually probably lots of crying, but I was going to hold it together.

The next morning, my road manager, Ja-Kee, and I boarded the cruise ship. I was so happy to have Ja-Kee with me. Another perk of becoming successful is being able to hire the best people to work with you. As I got more and more popular, I needed professional help. Not the shrink kind (that comes later). The business part was getting complicated, and I never even graduated community college. I needed someone who wasn't me to deal with the money, tickets, bonuses, and everything in between—the in-between being things like selling my merchandise and coordinating meet-and-greets.

By this point in our working relationship, Ja-Kee was more than a road manager. We spent more than two hundred days per year on the road, in airplanes and hotels together. Sometimes we'd have to share a room, because I'm not fancy, and if we're only in town for seven hours, why would I pay for two rooms? You can take the chola outta San Jose, but you can't make her pay for two hotel rooms.

Ja-Kee quickly became one of my closest confidants, even though we had totally opposite personalities. I can be very calm and quiet, and Ja-Kee has huge energy. She's the girl who laughs so loud at her own jokes, everyone turns and stares. She might come off as motherly and be syrupy sweet to your face, but deep down she is a beast, a boss lady who lays down the law. Like, don't even try it. When things went sideways, she'd say, "I'm handling it, don't worry about it." And I didn't worry.

I like to say that Ja-Kee has a "servant's heart." That doesn't mean she loved to give me sponge baths and feed me grapes. No, having a "servant's heart" meant that helping someone organically brought her joy. From the day I met her, Ja-Kee made me feel comfortable, happy, safe, and confident that I could take on the world. She knew all of my insecurities, and she knew how to keep me focused. Most important, she knew where to find us the best breakfast with five stars on Yelp in every town and remembered to pack Tums, sinus pills, and compression socks for long flights.

Even though we were so different, we became best friends. We were two personalities God put together that just worked.

Ja-Kee and I fit right in with the gaggles of giddy girlfriends all over Oprah's magical boat. As one would expect with anything having to do with Oprah, the next three days were phenomenal, uplifting, and life changing. We went to high-energy, emotional workouts with international fitness evangelist Angela Manuel-Davis, who made you sweat and weep out all of your toxins. We did the book clubs, dance parties, Super Soul lectures, you name it. She didn't give away any free cars—that ship had sailed. But the whole cruise was unreal. It was on a spiritual plane all its own.

The first day, I didn't perform, and I was still a little on edge. I walked into the cafeteria and talked to some of Oprah's fans. One woman named Giselle (who later became a friend of mine) sized me up, intuitively knew I was stressing out, and said, "Can I pray for you?"

"Sure!" I said, so grateful.

Giselle put her hands on me and prayed for me, and she rebuked and shut down all of the negative energy I was feeling. "I come against insecurity," she said with her eyes closed and her brow furrowed with purpose. "I come against any kind of fear." After, I really felt my worries had washed away. I was like, "Wow, that was so beautiful and so from God." There were so many things that happened on the cruise that made me feel like God was genuinely moving in that place.

"I have a favor to ask," Giselle said. "If you meet Oprah, can you tell her that I feel like God told me that we are supposed to have a special moment together?"

"Of course!" I lied. Are you kidding? If I got a chance to talk to Oprah, I didn't even know what I was gonna say on my own behalf.

Early the next morning, around six a.m., Giselle's friend texted her frantically that Oprah was working out in the gym and if she wanted her special moment, she better get her butt there before word got out and every human being on the boat and probably even a couple dolphins descended on the exercise room. Giselle rushed over, hopped on a treadmill right next to Oprah, and poured her heart out.

Oprah was so lovely about it, and when Giselle was finished talking to her, she said, "Get out your phone so we can take a picture."

"Oh no no," Giselle said. "That's not what this moment was for."

"You get it, girl," Oprah said.

Not quite a "You've got it," but close.

They had a moment. She just wanted to share her heart, and God kept telling her there was more to come. Later that night Oprah did a two-hour speech in the auditorium for a rapt audience. Suddenly, she started talking about her interaction with Giselle in the gym, then called her up to the stage, where she introduced Giselle to the crowd. Giselle was crying and in disbelief. This was her part of her moment. Like, the extended version. The to-be-continued moment. The moment at the end of the movie when you start walking out of the theater but then one last scene comes up on the screen.

In the end, Giselle's intuition was right. The gym interaction was only part of her moment. Being up onstage with Oprah in front of an entire cruise ship, that was the big grand finale God had for her special moment.

Transcendental, otherworldly, spiritual, spirit led, whatever you want to call it, that kind of stuff happened the whole weekend, to the point we all just kept shaking our heads. We were all existing in the moment on the highest vibration field. It was so crazy and powerful.

The second night was my first show. Oprah wasn't scheduled to come, but at a private dinner with her family, they all were talking about how they were going, then Gayle was like, "I'm going," and Oprah was like, "Wait, Gayle, you're going, too? Then I'm gonna go." So Oprah came to my show. Which was a big deal for me but also her security team, who had to remap her path for the night. It was as coordinated as the Secret Service details for the president of the United States. Oprah didn't just stroll over to the Dive In counter for a hot dog and a piña colada on a whim. It had to be preplanned and plotted out. So it was a big deal that she changed her plans to see me so last-minute.

I didn't know about this dinner conversation until her nieces filled me in later, but I did know when Oprah arrived at my show because the theater erupted like a World Cup championship match. I could not only hear it, I could feel her magnetic energy force field shaking the darn walls, all the way backstage in the greenroom. Ships twelve miles away could probably feel the ripple.

I was a little bit jittery, but my first show went great. Oprah sat in the back, and right before the end, her whole team got up to leave. I didn't see any of this happen, because it's dark out there. But this is what eyewitnesses on the scene told me later. They all got up and were walking out when Oprah stopped in the doorway, turned around, and watched me finish my set. I was honored she stayed until the end. I was honored she even came at all!

The next night was the private dinner and meet-and-greet. When I got my turn in line, Oprah was genuinely so excited to meet me. She recalled some of my jokes from the night before, like one I do about how when you're older your knee suddenly gives out when you're walking and you have to give it a pep talk. "You know how to do this, Knee, you got this." She also mentioned how she loved the joke I do about Ja-Kee, where I talk about our friendship and working relationship with all of our similarities and major differences. Like, I thought I was a happy-go-lucky person until I met Ja-Kee. Imagine taking a little kid to Disneyland for the very first time, then give them a bunch of sugar, and just when you think they're about to explode with excitement, give 'em a puppy. That's Ja-Kee...on a Monday morning.

Oprah and I posed for a quick photo as Ja-Kee was standing next to Gayle. When Gayle realized that Ja-Kee was my road manager, the one I do the joke about, she yelled to her bestie and said, "Oprah, this is Ja-Kee!" to which Oprah replied, *"Ja-Keeee!"* in the same voice she uses when she gives away cars. Gayle quickly ushered Ja-Kee over to Oprah, where the three of us took a photo that now hangs on the wall in my office.

I started to walk away. "Thank you so much. This was so amazing," I said.

"Hey," Oprah said, "You got it, girl."

Are. You. Kidding. Me? What is my life?!? I heard the three beautiful, affirming, stamp-of-approval-winning words from Oprah herself.

I somehow made it back to my cabin. Maybe I walked, or maybe I floated on air. I don't know. I may have blacked out.

I saw an Instagram video the other day that was a collage of different celebrities meeting a famous person they loved, like Chance the Rapper meeting Beyoncé on the red carpet. It's always important to maintain a little bit of your inner fandom. We don't have to prop up or worship celebrities. But how cool is it when you've seen someone in a movie or on TV, or you saw their hilarious video on YouTube, and then they're standing right in front of you?

I always maintain humility and gratitude but also make room to celebrate my wins and accomplishments. I never think I'm better than anybody for it. I've seen way too many episodes of *E! True Hollywood Story*. One minute you're riding high playing pool with Prince at a fancy mansion in the Hollywood Hills; the next minute you're flying high on bath salts and cleaning the pool at a sketchy motel on Hollywood Boulevard.

I cannot get too big for my britches (though I almost got too big to fit into the sweatpants I wore every single day of the pandemic). I will never allow myself, because there's always a chance I might roll up to the next red-carpet event in a poopmobile holding a big bag of greasy tortilla chips and Tupperware filled with homemade salsa.

CHAPTER 9

Manjelah

I promised God I was gonna do a six-month hiatus from dating. When the six months came and went, I was like, *Hmmm, lemme just finish out the year.* When the year was up, I finally felt like I'd paid my dues. I was hungry, but now I could buy my own food. I was ready to go out with guys but this time for the right reasons. If I sound like a contestant on *The Bachelor*, just know I'd never ever get in that hot tub without a hazmat suit on.

What I'm trying to say is that after a year in hibernation, the cuddle queen was back on the prowl. I went to a friend's wedding, and one of the first guys to catch my eye was an extremely good-looking, impeccably dressed mixed dude with the most luscious afro curls. He kind of looked like Maxwell or Lenny Kravitz, but his overall vibe was less hippie, more hip-hopster. I tried to get his attention over by the big bowl of shrimp cocktail, but he didn't even look my way. I was like, *That's weird—who does he think he is?* I didn't introduce myself because I was playing the pretend-not-to-notice-him game. I was the only player. I waited for one of my friends to introduce us, because obviously everyone noticed that he and I should totally be together, or at least make out and then pray about it later. But nobody did. When it was time for me to go home, I slowly walked toward the door to give him and everyone else one last chance to help us fall in love real quick. Right as I was about to walk out my friend shouted, "Anjelah, wait…you forgot your jacket." So I went home without even saying hi. *Oh well, he missed out,* I reassured myself. That night I did what any normal girl would do and stalked him on the internet. I checked out his social media, googled him, and found out that his name was Manwell Reyes. He was in a Christian hip-hop band called Group 1 Crew, and he was Puerto Rican and super hot in every picture I found of him. I remember thinking, *Wow, this guy is super hot and talented and loves the Lord! We should totally be together.* Only he didn't even look my way that night. So with all the pride my dad had taught me, I said out loud to no one, "Oh well, you missed out, dude. You should have said hi." And then I closed my computer and forgot about him.

After that, I dipped my toe in the dating pool, but I'd changed a lot in the past year. Taranjelah had been tamed, and I was sure she'd spun her last web. I was looking for something a little more serious, but I still wasn't exactly sure who that was or what that meant. God hadn't been that specific about it, so I was still flailing around a bit. I was not equally yoked with the first couple guys I dated, but I still went for it because it was fun, and let's face it, after a year alone, I was itching for a little attention and affection.

One night at the Hollywood Improv, I walked past a famous comedian in the hallway, and we locked eyes. We stopped to chat, and I don't know what it was, but we were drawn to each other like magnets. I can't say who it was, but I'll give you a hint: He was a white male comedian. That didn't help? Fine, I'll call him Jim because he definitely wasn't named Jim, but it'll make me laugh picturing you picturing Jim Gaffigan. (Don't worry, Jeannie. It wasn't really your husband!)

We had our own secret thing going on for a while. Nobody knew we were dating, and we both liked it that way. We were so comfortable with each other and had a lot in common, including our super-religious upbringings. Jimmy understood my world and that I wanted to wait until marriage to have sex, and he respected my decision. Like my first boyfriend, Paul, he never pressured me to do anything that I wasn't ready for. We were very communicative and had full-on dialogue and conversations about it, even in the daytime, when our hormones weren't going all wild.

"If we're going to have sex," Jimbalaya said, "I want to talk to you now about it. Not when it's in the moment and you regret it later. I know where you're coming from, and we aren't going to do anything until you're ready."

Jimportant was very kind and protective of me, and I appreciated that. Our biggest issue ironically turned out to be religion. I was still very Chrish, while he had grown out of it. Anytime I would bring up Christian music or praying, he laughed and poked fun. It triggered him because of his background and what was forced down his throat, and that was his response, to belittle it.

Throughout the whole relationship I had dreams about how he wasn't the right one for me. In one vivid dream, I was getting married, and I had my wedding dress on, and I asked my mom, "Who am I marrying?" And she told me it was Jimnastics. My face dropped.

"I can't," I said. "He's not the one." Then I woke up.

I have pages and pages in my journal processing the sadness I felt, and how I wished I could just go be with him. Ultimately, after several months of dating, I ended it with Jimple because we weren't on the same Christian page. I was somewhere between "In the beginning" and "Amen," and he had finished the book and misplaced it. We weren't equally yoked.

We did the whole dance of leave and come back and leave and come back until I finally begged him, "Please don't let me come back. I'm not strong enough to do this. Please don't answer my calls."

Jimpossible finally stopped answering my calls, and I stopped giving him hilarious pet names. I was so crushed, but it was what was needed. He was a real adult relationship that I wanted to take seriously. This guy was definitely a heart connection. Years later, I ran into him a couple times while I was working, and our chemistry was still there. The first time was after an audition on the Fox lot. I was so excited to see him, I ran over to say hi and fully tripped and almost face planted over my bag. Very sexy. Another time Jimenez snuck into my show in Denver and came into the greenroom to say hello. He texted me later and wanted me to come over and hang out at his hotel. I turned him down.

"Are you happy?" he asked me.

"I am, actually," I said. "I was caught off guard having you there and was excited to see you, but no, I can't come over."

I felt bad that I kept hurting Jimmunization. I was the one who said, "Hey, we can't date, we're on different pages." Then, within a few months of ending things, I started dating a new guy, also very successful in the entertainment industry, also not on the same page yoke-wise. I'm sure Jim heard about it and was probably not happy that I left him because he wasn't Christian enough only to immediately move on to another guy who clearly was not Christian at all. He was the opposite of Christian; he was atheist.

I met the new guy at a bar—I'll call him Guy, which he was. Guyote was so charming and funny, I gave him my number. He was very wealthy and wined and dined me, showering me with expensive gifts, purses, and wallets. I had never had that before, and I'm not gonna lie, being spoiled was intoxicating.

Maybe I got a little too spoiled. Guyding Light had a female best friend, and I was insecure about it. I was filming a movie at the time,

Alvin and the Chipmunks: The Squeakquel, and I remember feeling very confident about that, but for some reason, this friendship got under my skin and chipped away at my self-esteem. A big group of us met up to have dinner at a restaurant, and I was so jealous of their playful, natural banter that I acted cold and rude to both of them. Then, before dessert even came, I got up, announced dramatically, "I'm going home," and flounced. I left thinking, *He'll just call me later and we'll talk about it.* He never called me again. Not even to be like, "Oh yeah, we're done." I called him and he didn't call me back. I sent him an email apologizing, trying to be very mature, expecting him to at least respond with an "I get it. You were insecure. Thank you for apologizing. We're good." He never wrote back.

Guynocologist ghosted me hard, and I was devastated. Not because of him; I didn't even date him that long or like him that much yet. It was my first time feeling disposable. I felt so dumb and lost sight of my value and my worth. I kept replaying my stupid decision to leave the restaurant on a loop in my head. I was so heartbroken, my family was genuinely worried about me.

"What the heck happened?" my sister asked.

"Did you have sex with him?" my mom asked.

"Can I borrow $20?" my brother asked.

"Nothing happened," I mumbled. It was just the first time I was tossed aside like garbage, and it did not feel good. I imagine the same way cantaloupe feels. I felt ashamed of the way I acted and that it was being held against me. I wasn't given an opportunity to clear my name in this fiasco. We didn't have to be together or anything; I just wanted him to recognize and accept my apology. I never got either.

The silver lining to getting dumped is that it taught me empathy and how to recognize broken hearts in other people. The very next weekend I had shows in San Francisco, and I walked into a store and the girl behind the counter came off really rude. At first, I was offended. As I walked out of the store, though, suddenly I was like, wait a minute. I recognized sadness because I was sad. I turned around and went back in to find the girl, who was now folding clothes.

"I don't know what's going on in your life," I told her, "but I feel like you're sad. And I just want you to know that people care. I'm sad, too. I'm going through my own thing, too."

She started crying, and I gave her a hug. Hugs have magical powers, like Tia Mary's salsa.

It's possible that Guyro was a rebound from Jimmortal, but that didn't make either breakup any less painful. After two emotional splits back-to-back, I felt pretty low and vulnerable. Which of course was the perfect time for a manipulating narcissist to swoop in, work his sorcery, and destroy what little self-esteem I had left.

Enter Ben (again, not his real name), a model, public speaker, and aspiring actor who saw me perform at a Christian leadership conference. After the convention, he wrote me on Facebook and was so charming, gorgeous, and, more importantly, funny, which really got my attention.

We messaged back and forth, and he couldn't have been more perfect. He said all the right things to me, and used all the right Christianese language, too, like anything having to do with God guiding me. "I want to honor you," he wrote. He would quote Scripture in a hip way that made it feel relevant, and he sometimes ended our conversations with "Let me pray for you." *Well, if you insist...*

I showed our Facebook interactions to a few friends, and they agreed that he was pretty much the dreamiest dude any of us could have ever prayed for.

Benadryl and I messaged back and forth for a couple weeks and really started to connect. Then out of the blue one day my cousin Tisha called me. Remember Tisha from the earlier chapter where I mentioned her prophetic abilities to hear from God? Well, she left me a message one day that said, "Hey, Anj, I was riding my bike today and I felt the Lord tell me to tell you that the charming, good-looking guy isn't the one. Hope you're well, call me later, byyyye." I called her back.

"Girl, are you sure?" I cried. "Look at these messages."

I sent her our beautiful, spiritual chain of correspondence. Tisha called me back after reading our exchanges, exasperated and confused: "I don't know, maybe I heard wrong, because he sounds amazing."

Tisha was *not* wrong, and I should never question her gift again, because my relationship with Bench Press was not a dream, it was a nightmare. We only dated for about two months, but in that process, he destroyed the last of my already fragile psyche.

He criticized the way I dressed. More passive-aggressively than overtly—that was his way. "Why do you think you wear flats over heels?" he asked.

"I don't know," I shot back. "Because I'm comfortable?"

He gave me books to read, and it wasn't like Oprah recommending *The Seat of the Soul* because she loved it, like, "And you get a book! And you get a book!" Bentheredonethat handed me a book and instructed, "I think this book might help you." CliffsNotes version: "You need help because you're not quite as perfect as I'd like you to be."

Anytime Benign asked me a question, whether it was about my dreams or goals in life or about God and theology, it always felt like there was an invisible measuring stick next to me. He criticized my friends in a subtle, crafty way. Someone made a poop or a fart joke, and he said they were immature. "We're just being silly," I defended them. Who doesn't appreciate a good fart joke? Not only was I not good enough, but now my friends weren't either.

Every night I was dating him, I went to bed thinking, *Why do I feel like zero? Why do I feel like I spent a whole day trying to impress someone, but was never able to accomplish that?* I knew I was valuable. I knew I was impressive, but this guy was never truly impressed by me, only impressed enough to string me along.

I found out through the grapevine that I was not the only famous woman Benchwarmer had dated and that one of his conquests had been the star of a beloved sitcom that popped off her career. When I talked to her about Bento Box, she had creepy stories about him manipulating her, too. "He used me to get a part in my movie."

I definitely got a usey vibe from Fender Bender. I threw him a birthday barbecue and even threw on a pretty dress and some heels. Fine, they were wedges, but they were at least an inch off the ground. I got all the food and invited all his friends, and to show me how much he appreciated that, he ignored me the whole party. He didn't treat me like I was the girl he was seeing or even his hired help. I was invisible to him. I felt awful about myself when I was with him, and I didn't like feeling that way. I kept thinking, *Am I crazy? Maybe I'm just being oversensitive.* Later that night, one of his friends who was at the party reached out to me and told me I did a great job and was so kind to throw him that party, but she'd seen the way Bentertainment treated me, and I really deserved better. I wasn't crazy.

The final straw came when I flew Benefit up to San Francisco to come see one of my shows and meet my whole family. After my set, he milled around backstage talking to and networking with everyone but me. Ben Vogue was not affectionate toward me—he wouldn't even lay claim to me. And I was one of the stars of the show! What's a girl gotta do to get even a side hug around here?

My cousin's husband pulled me aside, raised his eyebrows, and said, "Who is this guy? Why is he acting like he's better than everyone else?" He could see it. Everyone could except me. "He's not the one," my sister whispered.

On the way home from that show, when we were in the car and no one could see us, he held my hand and wanted me to lay my head on his shoulder. When we got to my sister's house, he put the make-out moves on me, and even though I knew he didn't like me and this was purely physical to him, I let it happen.

After a miserable trip, we flew back to LA and I drove Benevolent home. "I don't think this is going to work," I said cautiously, expecting to have a difficult conversation.

"Yeah, you're probably right," he said nonchalantly.

A week passed, and I got a text from him just "checking in." I wrote Benchilada an honest email laying it all out. How he was manipulative and a womanizer. How he used his words to string women along to get what he wanted while he figured out what he wanted. I recently thought, *I wonder if I still have that email?* I had to try to remember my old email password to log in and find it. It was so interesting to read back over my thoughts. In my mind I had remembered being very direct and scathing; however, as I read back over it, I was like, *Man, I was too nice and gave him too much credit, but also very articulate in communicating my feelings,* so I was proud of myself.

He replied to me right away. "I'm pretty ashamed of myself after hearing your thoughts. Can we get together and talk it out before you cut me out?"

Oh. Wow. Very adult. I met him in public at the Americana in Glendale because at worst I thought I'd at least walk away with a piece of Linda's Fudge Cake from the Cheesecake Factory. But that was not the worst of it.

Bendometriosis did not apologize to me as I had assumed he would. He did his Jedi mind tricks on me and flipped my email and proceeded to lecture me about how wrong I was about him. That my insecurity was the big problem and that he wanted to remain friends with me.

"I don't want to be your friend," I said firmly.

"Why not?"

"Because I have a feeling toward you that you don't have back. It doesn't feel good."

"Why are you worshipping your feelings?"

When I tell you this guy was good at Jedi mind tricks, I mean he was the master. He could teach a course on it. Manipulation on, manipulation off.

"Worshipping my feelings" was a very Christianese, calculating thing to say. We're supposed to worship God only and not idolize money, career, or, sure, why not, feelings. He was trying to say that if I let my feelings dictate my life, I worshipped my feelings.

"I'm not worshipping my feelings," I said strongly but without emotion. "I just don't want to be friends with you."

"I'm friends with all my exes. They don't have a problem with it."

"Well, that's good for them, but not for me."

"Well, I think that's very cowardly of you."

I never talked to him again.

I dodged a bullet there and learned a lot of lessons in that relationship. Ben (I can't think of any more puns, so it's just Ben now) was so perfect on paper. He loved Jesus. He was involved in the church. He was a virgin (supposedly allegedly), and I was a virgin (for real). He was so handsome, so funny, and so charming. The whole package. But he was also sleazy and manipulative and made me feel ugly and worthless. Just an awful person to date, and yet he left a trail of beautiful, accomplished women behind him.

Hmm, reminds me of someone I know… *Taranjelah.* I had an epiphany that I'd almost come full circle—maybe my experience with Bentoxicated (I thought of one more) was me reaping what I'd sown. During that season of my life, I didn't treat some of my dates very respectfully. What if Ben was my karma? I thought that might be the case. I take responsibility for my actions and sincerely apologize to any guy I ever hurt and lost interest in. If I made you feel like you weren't good enough to date me, I am genuinely sorry and I hope you can forgive me.

After Benson, my guard went up. It was a Kevin Costner/Whitney

Houston situation like in *The Bodyguard*, except my protection was my own armor.

I reconnected with a handsome guy from my hometown who now played for a Major League Baseball team. We were both at a place in our careers where we were making a name for ourselves and making our hometown proud. We found each other on Facebook and started messaging and talking on the phone. We were just friends, but there was definitely a flirty vibe that would keep us talking on the phone for hours. While that was going on, my friend who got married at the beginning of this chapter rang me up.

"Hey," she said, "I want to hook you up with this guy, Manwell Reyes."

Well, well, well. Two years later and someone was finally ready to introduce us.

"Look him up on Facebook and see if he's your type."

"Okay, I'll check," I said, pretending that I didn't already know exactly who he was from all that social media stalking I did after her wedding.

Manny was a Christian rapper, so technically we were equally yoked. But so were Ben and I, or so I thought. I was skeptical. Manny lived in Florida, so we connected on Facebook. I was immediately triggered because his messages sounded just like Ben's, saying all the right things and the Christianese phrases. "How's your heart today?" Manny would write, or "Hey, I hope you're having a great day. I just want to pray for you. You have a blessed day." He even typed out a prayer for me for the day. I was so turned off. Like, I met a version of you last year, bro; these tricks do not work on me. I had no way of knowing that he was actually being legit. He wasn't making a move; this was his true heart. But I was freaked out.

Another time I noticed (aka stalking again) that he did a show somewhere with Ben on the bill, too. In a Facebook post, Ben left Manny a comment. I told Manny, "If y'all are friends, this is not

My bang game was strong. San Jose, CA, circa 1991 at the park by my house.
(Photo courtesy of my Uncle Ruben, who I think wanted to be a photographer at one point)

Fourth grade school photo. I dabbled in Hasidic Judaism that year. San Jose, CA.
(Photo courtesy of my mom)

Clearly, I had more questions, but the photographer had a job to do. Circa late 1980s, San Jose, CA.
(Photo courtesy of my mom)

Back when scrunchies looked like rolled-up gym socks. Circa early 1990s, San Jose, CA.
(Photo courtesy of...wait for it...my mom)

Me and my best friend in our puffy jackets, posing by a very handsome tree. Circa 1980s at some family member's house or one of my parents' friends who they definitely lost contact with.

(Photo courtesy of my dad this time)

I dressed up as Glinda the Good Witch for Halloween but took liberties with the umbrella part. San Jose, CA, circa 1990s.

(Photo and costume courtesy of my mom)

I wore my *Blossom* hat every single day and had no regrets. Also, I'd be good with spin-art coming back in style. Santa Clara, CA, circa 1990s.

(Photo courtesy of my mom)

We were a cute little Mexican American family. San Jose, CA, 1982.

(Photo courtesy of my mom)

Three generations of Lathees.
Circa 1980s, San Jose, CA.
(Photo courtesy of my mom)

The Get Along Gang: my sister
Veronica, brother Kennie, and our
cousin Michelle. Santa Clara, CA,
1980s.
(Photo courtesy of my mom)

Friends who chola together stay together. Me and Monica,
San Jose, CA, circa 1990s and 2021.

They wouldn't let me use my chola name,
Little Payasa Johnson. Hoover Middle
School ID 1996.

A very casual, natural, and unposed family photo with my dad. San Jose, CA, circa 1990s.
(Photo courtesy of Olan Mills)

Would we have paid full price for actual senior portraits if we knew I'd write a book one day and include it? Probably not. Lincoln High School, San Jose, CA, 2000.
(Photo courtesy of Sanford & Myers, clearly)

You could always find me sitting on my grandma's lap. San Jose, CA, 1998.
(Photo courtesy of my mom)

I get it from my Tia Mary. San Jose, CA, 2019.

Anjelah N. Johnson
SAG/AFTRA

My first "business card," which had my AOL email address on it. Los Angeles, CA, 2003.

I had just spotted my fan club in the audience, which consisted of my mom. Raider game, Oakland, CA, 2002.

(Photo courtesy of Mike Valencia)

This is my most favorite photo of me as a Raiderette. It says I'm feminine and pretty, but also I will cut you if I have to. Raiders home game, Oakland, CA, 2002.

(Photo courtesy of Mike Valencia)

Doing what I do. Austin, TX, 2019.

(Photo courtesy of Mal Hall)

Something about the crowd, the shadow, and Selena on my back doing the same pose feels so powerful. Fresno, CA, 2018.
(Photo courtesy of Mal Hall)

I didn't have bridesmaids, but if I did this would be them. Plus my sister, who for some reason is not in this picture. June 11, 2011, Half Moon Bay, CA.
(Photo courtesy of Grace and Hun Kim)

Mine and Manny's very first photo together. October 4, 2010, Los Angeles, CA.
(Photo courtesy of my cousin Joe)

My husband and I are not afraid of patterns. Los Angeles, CA, 2021.

Family photo backstage at the Wiltern.
Los Angeles, CA, 2019.
(Photo courtesy of Pablo Cabrera)

We both love peesha. Late-night green
room vibes, San Diego, CA, 2019.
(Photo courtesy Mal Hall)

Just a casual Tuesday night.
Unlikely Heroes Gala,
Dallas, TX, 2017.

Just two besties posing together.
Oprah's Girls' Getaway cruise, 2019.

Mom and me being fancy at a movie premiere. Los Angeles, CA, 2018.

My mom and her kids.
Los Angeles, CA, 2018.
(Photo courtesy of my sister Vero)

Three generations of funny. Grandpa, Dad, and me backstage at my show.
Odessa, TX, 2018.

My cousin Joe and me after eating the same serving size of food (also Penelope in the background).
Los Angeles, CA, 2004.

going to happen." He assured me they weren't friends, that he met him this one weekend at the show and never spoke to him again. Small World.

My guard was way up. I played hard to get, but not consciously. I just didn't dote over him. The first time we Skyped, the first time we saw each other's faces, I'd done a show in Nashville and was packing up my suitcase, getting ready to fly to another city and more shows. I had no makeup on, and my hair was pulled up in a ponytail. I walked around my hotel room picking up and folding things, totally multi-tasking him, and didn't put in any effort. I was signaling *Take it or leave it, buddy. I'm busy at life. I'm successful. If you want to be a part of this, this is what you gotta deal with. I'm real good at flirting.*

Manny clearly thought I was not into him but was still intrigued for some reason, so not long after that he flew from Florida to LA to come meet me. We did a double-date lunch in Hollywood with our mutual friends, then he walked me to my car.

"Do you want to hang out again tomorrow?" I asked, knowing he was only in town for a couple days.

"Yeah, let's go on our own tomorrow."

"Okay, I need to return some shoes," I said, not caring even slightly that it was the least romantic date idea ever. Hey, I could have taken him to the eye doctor. I mean I had stuff to do…you want to be a part of this or not?

The next afternoon, I picked Manny up. We went to DSW, and I made a beeline for the flats section. He kept trying to point out super-cute heels to me, which he didn't know was red flag numero uno because of Ben. I was kind of cold and standoffish. I'm sure he was used to women fawning all over him, but I wasn't about to do that, and I wasn't falling for the whole holier-than-thou act again. I was being cold but with a hint of warmth to try to keep him inter-ested. What I didn't know until years later is that he was seconds away from faking a stomachache and bailing on me. I would have deserved it. The truth was, I didn't want Manny to leave. He was so cute and nice and trying so hard. I realized he was paying for somebody else's mistakes, and he didn't deserve that.

We got in line to pay and, as he stood behind me, I nuzzled back into him like couples do in eighth grade prom photos. It was my apology for my being cold, and even though no words were spoken, that move melted both of us. I felt so connected to him in that moment.

After our snuggle, we spent the rest of the day together. We went to LaLa's Argentine Grill for dinner, then drove back to my condo in North Hollywood because I was dog-sitting Penelope's dogs and they needed to potty. When we walked in the door, my roommate Jean screamed, "How did it go? Did you DTR?" Which means *define the relationship*. It's the Christian version of DTF. Manny came walking around the corner, and Jean turned red. She didn't expect me to bring him back home. We all had a good laugh, then Manny and I walked the dogs in the neighborhood.

I didn't want the night to end, but I dropped him back off at our friend's house because he flew out early the next morning. When we said our goodbyes, we gave each other the warmest, most magical hug. You could feel magnetic sparks of energy transferring between us, and I knew at that moment that Manny was the man for me.

One big problem: I was still talking to the baseball player, and it became one of those overlapping situations. I didn't feel comfortable dating two guys at the same time. Who has the energy for that anyway? I had to call it off with one of them. I started pulling away from the baseball player, and he called me out on it.

"I feel like we kind of had a thing going for a while," he started, "and I haven't really talked to you that much lately."

"You know what, you're right," I said. "I'm sorry. I met someone, and I want to give this a shot right now. I didn't feel comfortable continuing our thing if I was trying to give this guy a shot."

"I totally understand. I'll be honest. I'm a little disappointed, because I would be lying if I said I wasn't hoping that something would happen between us."

It was a very mature conversation. A conversation that Taranjelah would never have been able to have and one that, just a few years earlier, Anjelah was incapable of having, too. But I'd grown so much since my solo time with God where I fasted dating.

I met Manny for the first time in August 2010. We dated long distance on Skype, and on October 4, we became an official couple, Manjelah (that's what couples did back then—remember Bennifer and Brangelina?). After that we would commemorate our anniversary by saying, "10-4 *crrsh*" as if we were speaking into a walkie-talkie. I picked him up at the airport and wore an outfit I knew he'd love—shorts, a cute top, and even high heels. That's how much I liked him. We said we weren't going to kiss until we were officially boyfriend and girlfriend, so we made it official and kissed for the first time in my car in the Glendale Galleria parking lot. Then we went to dinner at a Mexican restaurant, though at the time, Manny wasn't brave enough yet to tell me that he didn't like Mexican food because he had a weak stomach and couldn't eat spicy food. He was only in town for a few days before he went back on the road touring with his band. They would perform at churches and arenas and then get on the bus and drive to the next venue. Manny and I would Skype while he was in his dressing room with his band, and I gradually met all of them on a call one by one. He had his own little road family, and I wanted to be part of it.

Two and a half months after our first kiss, on Christmas Eve, Manny met my family for the first time in San Jose. He really wanted to go to San Francisco for the day, but I wanted to hang out with my family. It was tradition that on Christmas Eve all of us siblings just hang out together and then have dinner and play games with our dad.

"Just go," my sister Veronica said. "We're not even doing anything here."

Finnnnnnneee.

Manny and I went to Fisherman's Wharf and wandered into a souvenir store that sold cheap tchotchkes and trinkets. I picked up a giant fake diamond ring and put it on my own finger dramatically. "Could you imagine?! This thing is huge. Seriously, could you imagine, I do! I do!" and I just laughed as I put it back on the display.

Manny didn't think I was all that funny, and he always laughed at my jokes. In fact, he kind of looked like he was gonna puke. Maybe his belly hurt from all the Mexican spices he'd ingested from my family's cooking the last few days. At each stop we went to that day, Manny gave me another one of my Christmas gifts. Romance, am I right? On the way back to San Jose (yes, I know the way), we stopped to eat at one of my family's favorite restaurants in Half Moon Bay, a spot where the lovers go that held very special meaning to some of my family. When we got there, Manny and I walked down to the beach, and he surprised me with my last gift.

Manny handed me a blue Tiffany bag with a box inside, and I was really excited because I had wanted this Tiffany necklace with a little key on it. I knew that was what was in the box, which meant he was really good at taking hints, which was good news for our future happiness. As I was opening up the Tiffany box, I started joking around again, because I'm a comedian and clearly can't help myself.

"Oh, I do!" I squealed again, just being so dumb. "Yes, I do!"

When I opened the box, it wasn't the necklace, *dun-dun*, it was a diamond ring, as big as the one I was making fun of earlier. I was confused. Did he buy it as a gag gift when I wasn't looking?

"Is this real?" I said.

Manny got down on one knee.

"Is *that* real? What is happening?"

Manny proposed to me right there on the beach in Half Moon Bay. He mentioned Tia Mary and Tio Mike, who had been married for seventy-five years, and how he wanted a love like theirs. After my shock wore off, I wiped tears from my face and said yes. Six months later, we got married right across the street from the special spot of our engagement. My sister planned our whole wedding. I am so grateful that she did this for me, otherwise I probably would have just had everyone come over to the house for cake and ice cream. She really knocked it out of the park with organizing everything, from the flowers, to the venue, to the DJ, to the rehearsal dinner. I won the sister lottery. My in-laws flew in and got to meet my whole family. I'm so lucky that our families get along, because I have heard horror stories of overbearing mothers-in-law. My mother-in-law, Carmen, who I lovingly call Carmelita, loves me, and I love her. We joke that she loves me more than her own son now. Sorry, not sorry. My cousin Joe married us, which was so special to me. He was the first person I brought Manny to meet, and he had helped me navigate life as an adult. We wrote our own vows (I punched up Manny's with a couple of jokes so that I wasn't the only one doing funny vows), and we had mariachis play for us as we walked down the aisle.

Sounds like a fairy tale, right? I wish I could say I had the best time at my wedding, but it was a little disappointing. First of all, Manny and I had our first big fight about the guest list and how much money to spend on it. Manny was 100 percent opposed to spending a lot on a wedding. He would have been happy with the cake and ice cream idea.

"I've worked really hard for this money," I argued. "And if I want to spend it on a wedding, I should be able to."

"That's not gonna work," he argued back. "We're a team, and you're already starting with 'This is mine.'"

Manny was right, so we came to a happy medium of me cutting the list down from everyone I'd ever known in my entire life to 150 of our closest friends and family. I ixnayed every obligatory creepy uncle and distant aunt and used "It's a small wedding" as an excuse.

A few days before the wedding, I got a sinus infection and basically swallowed the entire drug aisle at Walgreens. The day of, I still felt under the weather, so I popped a multi-pack of vitamins, an allergy pill, three Advils for a headache, and an antibiotic. My body was not happy about it, to say the least. I put on my beautiful Mikaella wedding dress, a strapless number with a sweetheart neckline and ruched detailing, but suddenly I felt rumbles in my stomach. Uh-oh. Then I got sweaty chills, which made the makeup on my perfectly painted face drip down my temples. But I powered through, because it was my wedding day, and are you even kidding me?

We strolled around the property and took pre-wedding photos. Our photographers were amazing; however, I could barely focus because I was fourteen seconds away from having explosive diarrhea in my wedding dress.

I mini stepped as fast as I could toward the bathroom in my hotel room, careful not to launch into an all-out sprint, which would have split the form-fitting, Swarovski crystal–embellished bodice in half. I saw my dad and grandparents in the hotel foyer.

"Come say hi to Grandpa…"

"Not right now!" I yelled as I flew by them.

I made it to my room, my friends helped me shimmy out of my dress, and I jumped on the toilet just in the nick of time. I spent the next thirty or so minutes lying on the bathroom floor wearing only my sexy wedding-night undies and an updo. I got in and out of my dress three times and was therefore late to my own wedding ceremony, but I managed to make it before people thought I had runaway-brided it.

The rest of the wedding was a blur. I had a good time, like when my professional dancer friends and I did a choreographed routine for Manny to a mix of songs including one of his own. I definitely wasn't super in the moment and loving life, though. I was still feeling like I could have a *Bridesmaids*-level accident in my dress at any moment.

My queasy stomach had already dampened my big day, and now it was threatening to ruin the biggest night of my life. Um, remember,

I was supposed to lose my virginity in T-minus four hours. Imagine, I'd been such a good Christian girl for like a decade, and now the moment had finally arrived, and I felt like poo. Literally.

I felt all the pressure, every ounce, of this historic event bearing down on me. I was like, *I can't not have sex on my wedding night. I've been waiting for this forever. Like no way, I'm totally having sex.* Manny and I tried to make it romantic; we did all the clichéd things. We took a bubble bath and sashayed around in fluffy white, obscenely expensive robes in our beautiful hotel suite. But the actual act itself was awful. The *worst*. The closest I've ever gotten to being on an episode of *Law & Order: SVU*. It was so painful, and I felt like I was being attacked. I was crying, and poor Manny was like, "I can't do it if you're crying. Like, it doesn't work, you know?" I was able to hold in my tears and pretend I wasn't dying for long enough to let him finish his marital deed. See ya never, virginity.

In my family, after a big celebration, we usually have another party the very next day, and we all eat and drink again and talk about all the fun we had the night before. Well, I was very much looking forward to doing that. However, now that I was married, I had to share in decision-making. Manny's friends were in town for the wedding, and he wanted to show them around San Francisco. I was so upset that all my family was at a restaurant having the best time talking about my wedding, and I had to spend the day with two dodos. I ended up becoming really good friends with them, but at the time I just wanted to be with my family, so they were just Dodo One and Dodo Two.

To make matters worse, one of his friends, who was also very Christian, said to me, "There are so many gay people in your family."

"Yeah, I know," I said.

"Man, we gotta pray that off your family."

Excuse me? The truth is, I may have said something like that in my past, so I got what she was saying because I came from that church world. At the same time, I was thinking, *That's my family, how dare you*, which also just added to my "I'm so pissed that I'm here with you right now, while my gay family is having a gay old time without me" vibe. I was steaming but also gave myself an A+ for not causing a huge fight. I felt like I was already winning at being a wife and it was only day one. Go me!

Two days later, Manny and I flew to St. Lucia for our romantic honeymoon. When we landed on the island, people couldn't help but stare at Manny. I blend in wherever we go, but he's so handsome and looks like "somebody." He can't help but stand out with his big afro, chiseled face, and dark glasses. Everyone assumed he was famous, and we got special treatment everywhere we went. They would ask him, "What do you do?" and he would reply, "I do music." They would just assume he was famous, and we would let them assume. I mean he was kinda famous in the Christian music festival world. Next thing you know we were escorted to the front of the line. I was fine with that.

It was the first time Manny and I had ever been on vacation together, and we had a great time at our all-inclusive resort. We lazed on the beach, got seaside massages, and played naked Marco Polo in the little private pool that came with our room.

The best part of an all-inclusive resort is that everything is free, so I took the opportunity to reintroduce myself to alcohol. I was like, *Well, let me figure out what drinks I like now!* I tried wine and tequila and vodka and still didn't really like it, but I wanted to get my money's worth, so I gave it my best effort.

The booze was really helpful because everything was very new and we were still learning each other. In some ways, we were still strangers. Like, when my friend's mom, Margie, was so nice and gifted us a zip-lining excursion that was off the resort. We didn't know we would have to ride in a shuttle for two hours, so for the first time, I experienced Manny's major anxiety about riding in shuttle vans because he wasn't in control behind the wheel. The whole trip there he sat in silence and watched a movie on his phone with his earphones in. I don't know how he managed to be a touring musician for years, but at least they had bathrooms on those tour buses.

The other thing was, now we were allowed to have sex whenever we wanted, but something changed when all of a sudden having sex wasn't taboo.

The truth is, it took me a few years to figure out the whole sexuality thing. I had looked at sex like this thing I wasn't supposed to do, which made everything else really exciting, because I knew I was walking the line. But once the line was removed it was like, now what? Where do I go from here? I felt like purity culture had great intentions but really damaged my sexuality. Sex and sexuality were made out to be something to refrain from, not embrace. Like, cover up your chest, don't be proud of your body or your sensuality or your curves, because you might cause a man to stumble. Feeling sexy is not okay in purity culture. Then, when you get married, you're supposed to just throw that all out the window and be able to be a sexual being and know how to be confidently sexy, not shamefully sexy. Up to that point, I only knew how to be shamefully sexy. Now I was in a situation where having sex was not a shameful act, but I didn't know how to enjoy it. It was a whole process, and it took me a long time to even understand what was going on mentally. It's definitely been a journey to understand and get to know my body.

I was really resentful and also sad and depressed that I didn't have super-fun memories of my wedding and that my wedding night just wasn't what I expected. I didn't really have the best time at my wedding because I felt so sick, but I'm glad everybody else did. It took me a good year to get over it. I really had to do some inner work and process it and let it go. But at least I had a beautiful wedding video and photos! Now those I can brag about and say that I am very happy with how they came out.

Saying that the first year of marriage is the hardest is a cliché, but clichés exist for a reason: 'cuz they're true.

Because we're good Christians, Manny couldn't move into my condo with me until we were actually married. Neither of us had lived with a boyfriend/girlfriend before, so it took a minute to figure each other out, the things we do, the little "rules" we had. Like, when he first moved in, there was no room for him to put anything in my—sorry, *our* room. My closet was full, my dresser was full, and it's not like I was about to bring in another dresser because then the room would look like the opposite of whatever feng shui is. So, his stuff went down the hall. For the longest time, our room was actually *my* room, and it was like, *I'll just let you sleep in here with me.*

"Sharing" was a topic that came up a lot. For instance, my toothbrush. *I like to be the only one who uses my toothbrush.* This guy, I don't know how he grew up, like maybe they were on a budget or something. He'd come to me and say, "Hey babe, can I use your toothbrush real quick?"

"Wait, that's an option for you? Like you're thinking about it? Sick."

"What? It's just like kissing. We kiss. It's the same thing."

"Mmm, I do not scrape off your tartar with my tongue. I mean, I know I'm pretty amazing, but I'm pretty sure I cannot prevent cavities."

Maybe it really was a budget thing, because in the beginning, Manny bought all the cheapest brands of everything. We both came from humble beginnings, but he was a little extra humble. He bought all the generic knockoffs, so instead of Windex, it was just "window cleaner." We didn't get Fruity Pebbles, we got Fruity Stones. One time, he put a grocery bag in the bathroom garbage can to line it, and I said it looked ghetto. He got offended because that's what his mom did at home—he thought I was calling his mom ghetto. Not my Carmelita!

So, yeah, we had a bit of a learning curve. I was learning how to be a wife, and how to put somebody before myself. This was hard because I was single for a long time and didn't have the practice. In a marriage, if you put your spouse and their needs above yours, you're trusting that your partner is also doing the same and putting your needs above theirs. That way both of your needs are met. But at this point I was still in the mindset of "I need my needs met. I need what I need."

Our problems weren't all my fault (this time). We both had a lot of learning and adjusting to do. Especially because two weeks after our honeymoon, Manny and I both went on tour in different directions for months. We didn't see each other a lot right after we were married, and it really took a toll. Our phone calls ended up being:

"How was your show?"

"Good. How was yours?"

"Good. I'm tired."

"Me too."

"Talk to you tomorrow."

"Byeeeee."

That was it. And it was not good.

Early on in our marriage, communication was not our strong suit. If we got in an argument, I wouldn't talk to Manny for like two days. I shut him out. That was my way of trying to hurt him because I felt hurt. I wasn't capable of communicating my feelings in a healthy way. I came from a very prideful childhood background where we didn't talk about our feelings; we just closed off. I hurt you because you hurt me. Manny was very patient with me about that, but he also called me out when I gave him the silent treatment.

"You don't get to do that," he explained. "You don't get to just ignore me, because we're a team."

We were at a low point when a friend recommended a counselor/therapist based in Nashville whose ministry specialized in helping Christian musicians and artists pro bono. This therapist really understood the toll the touring life takes on a marriage. In one session with him, we learned techniques that we still apply to our relationship today.

First and foremost, he talked about how to cultivate intimacy when you're apart or far from each other. You ask your partner, "What is one thing that you thought today that you wouldn't have told me unless I asked you?" It causes you to pause and think about the internal dialogue you're not saying out loud, the stuff you're mulling over, like insecurities or dark thoughts. By sharing that, you're allowing your partner to see into you, which is intimacy. That has really helped us stay connected and not have the same boring conversations every day.

Another great exercise we learned was finding a special escape just for us, even if not a literal place. He asked us to think about New York City, how it's a bustling metropolis but right in the middle of it is this oasis called Central Park. That whoever decided to build it was a genius because they understood that sometimes you need to stop, take a deep breath, and pause, and that's what Central Park represented. We needed a Central Park in our marriage and our careers.

After our session, we decided that Manny would no longer do back-to-back tours. We decided he couldn't live on the road like he used to, because he was not single anymore. Which was a huge sacrifice he made, but after a lot of open and honest conversations about it, we both realized it would save our marriage.

I used to pray and ask God, "When do I get normal married time?" Because all you see in the movies and TV shows is nine-to-five marriages. Your parents go to work, they come home, you do dinner together, and on the weekends, you have birthday parties and baby showers and you go grocery shopping and you run errands. That's what a "regular, normal" marriage looked like.

I kept fighting my life, because I had this idea in my head of a perfect marriage. "God," I prayed, "when do I get to have this marriage? When do I get to be normal?"

Then I felt God say to me, "This is your normal."

When I felt that in my spirit, it really unlocked something. I stopped resisting what I had and started embracing it. I figured out how to not only make my normal work but how to make it stronger.

For a little while after we got married, Manny and I had an ongoing joke. He'd say, "Babe, do you wish you picked the baseball player? You could be in the players' wives suite right now eating a box of Cracker Jack."

I knew I made the right decision.

When we got married less than a year after meeting each other, everyone said we were moving too fast. But when you know, you know…you know? I thought I'd marry an ugly guy because at the end of the day personality was more important than looks, but Manny's so, so handsome. Like, his beauty takes my breath away, sometimes as if I need an inhaler. I don't even have asthma. With Manny, I'm not saying I'm chopped liver, but if we walked into a store together, nobody would notice me. Manny could commit a crime in said store and the police would ask the witnesses, "Was he with anyone?" and they would reply, "Nope. He was all alone. Could you please give him my number?"

I'm more than okay with that. Manny always talks about how he dated a girl one time who refused to ever tell him he was handsome because she said he heard it too much from everybody else. I thought that was so sad. That's the person you want to hear it from the most.

It is true that everybody loves Manny. Old people, young people, men, women, parents, and don't even get me started on flight attendants. They just love to flirt with him and touch his afro. His big hair definitely draws attention. He's also very fashionable, always in the coolest outfit with a hat and jewelry, and he always smells good.

I am so grateful for his hygiene because there are lots of stinky boys out there. You know, like when a guy has had his shirt in the closet for a long time, it smells like cilantro. As soon as Manny gets out of the shower, he sprays cologne, even if he's going to bed. That's his jam. Only problem is I have a very sensitive sense of smell, and we don't have the same taste. I like clean deodorant smells; he's into tobacco, musk, oud, and leather. I've grown to love his scents but I just need him to spray fifteen times less than he does. Hey, as long as he doesn't smell like cilantro, we're good.

Our individual strengths complement each other, and we let them shine. Manny does all the housework and picks out my outfits, and I love it. He wakes up early, around six a.m., and by the time I get up at eight, he's already mopped and swept the floors, done the laundry, and washed my car. I don't make him—he's not Cinderella—it's just his personality to do that. I just benefit from it.

He doesn't pick out my clothes to be controlling; he's just very into fashion and I don't love shopping because I'm too lazy to take off my clothes and try things on. But I do like getting cute new outfits and shoes, so Manny goes to the mall and brings so much stuff home to me, the salespeople have asked him what film production he's working on. They think he's a wardrobe stylist. "Nah, this is just for my wife," he tells them. I keep what I like—I swear he knows my body more than I do—and he returns the rest. Everybody wins. It's like subscribing to a personal styling service that also does the laundry, rubs my back, and complains if I get too sassy…

We don't subscribe to gender stereotypes in our marriage. Manny's a talented musician, but I'm the breadwinner. He is wise with money, so when I bring home a big check, he is figuring what percentage to invest and what percentage to save. He's emotional and can communicate; I'm emotional and am learning to communicate. Manny is very in touch with his feelings and loves Hallmark movies and romantic comedies like *My Best Friend's Wedding*. He also watches typical dude movies like *A Few Good Men* probably once a month. I'll come to the living room and say, "Didn't you just watch that?" "Yep."

Anyway, Manny has really helped me talk about my feelings, as hard as that once was for me. In the beginning I would ignore him for two days. Then it got to the point where I had to walk away, and a couple hours later, I could come back and talk about it. Now we're at a point where it's pretty immediate and I can come back to him without holding a grudge. I've seen the growth in myself as a human and as a wife and as a communicator.

I may provide financially, but Manny provides in so many other ways, especially spiritually and emotionally. I can't do what I do without the way he supports me. Manny is a natural born cheerleader. He lives to uplift and encourage. He's also very good at giving advice. But his biggest gripe with me is that he will give me advice, but I won't take it until I hear somebody else say it. "I told you that like two months ago!" he'll say, exasperated.

We can still get on each other's nerves, and of course that's normal. I say that he is the only one who knows the combination to the lock on my rage monster. For example, Manny likes to ask me questions to get to the bottom of why I'm mad, but his questions come off less as inquisitive and more like he is questioning me on the stand in a court of law and I have to defend myself. *Objection! Badgering the witness!* He is also the only person I know in the whole world who actually does mouthwash for the full minute, and that's always the exact time he wants to have an in-depth conversation with me.

"I don't speak mouthwash!" I say when he gargles through a story he's desperate to tell me. "I don't understand what you're saying. Just wait till you're done!" Manny also eats cereal in bed, slurping the milk and chewing with his mouth open, which grosses me out. He gets mad that I am so defensive, can still be prideful, and I'm kind of a hoarder who doesn't like throwing things away. I still have my high school cheerleading box that we would stand on to do cheers. It used to hold my pom-poms, but now it holds my shovels and soil for my garden. See? Good thing I kept it, so now we don't have to spend money on a garden box. You're welcome.

We have different personality types on the Enneagram scale. He's an 8 and Puerto Rican, so he is very passionate and loud. Eights are challengers, so he likes to ask questions and get to the bottom of things, no matter how long it takes. When he's super passionate and really embracing his Puerto Rican loudness, his nostrils flare. I'm a 9, a peacemaker who hates confrontation. God forbid I tap out of a conversation or argument with an "I don't want to talk about it" or an "I don't know." Ooh, girl, that really pushes his buttons.

But that's all just petty stuff. Overall Manny has taught me how to communicate my feelings and have healthy boundaries, and I've taught him lots of things, too, like how to eat sushi. I'm proud to say he's graduated from a chicken teriyaki roll to California roll to finally a spicy tuna roll. No wasabi, though. He's not there yet. I'm so proud that his palate has evolved since being with me.

People on the outside may think I'm the star and Manny's just my sidekick. They don't know I'm able to stand on this pedestal because he's holding it up. Manny and I are most definitely a team now. We inspire each other to strive to be the best version of ourselves.

At the end of the day, I know how lucky I am with Manny. I'm really blessed. When he finally crossed my path, he was more than I could ever hope for. He was beyond my greatest dreams or expectations. I wondered to myself if I even deserved him. I prayed to God and wrote in my journal, "Is he mine?…Do I get to keep him?" Like he was a puppy I found on the street.

We were both a surprise for each other. Before me Manny only dated white girls who liked hip-hop music. And before him I only dated guys who weren't right for me and were sometimes gay. It all happened so fast for us, but we followed peace. As my friend Laura once told me, "If you have peace in your spirit, follow that, no matter who thinks otherwise." Peace is how you can fall asleep at night. And it helps to have a hottie with excellent hair lying right next to you.

CHAPTER 10

Home Is Where the Hotel Is

I was bummed after I was let go from *MADtv*, but it turned out to be a blessing in disguise. I was able to move on with my career and toured the world as a stand-up headliner for the next thirteen years.

At first, I traveled all by myself. And the mere act of stepping foot outside my radius, my comfort zone, was a little overwhelming. I went to so many places I'd never even heard of in every corner of the country and met people from all walks of life. I remember sitting in so many airports, watching people go back and forth and wondering, *Who the heck are all of these people? Where do they come from? Where are they going? Are they sad? Are they happy? Do they like their carry-on bags? I needed a new one.*

I'm a street-smart city girl—I grew up in San Jose and lived in Hollywood—so I shouldn't have felt so naïve. But those early years on the road opened my eyes in so many ways. The first thing I learned was that in addition to traditional comedy clubs, I'd also be performing in really random places—from college cafeterias to corporate retreats.

Corporate gigs are notorious for being awful because you're in a situation where people are not expecting stand-up comedy. So it's usually a rough crowd. They're not really in the vibe of "Hey, let's laugh!" Like one time I performed at a trucking convention in a fancy hotel in Las Vegas. I knew a trucking convention was not really my jam when they booked me, but it was a nice paycheck, so I said, "Truck yeah, I'll do it!"

The audience was 85 percent male, and before the "show," they'd been schmoozing in a little lounge area in a nightclub, drinking, tipping their hats to the female bartenders, bobbing their heads to Garth Brooks or something (don't @ me, but he's the only country artist I can think of), and having a grand old time. Suddenly the music stopped, and they were shuffled into a conference room that had that yellow office lighting that makes everyone look like they have gangrene. "We have a comedy show for you!" the organizer announced to glassy-eyed blank stares. Maybe laughing wasn't their favorite.

Oh boy, I thought, *they're not gonna like me.* I was hoping my opener, Mal Hall, would at least get a few laughs because he was a dude, but he got crickets. They were itching to get back to the bar, but it was my turn. Sure enough, when I got up on the stage after him and did my material, I got zero laughs, not even one chuckle. Change of plans: Time to dig into my bag of tricks. I hit the mother truckers with my Raiderette jokes, because all guys like football, amiright? No. They apparently only liked Garth Brooks tonight, and all I heard was the sound of the figurative explosion that just went off—because I was bombing.

The truckers only laughed at me one time, when I made fun of myself. So, I switched gears again—see, I could speak their language—and launched into a self-deprecating monologue: "Listen, guys, I didn't book me for this show. You don't want me here. I don't want me here." I pointed at the lady who booked me, sitting right at the front table, and put her on blast. "Oh, she does this really funny nail salon joke," I said pretending to be her. "It's hilarious! All of these men who drive trucks for a living and have probably never been to a nail salon are going to love it!"

Finally, I got a big laugh. Maybe a knee slap or guffaw or snortle. However truckers laugh tepidly, that's what they did.

I could only make fun of myself for so long without it getting old for the audience and me needing to find a good therapist. It's not like I could just ad lib about trucker things. I didn't even own a trucker hat. I was supposed to be onstage for forty-five minutes, but after twenty-five minutes of torture, I glanced down at the lady booker and mouthed, "Do you want me to keep going? Or are we good with whatever just happened here?"

"That's fine," she whispered, giving me the invisible hook with her eyes.

"I'm Anjelah Johnson," I announced to the crowd. "Thank you and *goodnight*!"

I bolted offstage, collected my big ol' check, and escaped out the back door. On my way back to LA, I fist-pumped the air to get a big rig driver to honk his horn, my way of trying to prove to myself that not all truck drivers hate me. He didn't honk his horn. Clearly news travels fast in the trucker community over CB radio that Anjelah Johnson is *not* funny.

Obviously, truckers were not in my wheelhouse (see what I did there), but I discovered very quickly that I was a huge hit with my fellow evangelicals, especially because I always worked clean and could speak the Christian language. I did the whole church circuit as a comedian and as a speaker sharing my testimony. I got very close with a lot of the big famous pastors and worship leaders around the country.

My friend Tiffany Thurston Liftee-Kau started an amazing conference called BLOOM for young girls in Hawaii. Every year they put on this weekend event for girls and young women to be encouraged and inspired and learn how to bloom where they are planted. I hosted it multiple years in a row, and I was able to perform and share my testimony. I love being able to allow my story to uplift and encourage people—which is a big reason why I decided to write this book in the first place.

I've performed in many different Christian environments. Completely opposite of BLOOM is a place I like to call cholo church. Now, if you're a cholo and you're in church, that usually (not always) means you've done a 180 from living a life of bad things to living a life devoted to Jesus. To stay on the right track, some of these folks needed structure and rules and regulations. Some of the cholo churches were so strict and conservative, they didn't even allow dancing. At one of my shows, a rapper who performed after me tried to get the crowd to wave their arms in the air like they just didn't care, but they cared, a lot. Nobody would do it. It was like *Footloose*, but if Kevin Bacon's jeans were about five sizes bigger and creased up with starch.

Apparently I'm big with opposites because not only were the church people really into me, but I also noticed right off the bat that I had a huge following in the gay community. Weird, because those two circles usually didn't overlap, but for some reason I got love from *all* the Christians and *all* the gay people at my shows. Lisa Lampanelli and Kathy Griffin have their gay boys, Hannah Gadsby and Tig Notaro have their gay girls, but me? I got all the letters—L, G, B, T, Q, the plus sign, all of they/them.

I tried to dissect me and be like, what is it? Is it the sass of Bon Qui Qui that appeals to my gay boys? Is it my tomboy ponytail that reels in my lesties (aka lesbian besties)? The staff at clubs would tell me that the largest gay turnout was always at my shows. Clearly Ellen hadn't been in the building recently. I came to the conclusion that whether it was my sass or my ponytail didn't matter; God was using me to help show the LGBTQ+ community that a person like me, who is very vocal about loving God and Jesus, can also love and accept them. They hear too much from people who look and sound like me that they're not accepted, that they're not good enough, and that they need to change. At my show, they see a person who loves them as is. Who tells them, "You are enough. You are loved just the way you are. We are all the same. Come sit at my table and laugh with me."

I'm completely accepting of all people (except drunk heckler people), and my audience reflects that in their diversity. The best audiences are a mix of race, gender, class, and sexuality. When you get straight, gay, Black, white, Latino, Asian, rich, poor together under one roof, it's always a beautiful show. The only common thread that matters is that my audience loves to laugh. My material is very universal. I'm not a political comedian. I'm not angry, and I don't want to get my opinion out on touchy subjects. I don't have an aggressive energy. Don't get me wrong, I do have sass and I talk about things like how I love Jesus, but I will punch a ho if I need to. But I put out a very playful, inclusive vibe. That's who I am.

When I go to comedy clubs, I always get compliments from the staff that my fans are "the best." They're a happy bunch. They eat food, drink a lot, and tip well. Servers live off their tips and, after my shows, I always see them counting their well-earned money. That always makes me feel good because it's a reflection of who I am and the energy I put out and attract to me. And people outside of me see it and feel it. It never gets old hearing "I love when you come here" from the comedy club employees.

Now, that's not to say it was always kumbaya at da club. When I first started, I was very young and innocent and got taken advantage of a bunch. I didn't know the ins and outs of the business side of stand-up comedy. For example, there are different ways to get paid. You can get a flat fee, percentages, bonus deals—there are lots of ways to structure it. Early in my career, I was on bonus deals. That meant I got extra money for selling out a club. But what happened was, a certain club was 450 seats, and this one manager told me after the show, "Oooh, you were so close, you sold 443!"

"Darn!" I said. "If I'd only sold seven more!"

I didn't know I'd been had until my friend the comedian Gabriel "Fluffy" Iglesias pointed it out. "Why didn't you just buy those tickets?" he said.

"What, I can do that?"

"Yeah, if those seven tickets are going to cost you two hundred bucks, you can get your thousand-dollar bonus buying the seven tickets," Fluffy explained. "You still make $800."

I didn't know I could do that. I didn't realize and couldn't stomach that some clubs would take advantage of me if they could. Others were totally aboveboard and extremely generous, like the manager at the Ontario Improv, who still gave me my bonus even if I was short a few tickets. "I want you to come back to my club," he told me.

I became a road warrior by trial and error. Like, I could be super hot in one market and ice-cold in another. I once did eight sold-out shows in San Jose, my hometown, only to sell *seventeen tickets* the next weekend in Pittsburgh. They gave away free tickets just to get people inside the club. Talk about keeping a girl humble.

Luckily, I had way more sold-out shows than empty houses. I never took for granted that people were willing to pay their hard-earned money to see me perform. That was and is so special to me. I was always so grateful to get the email or phone call that said, "You're sold out. Do you want to add a show?" My road family eventually became Ja-Kee; my go-to openers, Mal Hall, Rahn Hortman, and Eddie Sisneros; and my real brother Mitchell, aka Sonny, who I'd sometimes bring along as my security. Sonny looks like a UFC fighter, but—don't tell anyone—he still sleeps with a teddy bear and he's in his thirties. My fans are not aggressive—they're usually happy and friendly—but I do have an online stalker or two, and weird things have happened at my meet-and-greets backstage. Like, I've had fans sneak into my greenroom. At Caroline's in New York City, a seventy-year-old lady wandered in after my show and started schmoozing with everyone. She introduced herself to me, but there was no need. I instantly recognized her. She'd been sitting in the second row, and the waitress visited her a few more times than the two-drink minimum.

"And what's your name, dear?" she slurred.

"Hi, I'm Anjelah. You just watched my show."

"Who?" Her drunken dragon breath almost knocked me over.

There's another comedy fan who takes pictures with celebrities and asks them if she can smell their head. This was probably the weirdest request I've gotten, and reluctantly I did it. I knew I had just washed my hair so at least I would smell good. One thing I definitely will not do is take a picture while I'm eating. I'm touching my food and usually with family or loved ones, so it's not the time to be shaking hands or pausing from chewing so I can smile for the 'Gram. One time in San Jose I'd just done a group workout with my cousins and my sister, and we decided to grab breakfast and gain back all of the calories we'd just burned off. We were all sweaty and nasty when this woman came up to our table and asked for a picture. She already had her phone out.

"Oh no, not right now," I said as pleasantly as possible. "I'm eating with my family."

"Come on, real quick!" *Click.* She took the picture.

I lost it. I grabbed her phone, deleted the photo, and threw it back at her.

"You're rude!" she whined. "You need to learn how to appreciate your fans!"

"You need to learn respect for people," I sniped back. "I said no, and you took your picture anyway. That is not okay."

It's extremely rare that I melt down like that. I'm hypervigilant about treating my fans like the kings and queens they are, because I've been around other celebs who don't, and it's hugely disappointing.

One time I ran into someone I admired (not the chain-smoking girl who told me to have lots of sex, someone else) and asked, "Can I take a picture with you?"

"I'm in a hurry, come on, let's go," the famous person said curtly. Then she barely leaned in and mustered up a half smile. It was so awkward.

Small world: I ended up working with her down the road and we became friends, but I never forgot that nasty moment. She gave me a master class on how *not* to handle fans. Nobody teaches you how to be a celebrity, how to be famous, what to do, what not to do. She actually taught me that it's okay to have boundaries with fans and that they should know when you're uncomfortable and you don't want to take a photo. They don't own you. But I also learned from her how not to communicate. Note to self: Don't do what she did. Except for that one time when I threw a phone.

That wasn't my finest moment. Or was it actually the greatest moment ever? Who do I think I am? One time I got a comment on a post from a girl who said she saw me in Target that I "did not look nice at all." That's probably because I have RBF, resting bitch face. That's just what I look like all the time. I might not look friendly, but I swear I am—99.9 percent of the time, I'm thrilled to meet fans. And by the way, who walks around Target smiling and chitchatting with strangers anyway? I love to hug my fans, except when I find myself in the crook of their sweaty armpit. I'm little, so that's where I always end up with people taller than me, wedged into stinky pits. Please, I just ask that you put some deodorant on before a show, with a clean and fresh scent, nothing powdery or flowery if it's gonna end up on my shoulder for the rest of the night. Please and thank you.

My brother Sonny is more of a security blanket for me than an actual security guard. He would protect me in a heartbeat and has had to settle down a few people, but really I just loved being able to take people I love on my journey with me whenever possible. My brother

Kennie comes on the road as my hairstylist sometimes, too. And actually, if we take it all the way back, my sister, Veronica, was really my very first assistant. I've brought her out on the road a couple times to sell my merch and look for people recording me in the audience with their cell phones. She always wanted to be a police officer, but she is only four-eleven and weighs a hundred pounds fully grown. So when she applied for criminal justice classes, they were like, "Aww, how cute." When she got to catch people recording me and flash her flashlight at them to put it away, it was like she was living her wildest law enforcement dream. Having my peeps around me and traveling around the world together makes all of my incredible experiences that much more special.

I've been to too many random places to list them all—from small-town family-owned clubs across the United States to big theaters in Australia—so I'll just describe the most memorable places I've been, good, bad, and WTH.

The most intense but fulfilling experience of my career was going on an USO tour with a five-star general and some incredible people like actress Mayim Bialik, Miss America 2019 Nia Franklin, MMA star Rampage Jackson, country singers Cassadee Pope and Laura Bryna, and actress Toni Trucks. We flew to six countries on four continents in nine days on a private plane usually reserved for members of Congress. Like, the plane said THE UNITED STATES OF AMERICA on the side and had a couch on it, and we got three-course meals. Yes, we fancy by association.

I can't tell you everywhere I went because then I'd have to kill you, but a few of the hotspots were Africa, Kosovo, Germany, Kuwait, and "undisclosed location." I got to sit in the cockpit when we circled above said undisclosed location and kind of overheard on their pilots' radio that if we landed in the wrong place, we were gonna start World War III. I got it all on an iPhone video, but if I showed it to you, it might cause an international incident and I'd have to kill you again.

I hosted the variety show, which also included my stand-up act, so I was doing double duty, aye-aye, sir. I'm not gonna sugarcoat it: I bombed the first three shows, which I believe is a rite of passage, and I had to learn how to craft my set for a military audience, which of course had female soldiers but overall was an extremely masculine environment. All I know is they liked it a lot when I beat boxed—always a crowd pleaser when it's a room full of mostly dudes.

I'll try to explain the reason for my poor performances, but I'm afraid you can't handle the truth (I've watched *A Few Good Men* with Manny way too many times). Listen, in Kuwait it was 125 degrees at six p.m. I didn't even know thermometers went that high. I did as little exertion as humanly possible. It was too hot to even go sight-seeing at the magical street markets because I had to conserve all of my energy for the show. I always appreciated our troops, but after that trip, it was like a whole different level of gratitude. Like, *Wow, I'm in shorts and a T-shirt complaining, and you guys do all this in full fatigues without complaining. All while you're away from your families. I'm fatigued and complaining just sitting in a chair out here.*

The hardest thing about being on the road, whether a soldier or a stand-up, is leaving your family, leaving your comfort, leaving your bed, leaving your shower, leaving two-ply toilet paper, and leaving your favorite grocery store. So, you really gotta try to make your time away count and not just lie in a cot motionless in the desert heat, even though that's what every part of you desires.

Hands-down the best trip of my career so far was touring Australia and New Zealand for a month. I went to Sydney, Brisbane, Melbourne, and Perth. I filled myself to the rim with meat pies and went to a drag club—both were existential, spiritual experiences. What? Meat pies are spiritual.

In New Zealand, we spent an afternoon at the legendary Piha Beach, and as I ran in and out of the freezing surf like a little kid, I felt unexplainable joy radiating throughout my body. I thought the meat pie was heavenly, but this misty mysterious beach, with its black sparkly sand and giant waves, made my heart soar. As we were walking back to the car, I walked up a hill and a little puppy came running toward me. I remember laughing and thinking, *Of course God would do that.* Top off the most ethereal day with the cutest most random thing ever that God knew I would love. It was like a director secretly yelled, "Action! Cue the puppy!" Like, are you kidding me?

We finished that day by going to a fabulous Indian restaurant and we cheers'd to living our best life. We all felt very grateful for each other, for our friendships, and that this was what we got to do for a living. It was a very special dinner.

Dinners on the road were always different. Sometimes it's a vending machine night at the Quality Inn; other times it's a five-star meal by the hottest chef in Chicago. Japan was my favorite food city. I had the best pizza I've ever had in Tokyo. I know, I know, you don't go to Japan to eat pizza, but we were told to try this one particular pizza, and it truly was Tokyo's finest. By the way, I've never felt more like the "loud American" than I did in Japan. It was so quiet on the streets. Nobody talks. Nobody eats food on the street. You don't see people drinking a Starbucks or walking and eating on the way to work. We realized that even in the intersection, where there were thousands of people crossing the street, it was silent. Was this some sort of Emily Blunt/John Krasinski *A Quiet Place* movie situation where, at the sound of a pin drop, a monster would appear out of nowhere and murder everyone? As it turns out, no, but it could have gone either way. And of course it would happen in Japan, because most of the best scary movies come out in Asia first and then we remake them in America with a white lady.

Anyway, don't worry, I didn't die, but I did eat plenty of ramen. Some people go bar hopping; we went soup strolling. We looked up the best ramen, ate one, settled our stomachs, then made our way to the next ramen spot. I also ate as much top-notch sushi as I could fit in my body. Ja-Kee isn't the most adventurous eater; she has a self-proclaimed "toddler diet," which usually consists of chicken fingers and mac and cheese. So, we all had a good laugh when she ordered a Philadelphia roll at one of the best sushi bars in Japan. "That's American sushi!" I whispered.

"They don't have cream cheese here?" Ja-Kee said innocently.

I'm aware that gluttony is a sin, but it's a delicious sin. Whenever I'm on tour, I must seek out the best local cuisine in each city. In Boston, restaurateur Nick Varano became a fan of mine, and anytime I came to town, he spoiled my gang with dish after dish at one of his many Italian joints. All the pasta and desserts and limoncello a girl could dream of. I now call him my Boston godfather, and I love to spend time with him and his family anytime I'm in Boston.

Sometimes I get gourmet; sometimes not so much. For example, a girl in Birmingham, Alabama, recommended a Mexican restaurant. I was like, "Oh that's so cute…but no thank you. We're in the South! I need biscuits and gravy." But I wanted to be open-minded, so we went, and there wasn't one Mexican person in the entire restaurant. *I was the Mexican person.* We asked for chips and salsa and they said, "That'll be $2.75." First of all, chips and salsa are free. Everybody knows that is Mexicans' gift to humanity! *How dare you.* I noticed something called "Seasonal Guacamole" on the menu. So I asked the waiter, "Excuse me, Chad, uh, what's in the seasonal guacamole?" And he said, "Walnuts and candied apples."

It was my "Sí se puede" moment. I needed to stand up for my people. I wanted to scream, "I rebuke you in the name of Jesus! You take that guacamole back to the pit of hell!" Instead, I just ate my white people Mexican food and left.

I grew up a city girl, so I enjoy city life. I admit that when I go to a place that is a more small-town vibe, I do get a little uncomfortable, just because I know I'm different. But it's okay if you only have one Applebee's in your city; I'm not judgmental. I feel like each city has its own heartbeat and its own vibe based on its history, the type of people that live there, the economics, a lot of things. But there is an unspoken, unseen energy in each city for sure.

I can be sensitive to those vibes. If I pick up on it and feel a type of way, I actively remind myself why I'm there, especially when it's a city that has a lower vibrational energy or feels a little sad, oppressed, or small minded. Even if I don't jibe with the heartbeat of the city, I'm there for a purpose. My job is to bring joy to people, even if I feel uncomfortable or things move or work differently there. And when I tap into that purpose, I'm able to bypass whatever vibe is happening and bring in my own vibe.

I sometimes pray over my venues and seats. I acknowledge the energy that existed before I got there but say, "However, I'm here now. I bring in joy. I bring in the spirit of God. Let joy marinate in this theater right now." When people dealing with depression, anxiety, divorce, health, whatever walk in, I offer this joy that is medicine. They come into a place that I made mine. If I am able to tap into that, it's very powerful.

Sometimes the crowd is just straight-up wack, and there's nothing I can do about it. I've heard comedians say that there are no bad audiences, just bad comedians. I completely fully and 100 percent disagree. Sometimes an audience can be disastrous. Like they all met up and decided to be in a bad mood or tired by the time they walked into the show. The crazy part is usually an audience has no clue that they're terrible. They just think they're laughing and having a good time as they chuckle underneath their breath, but they have no idea that the show before them was roaring with laughter.

Sometimes I walk onstage and my personality, my voice, my inflection, my timing, my opinions change the vibe. Before I did a Bon Qui Qui show in the panhandle of Florida, my backup dancer and backup singer, who are Black, went to go get their nails done and were refused service. I was so upset and offended for them that when

I got onstage, I was almost mad at the audience. But they were hype, they were standing, they were dancing. They flipped the energy and reminded me that I came here to help bring joy and help people have a good time. Just because the history and the energy of the city may be rooted in ugliness, not everyone there was about that.

All small towns are not the same. You shouldn't stereotype, and when I say *you* I mean *me*. One of my favorite little towns of all is Hanford, California, between Fresno and Bakersfield. They have the cutest antique shops and the cutest little theater, and it has its own dairy. You literally get ice cream right from their cows standing right there. My other favorite venue is Tommy T's Comedy Club in Pleasanton, not far from where I grew up. Tommy T owns the club, and his wife, daughter, and son all run the place. It's a very family environment, and I've been performing there since I started. I almost always do my New Year's Eve show at Tommy T's. I love that I support them, and they support me.

My favorite places to visit are the cities where I have family, and I'm Mexican, so that's a lot of cities. I also love the tropical feel of Miami and the hustle and dreamy heartbeat of New York. I love the Bay Area, where I'm from, and Los Angeles and Nashville. My husband has been going to Nashville for his music business for years, and we spent so much time there that we decided to move there part time. We now go back and forth from Los Angeles to Nash-Vegas depending on our tour dates. We have built a community of friends there that we can count on and do life with, which is very important to me. San Diego is my favorite big city, period. It's sunny, the downtown is clean, it has a laid-back California beach vibe, and it's close to Mexico, so the food is really authentic.

More than anything, I love any city that has a good crowd. For some reason, Texas is my sweet spot. The craziest, most energetic show I've ever done was in McAllen, a small town right on the border of Mexico. The laughter and the vibration was so high, it scared me. I am not joking. The first laugh I got, I wasn't expecting it. It came back and hit my body like a truck. I still get chills thinking about it because it was so powerful. I had never felt that before—or since.

I always get so excited to come to Houston, because I know my shows are going to be fire, which is why when it came down to filming my very first hour-long special for Comedy Central, *That's How We Do It*, I chose to film it in Houston. One time I said onstage, "Where's the best place to eat in Houston?" Because you know, priorities. And a fan responded, "My grandma's house." So, guess what? We went to her grandma's house for lunch.

"It'll just be my immediate family," the girl promised. By the time we got there, there were thirty people in her house. It was a full-on Mexican-style immediate family. There were cars parked up on the grass, the whole deal. But she didn't lie: Her grandma's tamales and menudo were bomb.

Traveling all over the country and eating the best food and seeing historical sites is good for my brain and my soul, if not my butt and thighs. I love being introduced to new cultures and cuisines and touring Paul Revere's house. But the best part about my job, the life-changing part, has nothing to do with places or things. It's the people. Meeting you after my shows and hearing your personal stories.

Some of my fans come up to me at meet-and-greets, and they're already bawling before they've even said a word. Then I get overcome with emotion too. I try to be disarming and say, "This is our moment. Let's talk." And these complete strangers, who feel they know my heart because they've seen me on YouTube or TV or in the movies, pour their hearts out to me.

Mothers and daughters come to my show together a lot. "I don't get along with my mom," the daughter will whisper, "but we bond over your comedy." Too many people tell me they've watched me while they're doing chemo treatments or when a family member was in the hospital. "We watch your videos over and over. Sometimes it's the only thing that makes life more bearable."

I have loyal "regulars," who I've seen year after year at my shows, and I'm so happy to see their faces in the crowd. I've had people who bought their tickets well in advance come to the show even though one of their friends ended up passing away. And they all still come in honor of that friend. I have fans who I'd met with their spouse when they would come year after year to my show, and then suddenly only one is at my meet-and-greet. I have so much empathy for anyone experiencing the loss of a loved one. I get in my head and think, *Wow, there was a human being, a soul on this earth, that knew of me, that laughed at my jokes, that shared me with their friends, and now they're not here anymore.* It hits a little differently.

I pray with fans a lot, whenever and however I feel it in my heart. Sometimes it's an obvious prayer; sometimes I just say what I hear in my heart; sometimes it's just an extended hug and I whisper nice words in their ears. I've had people message me and write, "You may not remember me, but you prayed for me five years ago in your meet-and-greet line. And it was really life changing. Thank you for doing that."

Some people will come through the meet-and-greet line and take a picture, and I say, "Thanks for being here, get home safe!" and that will be the end of our convo. And then there'll be people that come up who I feel in my spirit that I need to take a little more time with. Words do mean everything to people, so I take that opportunity to figure out the perfect thing to say to them. I use my intuition, I listen to God speak to me, and I repeat it. God gives me one-on-one time with His soul creations. And I'm like, *What do You want to say to them? What do they need to hear? What is going to help their life? What is going to motivate them? What is going to be the key that unlocks whatever has been keeping them down?*

It can be profound, or it can just be me telling a woman that her sweater is beautiful and looks great on her. When anyone, let alone a well-known person or someone you admire, says something like that, it carries weight. The memory lasts a lifetime. I mean, I'm still talking about Lisa Kudrow telling me the teacakes on the craft services table were good fifteen years later. And I didn't even bake them.

I got into stand-up comedy by accident, but my chosen profession has given me the greatest gift. I'm not talking about eating paella in Spain or finding a really cool mop that effortlessly picks up hair off the floor in Japan. The emotional connection I have with my audience is priceless. I need them as much as they need me. Especially if their grandma will make me a delicious homemade lunch.

CHAPTER 11

A Sucker for Stray Dogs

Growing up, we always had animals in my house—dogs, turtles, rabbits, and a bird I named after my nina. I actually have two ninas. One on my mom's side of the family, Irene, and one on my dad's side, Rosemarie. I won't tell you which one I named the bird after because I still use her name as a pseudonym when I check into hotels today. But don't tell anyone.

We had lots of dogs and not surprisingly, my dad made sure they were very obedient. He trained one of his Rottweilers, Baby, to pray before she ate her food. Baby would put her little head down, my dad would say grace, and after the command of "Amen," the dog could go ahead and chow down. My dad finally had an obedient child.

In high school, I got my own pet just for me. A friend had a litter of baby kittens, and when I went to go pick one out, all of the cats were just sitting there except for one climbing up a bike tire. He was showing off, like, "Ooh look at me! Pick me!" So, I took him home and named him Tah-Nes, baby talk for "Tiny." He was gorgeous and amazing, and we were in love—well, me more so than him because, you know, cats. One day he walked out on me and went missing. I was crushed and stapled posters with his picture on it on all the telephone poles in the neighborhood.

After a couple of weeks, I gave up looking for my beloved kitty, not because I didn't love him, because I had appendicitis and had to go to the hospital for emergency surgery to have my appendix removed. The day I got home, Tah-Nes came strolling through the front door casually, as cats do, as if to say, "I've been busy, but I felt like you might need me."

I really did. I've always loved animals. After I left home, when I was younger, I really wanted to get a dog, but I was too poor. I could barely pay my own bills and buy my own food. Then I became successful and could finally afford a dog, but I was too busy traveling all the time. There was no way. But God has a way of arranging things and always made sure there were sweet puppers in my life in so many unexpected ways. I'm not saying it means anything, but let's not forget that *God* backward is *dog*.

In my twenties, when I lived with Penelope, she had a white Maltipoo mix named JoJo. But she was always on back-to-back tours, dancing around the world (Pen, not JoJo). So JoJo ended up basically becoming my dog. Our bond was so strong, she followed me everywhere. If I wanted to clean the house, I put on a zip-up hoodie and tied the waist tight with a scarf. I placed JoJo inside my hoodie like a pouch, so her little head could pop out of the hoodie. That way she could be with me 24/7, even when I did my chores. This was before *Shark Tank*, otherwise I'd for sure be a bajillionaire by now.

JoJo was my special booboo, but my heart was never meant to belong to just one. I stopped by a friend's house in Orange County once to say hi, and he showed me the cutest fluffy puppy tied up in the garage. It couldn't have been more than a year old and looked like Chewbacca.

"Why do you have your dog in the garage?" I asked furiously.

"My mom doesn't really want him."

"Then I'm taking him. You can't do that. This does not make sense."

I scooped the dog up in my arms and took him back to Penelope's. I promised her I would find him a new home ASAP and called every cousin in my family's phone book. Meanwhile, this little guy was tugging at our heartstrings, with every head tilt. He was an adorable angel, licked your face uncontrollably, and played dead with the command *bang*. He was only there a few days when Penelope looked into his beautiful eyes and blurted out, "I'm going to keep him! His name is Smokey." It kind of felt like we were new parents. We wanted to have a puppy reveal party but didn't want to accidentally blow up the neighborhood.

JoJo and Smokey, who became blind in his later years, were our babies for the next decade of our lives. We shared custody, even after she married Steelo and I moved out and eventually married Manny. During this season of my life, I was dogless more often than not, and at first that was hard and sad. But then this strange thing started happening wherever I went. Stray dogs found me. Like, at least once a month.

I'm a sucker for stray dogs. Let me clarify. I don't like to keep them. I just like to save them. It's physically impossible for me not to help when I see a dog wandering around outside alone.

Here's the thing though—it happens a lot. I can't seem to stop finding stray dogs. It's like all the local stray dogs know when I'm nearby and decide among themselves whose turn it is to get saved. "Hey, Brewster, you're up."

Once on a walk in my neighborhood I found a giant Chow Chow. As I got close enough to check for a name and number on her collar, she tried to bite me. I understood where she was coming from, because to her, I was probably just a stray lady. I would have tried to bite me too.

Needless to say, my adrenaline was pumping. A normal human would have just been like, "K, well, good luck then, Chow." But not Anjelah Dog-Rescuer Johnson. Quite the opposite, actually.

I chased the dog for forty-five minutes up and down a very hilly road and rounded up six of my neighbors to help until I got the dog to her owner.

It was exhausting, and everyone was happy, but that's nothing compared to the one time I spent four hours in the rain to rescue another dog.

I was with my husband in Nashville at one of his songwriting sessions. We were hungry, so I ordered us some food from the Italian place around the block. I left to go get it, and as soon as I turned down the street in my car, I saw a dog running through the rain like she was channeling Rachel McAdams in *The Notebook*.

I thought, *OMG, someone should help that dog. Not me though, because mud and wet and no, but someone seriously should.* Then I remembered I was in a rental car, so I was like, *Okay, I'm the person for this job.*

Sorry, Enterprise. This is why I pay for insurance.

I pulled over, reached over to open the passenger door, and was like, "Come on, dog, get in." She didn't get in. It was in that moment that I realized most dogs won't just jump into a rando stranger's car. What a creep I must have looked like to her. "Hey doggy, you like treats? Come on in, I got some treats for ya."

She wasn't falling for my sleazy tricks, so I pulled over and got out in the rain. She apparently preferred the rain to my dry stranger-danger car, so I had to aggressively attempt to kidnap her in the rain. (I'm going to say "in the rain" several more times in this story just so you guys really grasp the trauma I went through.)

I kept trying to get her to come to me, but she wouldn't. I'd get a little closer to her, then she'd take off running in the street. In the rain. Cars were driving by at an alarming speed for a residential neighborhood in the middle of the day, so I had to risk my life by jumping in the street to scream from the depths of my dog-saving soul, "Stop! Don't hit her! She's just a dog." Then I had to switch back to "Come on, cute little puppy. Come to me. I'm very safe and trustworthy, and I'm just trying to help you." Then she would bolt again, and I'd chase her in the street, and do the whole thing again. This went on about twenty more times. In the rain.

At that point, we both needed a break from each other, and I needed to get my husband some food before I had to deal with a hangry songwriter. So, I went to get the food I ordered, and made a pact with myself that if she was still there when I got back, I'd try again. If not, then I'd choose to believe her owner found her and they lived happily ever after.

I came back and she was still there. Ugh. (I'll be honest, part of me was happy to see her again even though I knew this was going to take up the rest of my day, maybe the rest of my life, and my husband was going to be hangry to the point of no return.) So, for the next two hours, I tried to get this wet dog into my rental car.

My kidnapper tactics were not working, so I thought, *Maybe a treat?* That's when I remembered I had Manny's chicken alfredo pasta sitting in the car. Go, me.

I tried tossing her some chicken. That didn't work. I placed a trail of chicken leading back to my car. That didn't work. Instead, she grabbed the chicken and took off running. Clearly no dummy. So, then I resorted to throwing chicken at her, yelling, "Wait, I have more chicken!" To any passerby, I just looked like a crazy woman throwing the best part of her pasta in the street. In the rain.

Two brave girls driving by saw beyond my crazy and noticed I was struggling, so they pulled over to help. I asked if they had anything to entice the dog to get in my car. They said they had tape, a spare tire, and reusable grocery bags in their trunk, which reminded me of an episode I saw on *SVU* but probably wouldn't work in this situation.

Then one of the girls remembered she had a blanket in the back seat. That got my wheels turning. What if I mixed together some *SVU* moves along with some Cesar "Dog Whisperer" Millan techniques to capture this dog once and for all?

I said to the girls, "Okay, I'll distract her with chicken and tell her she's pretty. You know, gain her trust. And you sneak up from around the car and throw the blanket over her."

It quickly turned into a super-intense scene from a high school football movie. It was practically monsooning at this point but in slow motion in my mind, and I was talking to the girls like I was their coach and we were in the red zone with five seconds left on the clock.

I shouted, "You block the cars! You come up from behind, can you do that?!" "Yes." "Can I trust you?!" "Yes!" "The whole town is counting on you, kid. This is your time. Nothing in life matters after this."

So we went for it.

Our play ended up working out perfectly. The dog was as good as kidnapped. Not even Olivia Benson could have stopped this mission from happening.

We finally got the dog in my car, and it felt victorious. Like, wow, we just saved her life. But as I was feeling all the feels, I thought, "Wait, now what do I do with her?"

I called every shelter, vet, groomer—anything in the phone book that had the word *animal* in the title. No one would take her. At that point, it had been almost four hours, but it felt like four days. I hadn't even told my husband about my rescue mission, and I assumed I'd have millions of texts from him like, "Where are you? I'm worried. Call me!" But no. I had one text from him: "I'm hungry."

I could have been dead. My husband was in the comfort of his very dry recording studio drinking Throat Coat, singing his song, oblivious to my Liam Neeson kinda day. When I made it back to the recording studio, his biggest concern was why his pasta was cold and vegetarian.

What happened to the dog, you ask? Well, I'll tell you. After I took the dog to a vet to get her checked out (she had fleas and was severely malnourished), I posted my entire journey of the day on Facebook along with her picture. I asked my fans to help me find her owner.

Someone recognized the dog from their neighborhood, where some awful human kept her outside tied to a tree 24/7. It's a good thing that person never showed up to claim her, because I would have Charlize Theron–ed them so hard. Not Charlize from the Dior commercials; Charlize from *Mad Max: Fury Road* or *Monster*. Anything to save a dog. There was no way I would have let her go back to those conditions. Otherwise, I'd have to save her all over again.

Instead, a woman reached out to say that she and her husband saw my post and wanted to adopt her. And they did! They named her Reba (not sure if it's after the TV show or the singer…you can't see my face, but that's a joke), and they lived happily ever after. We have since kept in touch, and every now and then she sends pictures and videos of their sweet and happy dog, along with their children they've since adopted. (They're super into adopting.) I'm so grateful that I didn't give up that day, because who knows what could have happened. It was all worth it.

I've always gotten signs that I was meant to have my own dog, but it never seemed like the right time. I'd been killing it in my career for more than a decade and was on a high the entire ride so far. I was so busy, it just didn't make sense to be like, "Yes, in between my eight sold-out shows this weekend and the four auditions I have next week, right now is a great time to add a dog into the mix."

Eventually, the lifestyle of being a stand-up—all the traveling, late nights, lack of sleep, hustling, airport food—started to wear me down.

A couple years ago, I noticed I'd always get melancholy around three days before I had to leave for tour. I didn't even whistle anymore when I packed; it started to feel like a slog, doing the whole car-airport-car-hotel thing I'd done a million times before. I tried everything to pump up my spirit, like listen to worship music or watch my favorite preachers' videos. All I could do was pray, but in that sort of head-space sometimes that didn't even work. I knew nothing about anxiety yet; I just thought I had a case of the what-ifs. *What if Starbucks runs out of cold brew by the time I get there? What if I forget my hoop earrings? What if everybody I love dies?* Ya know, normal stuff. What-ifs all day long, creeping up on me until it was time to go.

My anxiety and overall malaise around touring deepened. I had a show in Virginia Beach one weekend and was not myself. I'd felt depression before; this wasn't quite depression, just a heaviness I couldn't shake. I just felt blah and melancholy. None of the things that typically helped me break out of that were working—praying, jour-naling, watching something comforting on TV like a murder show.

I was invited to a friend's house for lunch, and even though I wasn't feeling myself, I reluctantly agreed to go. Maybe getting out of the hotel room would help. As soon as I walked through their front door, their little dog came running up to me. It was like how in New Zealand the puppy came running up to me from out of nowhere. I picked up the dog and I felt *the melt.* All the heaviness I'd been feeling evaporated off my shoulders. I could see clearly, and I could suddenly feel my feelings again. I actually felt happy. Whoa, how did this dog know that I needed that? I looked into the dogs eyes and thought, Tah-Nes, are you in there?

From that moment on, I knew I needed an emotional support animal to bring with me on the road. I researched how to fly with an emotional support animal. The process of getting a pet officially certi-fied was complicated and overwhelming. I am a rule follower; I wasn't the type to get a fake doctor's note so I could take a giant peacock on a plane with me, although I'm sure peacocks can be very soothing when they aren't screaming. If I was gonna do this, I was gonna be legit about it.

My friend Iliza Shlesinger always traveled with her sweet dog, Blanche. I went to her for advice and asked so many questions. Most importantly, where do they go to the bathroom on the plane? And I was always on the go, go, go, so how would I make connecting flights carrying a dog bag, my luggage, my purse, *and* a Cinnabon?

It seemed like a giant headache but more than worth the trouble. And if Iliza could do it, I could figure out how to do it, too. There was only one problem: Manny did not want a dog. He didn't grow up with animals, and his attitude was, "If we get a dog, it's your dog. You have to take care of it."

"Oh no, I don't want that life," I argued. "*We* are getting a dog. I'm not going to get one until you actually want one too."

Luckily, not long after, Penelope needed a babysitter for Smokey, but I was out of town. Manny was on Smokey duty by himself. He sent me a message:

"If we ever got a dog, I would want him to be like Smokey."

That was all I needed to hear. Manny opened the floodgates and unleashed the hounds. I texted Manny all the photos of dogs I had saved on my phone from local rescue organizations. I had a whole album on my phone, like a doggie vision board. My friend Maya and I follow all of the rescue organizations on Instagram, and we sent the cutest ones to each other with the caption "Get this one!"

As time went on, I kept touring dogless but with an open heart, wondering when I would actually get one. This one weekend I was on the road doing one of those brutal back-to-back-to-back cities tours, where you finish a show and sleep for three hours, then wake up early to fly to the next city and do the same thing two more times. One late afternoon in the last city, Biloxi, Mississippi, lying down in my hotel room resting before my last show, I was scrolling mindlessly through

Instagram when Maya sent me a post of the most precious dog at a rescue shelter in Burbank, about fifteen minutes from my house in LA.

"Oh my God, look at this dog," she wrote.

"Oh my God, that's my dog," I wrote back immediately.

He was so cute, I figured he already had like ten applications. But then I noticed the post had only been up for an hour. I messaged the shelter right away and he was still available.

"I'm in Biloxi, Mississippi, until tomorrow," I explained. "Please don't give this dog away. As soon as I land, I will come straight to you. But I just need you to hold on to him until I get there. One more thing: It probably won't be until the late afternoon. Which is why I need you to just not let him get adopted by anybody else."

"We will hold on to him for you," she said, "but are you for sure coming in?"

"I promise I'll be there," I said as calmly as possible, which was not calm at all.

The next day, after I landed, Manny and I drove to Burbank, and I prayed the whole way there. I knew I could bond with any animal walking down the street very easily. I bond with them before I even recognize there's a human attached to the other end of the leash. There was no question in my mind that I'd be okay. But I needed Manny to have a connection with this dog to really show me that he was meant to be *our* dog. I just needed this dog to kiss Manny, and that would be my sign. I prayed harder.

At the shelter, all of the dogs were barking like crazy, but off in one little corner of a kennel, sitting quietly, was my guy, Garbanzo. I believe I gasped, if I remember correctly. The worker picked him up out of the crate and put him in my lap. Garbanzo immediately snuggled into me and gave me kisses. Manny put his hand toward Garbanzo, but he turned his head away dismissively, as if he had been offered burnt eggs or raisins.

"Oh, I don't think he likes my cologne," Manny said.

"Nobody likes your cologne," I said. That wasn't nice. Manny does smell good all the time, but a lot of times he just overdoes it. One spritz is ideal, not sixteen. You aren't an Abercrombie & Fitch store. "Do you want to hold him?"

"Sure."

I put the dog in Manny's lap, and they sat face-to-face. There was a slight pause and head tilt, then Garbanzo licked the end of Manny's nose.

"We'll take him!" I shouted.

I found my Banzo. Garbanzo Bean Reyes. He's Yorkie–Maltese–Shih Tzu–Cocker Spaniel–Miniature Schnauzer–Mexican–Puerto Rican. His accent's *all* messed up. We wanted to rename him, but nothing made sense. My first choice was Chandler after Chandler Bing on *Friends*, but you could really only shorten that to Chandy as a nickname, and that sounded like a girl's name to me. We tried all the *Friends* names—Ross, Joey, even Gunther—but they fell flat. Manny wanted Sinatra, but that seemed like a better name for a big dog like a Great Dane. So Garbanzo remained his name-o.

Banzo is the most perfect dog. He's so soft, very communicative, smart, and intuitive. He has a great personality. He's silly and funny. He loves to do zoomies and show off by dancing on his hind legs. He's so sweet and loves to love people. I love how he leans in and snuggles strangers. He follows me everywhere, I mean everywhere, even into the bathroom when I'm going number two. I'm like, *You really don't need to be here for this, I got this*, but he has to stand guard at my feet. As soon as I reach for the toilet paper, he knows he can stand down. Mission accomplished. Then he walks away.

Banzo has no problem waiting patiently while I drop the kids off at the pool, but God forbid he accidentally poops inside the house. It's not that I'll yell at him; I don't even need to. Banzo cannot take disappointing me, so he punishes himself. He gets super emo about it.

As soon as he spots me cleaning it up, he runs and hides in his travel bag with his ears down. He's so sad and so ashamed, he can't even look at me. Then, even though he pooed in my office and I have to clean it up, I end up soothing him. "Momma's not mad atchoo," I say in the most embarrassing baby voice. "Iz okay. You're not in twouble."

Baby talk, T-shirts and mugs with Banzo's picture on it—yes, I do all of it, and I'm now that crazy dog person. I take him everywhere with me—the mall, hospitals, on hikes, the gynecologist, restaurants. He even joins me onstage on my shows. It's possible people are paying to see him at this point. At first, I was self-conscious and insecure about bringing him everywhere, but my friend Iliza taught me to have confidence when I walked in anywhere with Banzo. "Who cares?" she said. "This is your animal that you need and provides support for you. Just act like you know what you're doing. Say, 'Table for two, please!'"

Of course, I take Banzo on the road with me. His very first trip was Houston, Texas, and since then, he's gone on well over seventy flights and tour bus rides. I love coming offstage and walking into the greenroom and seeing his face. He really helps me with my anxiety. Everybody has their own stuff they deal with. Mine was traveling and constantly being away from not only my family and the people that I love, but my comfort, my home, my bedroom, my bathroom, my car, my favorite grocery store. I missed the big stuff, like birthday parties and quinceañeras and weddings (still sent a gift) and the little stuff, like weekend errands and going to movies. Even though some people think they would give their left arm to live my life, I lived in a constant state of FOMO in the opposite direction. I longed to do "normal" people stuff again. Banzo helped balance that out. And in return he got his own fans—seventeen thousand followers on Instagram plus tons of cute gifts at my meet-and-greets. When he sees a bag with tissue coming out of the top, he knows it's for him and can't wait to rip it to shreds.

I admit Banzo is a teensy tiny bit spoiled. I have a bed for him in every room of my house, but he still climbs up on all the furniture, and I'm okay with it because he doesn't shed and also I like to cuddle. He gets top-of-the-line treats, such as the odor-free bully sticks. You tell me, but it seems fancy to have the stanky part removed. All of his food is organic and sustainable and freshly made with real ingredients; meanwhile I'm over here eating my Flamin' Hot Cheetos. Every night, Banzo gets dinner and a show. It's kinda like being at Medieval Times—he eats with no utensils, but instead of jousting, we have a fierce tug of war with a Kong rope toy.

I am my father's daughter. My dad taught his Rottweiler to say grace before he ate. I've trained Banzo to wait for my special song I sing to him to be done, then I say, "On your mark, get set, eat your food!" The song I sing goes like this:

If you're hungry and you know it, lick your chops.
If you're hungry and you know it, lick your chops.
If you're hungry and you know it
Then your face will surely show it.
If you're hungry and you know it, lick your chops.

I'll stick to my day job. Banzo prefers my stand-up anyway. He actually knows my set. When he hears me finishing my last joke, he gets up and starts pacing for me to come in, I've been told. Either that or he's ready for someone to take him out to pee.

I perform for Banzo, and I shower him with gifts. He has about forty thousand toys and doesn't need any more. But anytime I'm at TJMaxx looking for new pajamas, random spices you can't find anywhere else, or holiday-scented candles, which is quite often—they should really sponsor me, but that's neither here nor there—I have to stop in the dog aisle and get him another toy. Sometimes I let him pick one out. Which means the first one he smells.

He's so good when I take him shopping. Unlike human babies,

he never throws a tantrum in the store or freaks out when I don't buy him all the ice cream. Kids are great, some of them, but I'm very happy that my only child walks on four legs and doesn't talk back to me when I tell him it's time for bed.

I gave Banzo a first birthday party, and it was the best first birthday party ever. We had balloons, a human cake (no chocolate allowed), a dog cake shaped like a bone, and goody bags with toys, treats, and poop bags for all the dogs we invited. Banzo and all his puppy friends ran around in the backyard while the adults stayed inside and did a tequila tasting. All birthday parties are better with tequila, even dog ones.

Banzo is like my son. I am already a godmother/nina to a lot of children and a few dogs too. However, Banzo does not have a godmother and godfather yet because I am still torn on who I would leave him with. The first person you'd think of is Penelope, because we've already co-parented dogs before. But Penelope doesn't like licks to the face. I'm like, "Wait a minute. If I die, you're not going to let my dog lick your face? You're out of the running." Nobody's good enough.

Manny has bonded with Banzo for sure, but I'm clearly Banzo's person. Some people let their dog play in the backyard alone, and I would never let Banzo outside without adult supervision (unless he has twelve of his closest dog friends with him and tequila is involved, like at his birthday party). I guess you could say that's why I'm a helicopter parent, always hovering around my boy. I mean, coyotes were a real threat in my neighborhood, plus he looks like a tasty snack to the crows hovering above. I bought him a tricked-out coyote vest that had all the things—LCD blinkers, a shocker, pointy bristles, and a spiked collar. I thought he looked like an adorable punk rocker, but he hated it. I think he wore it once, and after that, he ran and hid in his crate when I brought it out.

I miss him when he naps curled up like a croissant, which is like twenty hours a day. He loves people, and I'm so proud that he brings everyone so much joy, but he's a stage 5 clinger at the dog park. He's more of a people-loving dog than a dog-loving dog, and I'm not mad about it. On a road trip across the country, he sat on my lap for five days straight. He would pop his head out the window for some fresh freeway air and then curl back in his croissant position for a few more hours.

Banzo loves his kennel from back in his training days, but I'm so enmeshed in his life, I actually get offended when he chooses to sleep in his crate instead of in our bed. *Excuse me? What did I do to deserve this?* "Mom, you've been helicoptering me all day," he's probably thinking. "Can I get some space?"

All dog owners are dying to know what's happening inside the minds of our fur babies. That's why I paid far too much money so Banzo and I could chat with an "animal communicator." My friend Aimee and her dog Moose had a session with this woman and told me I should definitely give it a go. "You have to talk to my dog communicator," she implored. "She gets on the phone with you and then talks to your dog. She will tell you everything you need to know."

I made an appointment because I was very curious about two things:

1. Where was Banzo before me? The story I got from the shelter was that a man came in and said he found two stray dogs on the street, one being Banzo.
2. Most important, does he understand how much I love him? Like, *does he get it?* Because sometimes I'll be right in his face pouring out my heart. Does he know? I needed to know that he knows.

So, I booked an appointment, and right off the bat, I loved the animal communicator on the phone. She had kindness in her voice, and she felt like a momma from the South who just wanted to serve you sweet tea and chitchat. She explained how it worked, took a deep inhale, then announced, "Okay, I want to talk to your dog. I'm going to ask him what he says about himself. And I'm going to ask him what he says other people say about him."

I was quiet and she was quiet.

"Wow, he's so soft."

She had only seen a picture of Banzo, and sure, she could guess that he looks very soft, but the weird thing was that every single person who has ever touched my dog—the skycap at the airport, the Starbucks barista, fans at meet-and-greets, every single one of my cousins—the first words out of their mouths are "Wow, he's so soft. I've never met a dog as soft as this."

"Wow, you're so fast," the animal lady said next.

That's exactly what we said to him when he did his zoomies in the backyard. She was copying what Banzo heard people say to him!

"He's calm, but confident for a small dog," she added, then started laughing. "He's definitely got a personality. I can see him as if he was putting his hands on his hips like, 'What do you mean, *small dog*?'"

"Where was he before me?" I asked.

"He was not a street dog. I feel like he lived with an older woman and she couldn't take care of him anymore, because he's telling me that the house he's at now is way more energetic than where he was before. The person who dropped him off was not his person. The man who dropped him off was her son. She couldn't take care of him. He was very confused when he was getting dropped off."

Now this was way different than what the shelter said. They said he was found as a stray on the streets of South Central LA. So I assumed I had the most gentle, loving, and kind thug dog. If you follow him on Instagram you will see that his online persona is very much a street-smart homie dog from South Central. This news was stripping him of all his street cred. Not only was I disappointed as a kid that I wasn't a real chola, but now I was disappointed that my dog wasn't a real thug dog.

"Does he know how much I love him?"

I concentrated really hard in case I could telepathically channel my thoughts into Banzo's brain so he could say the right thing. How I tell him all the time that I'm very lucky to have him. That because of him, I'm more nurturing, I'm more present in the moment. I spend less time in my head and on my phone because I have a living being to take care of. (Don't get me wrong, I still spend way too much time on my phone.) My love language is physical touch and words of affirmation. Sometimes I will just communicate the heck out of it to Banzo. I'll say, "You make me so happy. You are the best dog. I love how you love people. I love how smart you are. You're so generous with your unconditional love, and I really do appreciate you." I tell him every single day, "I'm so so grateful for you."

"Okay, let me ask him if he has anything he wants to say to you about your love."

More silence. This time it felt like an eternity.

"He says…'*Grateful.*'"

I told the woman how I always tell him that I'm grateful for him and she said, "Well, he feels the same way about you."

It was the best mortgage payment I'd ever spent in one hour in my entire life. Ever since our session, I feel even more connected to Banzo, and I didn't think that was possible. I feel like now I know a little more of what's going on in his mind. I still wish I could understand his barks, though. Whenever the neighborhood dogs start up and Banzo's ears perk up, I ask him, "What are they saying? What's going down? Translate it to me!"

He doesn't translate it to me. But he does settle down, look into my eyes, and curl up into his trademark croissant position right next to me, and all that matters is him and me together forever. Oh, and Manny too.

CHAPTER 12

Please Don't Die, Okay?

Loving people and animals is great and all…until they die. Hi, my name's Anjelah, and I have an irrational fear of death. I've had this since childhood; it started when my mom would drop me off at school and every day I'd cry because I thought she was gonna die. She'd be like "Bye! Have fun!" and I'd say, "Bye! Don't die, okay?" The teachers sent me to a therapist and said, "Listen, her mom is a trigger. We think she might be beating her." *What?! No! That's stupid!* My mom's not beating me…that's my dad, but that's *not* why I'm crying.

When I was seven, one of my best friends died in a car crash. Lisa Lykam lived across the street from my grandma, and we had "gentle and kind" play dates, according to my mom, "because neither of you were bossy." Lisa was really shy and so was I, so we'd spend most of our time smiling at each other until it was time for dinner. We were in Camp Fire together, which some people may consider to be the poor man's Girl Scouts, but fun fact, Camp Fire was created first so, in your face, Thin Mints. I remember entering a cake decorating competition with Lisa, and our team leader had the life hack of the century.

Instead of wasting all that time baking a cake, we used a cardboard box and layered frosting all over it and topped it with cute decorations. I don't know if it was the sharp edges of our "cake" that gave it away, but we ended up being disqualified from the competition. No one told us it would be a *Great British Baking Show* situation where they actually taste the cake. We should have at least been given extra bonus points for creativity and ingenuity!

I remember very vividly being very confused and scared after Lisa died. It was the first time I ever went to a funeral, and I can still see the pink and purple balloons everywhere, her favorite colors. Lisa's favorite song, Tiffany's "I Think We're Alone Now," played on a loop, over and over and over again.

As I was writing this chapter, I decided that I wanted to reach out to Lisa's mom, Stephanie. I found her email address online but was too scared to write the email. A week later my mom asked if I had written to her yet. I said, "No, I don't really know what to say." A few weeks went by and one day I finally said to myself, "Just write it, Anjelah! Write it and send it." So I put an email together, and I prayed before I sent it. I asked God to prepare her to receive it and that it would spark joy in her and not sorrow. I wanted her to feel love knowing that her daughter is still thought of.

Stephanie replied pretty much immediately with gratitude and love. She said that the email brought her tears of joy, which made me happy because that's what I prayed for. We emailed back and forth a bit and she ended her last email by telling me this: "Your email made my day. Lisa's birthday is tomorrow and she will be 39." I had no idea. The fact that I googled her weeks prior but didn't actually email her until the eve of Lisa's birthday shows me that our interaction was a gift from God or from Lisa herself for her mom. What a blessing.

Lisa's death had a profound influence on who I am today. Which is someone who worries about everyone dying 24/7.

Every time I see an ambulance go by, if it's heading west, I think,

Who do I know who lives west? Who could they be going to that I love? Are they going toward my aunt's house? And then I text her to make sure she's not dead or dying. Which sounds very caring on one hand but on the other more important hand is unnecessary and a lil' crazy.

Anytime I see an ambulance or fire truck fly by, sirens blaring, I pray for them and the people they'll hopefully save. If somebody in a car speeds past me, I usually scream, "You idiot!" and then I pray for them and that they don't hurt anybody else. After I pray for them, I pray for my husband. "Jesus, please don't let my husband get in an accident, please don't let my mom, please don't let my sister," then I feel guilty if I don't name every single person I know. Wherever I'm going, I'm fifteen minutes late because I have to sit in my car and finish my prayer. Then I feel even worse if I run out of time and leave my husband's family all vulnerable with no prayers, so then I'm eighteen minutes late. Wait, my dog too. Twenty minutes late.

You don't pray for your dog? I hope they don't die then. I pray for my dog. I look over at Banzo constantly when he's sleeping to make sure he's still breathing. If it doesn't look like his stomach is moving up and down, I shout, "Banzo!" He bolts up panting like, "Huh? Wut? Why? Where?"

"Thank God," I'll coo to him, then cover him in a million kisses. All dogs go to heaven, but not today. Not on my watch.

I got an emotional support animal for my anxiety and fear of death, and now I'm afraid that my emotional support animal will die. Actually, not just my animal, any animal. Dogs that aren't mine, squirrels that dart into traffic, goldfish in plastic bags at carnivals, wildlife in the jungle. I can't watch animals attacking each other on the National Geographic channel. I get that they need to eat and they can't Postmates their meal, but I can't handle the circle of life and how it works. They have family, too, and after they're killed their loved ones have no idea where they are or that today was their last day drinking from the pond. Did they even get to say I love you with their eyes one last time before they wandered away from the pack?

It's all so much worse when you really truly, madly, deeply care about someone. I always think my husband is going to die. Even when we're both at home my mind plays tricks on me. If I don't see him for a while, I start asking questions. I think, *Maybe he slipped in the bathroom? Maybe he hurt himself in the garage with his tools…Nah, he don't have any tools.* He gets three "Babes" before I freak out.

"Babe! BABE! *BABE!*"

By the time he responds, I've already imagined his death, his funeral, the outfit I'm gonna wear to it, and the next guy I'm gonna date, who never measures up to Manny.

My husband goes to the gym every day, and every day I say the same thing: "Bye! Have a good workout!…Don't die, okay?!" Then I run to the window and watch him drive away, just in case it was my last time seeing him alive. I need to see him for as many seconds as I can.

If Manny's out and about enjoying his life and I text him, he has three minutes to reply. Then if I call him and he doesn't answer the phone within three calls, I stalk him on social media. Not because I'm jealous, but because he's dead somewhere. What I'm doing is technically *not* stalking because we're married. I just care as much as a stalker would. First, I'll check his Instagram and see if he posted anything. Dammit, where is he? Then I'll check Find My Friends. The app allows you to share your location with someone so they will always know where you're at. So I shared my husband's location with me, and now I always know. I'm still waiting for him to figure it out.

Sometimes he'll come home, and I'll say, "What did you get at the grocery store?"

"How did you know I was at the grocery store?"

"You told me."

"I did?"

"You don't remember? You must be losing your mind."

Warning: Before you use this app and have all kinds of fun, you need to know it's not 100 percent accurate and may lead you to jump to unfortunate conclusions. One dark and stormy night—okay, it wasn't raining, but it's good for the story's dramatic effect—Manny went to the movies with friends and was supposed to be home around eleven p.m. I fell asleep and woke up, and my husband was not next to me in bed. My first thought was *Oh my God, he's dead.* It wasn't *Ooh, he's out there cheating.* Although that would also mean *Oh my god, he's dead.*

It was two a.m., and I started freaking out with the what-ifs. I called him. No answer. I texted a bunch of times. No replies. I checked Instagram, and he hadn't posted anything. Then I went scrolling down a rabbit hole for thirty-five minutes. I bought a cute top from a targeted Instagram ad (they get me every time) and learned a couple of good recipes, recipes I'm never gonna try, but they do make it look so easy. That's how you make twelve-cheese macaroni? I didn't even know there were twelve cheeses. Cheddar, gouda, blue, Whiz, I see you string, queso fresco…wait, I just remembered…Oh my God, *Manny is dead.*

I checked the Find My Friends app, which showed Manny's car stopped on the side of a freeway not far from our house. *What if* he was in an accident and the car turned over and he was just lying there? I immediately (finally) jumped out of bed because Manny was dead, and I needed to go to the location because that's what people do on TV. I had to ID the body. I went to brush my teeth, because if first responders were there, they'd tell me the bad news, and my response would be a guttural wail, like, "Uahhhghhh nooooooo!" with my mouth wide open, my breath fumes everywhere. They didn't deserve that. They put their lives on the line. I brushed my teeth first because I'm a good person.

So, I started brushing my teeth and thinking all the thoughts.

I knew it.

This is my fault.

I should have prayed for him that one time instead of that antelope being eaten by a lion in Zimbabwe on Animal Fight Night.

I was thinking about how I was a widow now, and I couldn't believe it. Then I walked down the stairs, practicing my solemn head nod and silent "Thank you" for the funeral, which was very similar in tone and volume to the "I'm sorry for your loss" condolence phrase I'd be getting back from everyone. Pro tip: You have to whisper "I'm sorry" quietly or even silently, because if you say "I'm sorry" at regular volume, that communicates that you had something to do with the death. Try it—you'll see what I mean.

I got downstairs and went into the kitchen to grab a glass of water—*Manny used to love water*—and walked over to the living room. I stared at his favorite spot in the living room, the couch, to mourn him. I noticed a couple of pillows were askew and a blanket had fallen off to one side. Sigh, that was so Manny. I gave the couch a knowing smile. Oh, how he loved to watch UFC, Hallmark movies, and *A Few Good Men*. Manny's TV choices were so diverse.

I turned on the light…and there he was. Manny was sleeping on the couch. The audacity! The Find My Friends app lied to me. It told me I was a widow. I'd already downloaded a dating app on my phone! Don't judge me; we all grieve differently.

My husband and I decided that we did not want kids. We had a few reasons: We loved our life just the way it was, and we were so focused on work. But also, one of the other reasons was because what if they die? I don't want that pain. I can't imagine the pain my friend Lisa's mom went through having lost her child in a tragic car accident.

I'm worried about everyone dying, including myself. I get sad thinking about my family, my husband, and my dog being sad without me. But I also get major FOMO thinking about them going on without me and making memories I don't get to be a part of.

I think about my own unfortunate, untimely demise often. When I walk out the front door, I can be a little dramatic. Even if I'm just going to the mailbox at the end of the driveway, I'm all, "If anything happens to me, I love you. I'll see you later, God willing."

After a great deal of thought, I've come to the conclusion that I will not be murdered like on my favorite show, *Law & Order: SVU*. That's just too predictable. Since I was young, I always thought that I was going to die in a car accident. Sometimes when I'm driving, I look around, visualize a mangled crash, and get a vibe of *Yeah, that feels about right*. I mean, I hope not. Perhaps I feel that way because the first person I knew to die did so in a car accident. She was like me, so why not me? Again, I hope not. I hope I die in my sleep at a very old age cuddling with Manny, and we both just sleep die at the same time.

We should hold fake funerals instead of birthday parties, because that's where people actually say what they really feel about you. If we had funerals every year instead of birthday parties, we would get to hear all the lovely things that people think about us. It would be hard to breathe in the casket but worth it. After everyone said nice things about me, I'd swing open the casket and be like, "Awww, thank you so much for coming, you guys. You know how to make a girl feel special. Joe, I honestly thought you would be a little more sad than this, but that's fine. We all grieve differently." Then I'd look around to see who didn't show up and unfollow them on social media.

But after I die for real, I don't want to be turned into a diamond or an orange tree or anything extra like that. Or do I? I've seen creepy stuff online of people stuffed up like animal taxidermy. This one guy died in Puerto Rico, and at his funeral he was propped up on his motorcycle wearing his motorcycle outfit.

I worry about things I can't control, like dying, but also aging. Forever 21? No, I am not. I can't even shop there anymore. I can't be standing behind some Gen Zer buying the same miniskirt. She's living her best wrinkleless life, and I'm trying to remember to take my vitamins. I should put the crop top down and go to Ann Taylor Loft, where I belong. Actually, maybe more like Nordstrom Rack. Let's not get carried away. I'm not there yet, but I am approaching the age where I'll start to buy my clothes at the same place I buy my groceries. Kirkland jeans are very practical and get the job done. Getting older is scary. The more I age, the closer I am to death. These are just facts.

Nobody really knows what happens when you die. We can say all these things to make us feel better about it—oh, it's a better place, it's the pearly gates of heaven and your mansion on a street of gold and all of that. Well, what if you don't value gold? What if you just value your loved ones? How is that good for me? I just want to be with my family, you know? We're supposed to feel comforted that we'll be reunited with other loved ones who have passed away, but I have so many questions. Like will my grandma be eighty or Grandma in her prime, like hot and thirty? Will she just be a light orb of Grandma? If so, then how does she get to hug Grandpa? Do hugs not matter anymore? I still want hugs to matter. Will I look bomb in heaven, or will my face be ridden with hormonal acne? It's the great unknown that's so scary to me.

People will argue that the Bible gives you exact answers and there are no unknowns. Like if you live this way you go to heaven, and if you live this way you go to hell. And I'm realizing that I don't fully subscribe to that. I personally don't believe the Bible gives you exact answers. The Bible gives you beautiful (and some scary) stories to learn lessons from as you figure out your own journey of life.

My thoughts on what happens when we die are changing. I used to be so sure that it was very black and white. You were either in or out, you go up or you go down. I've recently been asking more questions about this and learning different schools of thought. What if we are all just energy? And what if when you die that energy continues on in the nonphysical? What if when we die our soul goes to a waiting room until the big judgment day? What if when we transition out of this body our soul jumps over to a new body, or plant, or butterfly? Every time I see a monarch butterfly, I always say hello to my grandma. Now, do I believe that the butterfly is actually my grandma's soul? Not really, but it makes me happy to think about her coming to visit me and fluttering uncomfortably close to my face, as butterflies do, to remind me of her love for me.

I like to think that my grandma and loved ones are in heaven, waiting for me. And then when I die I get to hug them and be with them and hang out and have my grandma's cooking. That feels comforting, but it doesn't feel exactly right to me. I think about all this stuff a lot, and I know not everybody does or wants to. Who are the people who don't think about it at all? They're just like, "Live free. Do whatever." And they don't even care about what happens when you die. Sometimes I do jokes about dying onstage and talk about my fear of death, and I see people's faces and they're so disturbed like, "Oh, she's weird." Or maybe the nachos were bad. But I have to think about this because I want to know that not just me but also my loved ones are going to be all right in the afterlife, whatever form that might take.

My fear of death really boils down to one thing: I don't want to be sad. There's the old proverb "'Tis better to have loved and lost than never to have loved at all." Would I rather not have a husband or a dog because they might die one day and I'll be sad? Absolutely not. I'd rather experience love. In the meantime, they're just gonna have to deal with me putting trackers on them and shaking them awake in the middle of the night to make sure they're alive. Hopefully they won't have a heart attack and die.

CHAPTER 13

Do You & Do You Well

I try my hardest not to play comparison roulette—that is, compare myself, or my journey, to anyone else's. Comparing your life, your faith, your Instagram followers, adult acne, etc., steals your joy. I trust that my path is specific for me and I live fully in that. Well, *now I do*. It took a minute.

In the beginning, when I didn't have a career yet, I was just a dreamer. Anytime I looked at someone else's life, I just admired it and wanted to do that one day myself. As I started making a name for myself in the entertainment world, things started to shift, and I started looking over my shoulder. That's when the comparison syndrome seeped into my brain and infected me with envy. Because here were all these other people I saw, also stand-up comedians and actors, but they were doing XYZ. So, then it became, *Oh, should I be doing ABCDEFGHIJKLMNOPQRSTUVW, too? They're my age, but they've already done this. Should I be doing that?*

Ten years into my career, I'd sold out tours, appeared in movies and TV shows, and starred in my own hour-long comedy specials, but

I still hadn't fulfilled my biggest dream yet: starring in my own multi-cam sitcom. The dream was even more specific than that: I wanted the show to be filmed on the Warner Bros. studio lot because that's where I got my start on *Friends* as an extra. There was just something so romantic about thinking of my career coming full circle to where I started as an extra. At this point I was coming up on the ten-year milestone in LA, and that felt like the perfect time to get my own show. Unfortunately, reality had other plans.

I pitched so many shows and got so close but no cigar. I would have loved to co-star in someone else's show, too. I auditioned for one of the lead characters of *Brooklyn Nine-Nine*, and they loved me so much, they tested me for another role, too. *Which one am I going to get?* I thought. *Who cares? I'm going to get one!* In the biz, *testing* means they've narrowed it down to their top choices and you are one of them. At this point they have negotiated a contract for you in the event that you book the role. It's like the last stop before you get to destination "dream come true." The script was so funny, and it was perfect for me—a crime show but also a silly comedy. After I screen tested with Andy Samberg and we improvised a bit, I was sure this was the show I wanted to be on.

I remember being in the audition room with other Latina actresses, and I had such swagger and so much confidence in myself. *Oh, you're testing for only one part?* I thought. *I'm testing for two, but don't worry, girl, your time will come.*

As it turns out, testing for two roles doesn't increase your chances of getting a part, but it does give them two reasons not to hire you. Needless to say, when I found out that I didn't get either role, I was shocked and heartbroken. Instead, I booked a different pilot, the TV version of the movie *About a Boy*. All my agents, my whole team told me, "You booked the right one! This is the one that everyone's talking about!" I'd play Al Madrigal's wife, and Minnie Driver was in it, and everyone always told me I looked like her, and I could kind of see that, but she's British and I'm Mexican, but cool, I guess?

"Yeah, but I wanted to be on *Brooklyn Nine-Nine*," I said sadly. The truth is, I would have been thrilled to get cast on *About a Boy* if a comedy cop show wasn't initially on the table. It's as if they wrote the show specifically for me and my interests, but then they forgot and hired someone else.

About a Boy was directed by Jon Favreau, who's been in, directed, and executive produced a million things like *The Mandalorian*, but you might know him best from *Swingers*. I like to remember him as Monica's boyfriend Pete on *Friends*. When I showed up to the audition, he said, "I'm a big fan of yours."

Record scratch...a fan of *mine*?

"My kid showed me all of your videos. We love you."

It never gets old hearing that, whether from a regular fan or a Jon Favreau fan, a Jon Fan-vreau if you will.

What does get old is constant rejection. When the network announced that the show got greenlit, my agent called me.

"They picked up *About a Boy*..."

"Yay!"

"...but they didn't pick up *you*. You're getting recast."

I was still devastated about *Brooklyn Nine-Nine*, and now this? I woke up early not long after I got the bad news, like six a.m., and went for a jog to clear my head. I put my worship music on, trying to spend some time with God. I was jogging down the street, and I was praying as I was jogging, telling God, "Man, I'm so disappointed. I really, really wanted *Brooklyn Nine-Nine*. That was such a fun script, and it's going to be a great show. I really wanted that show." As I was praying and talking to God, a bus drove by me with a giant *Brooklyn Nine-Nine* poster plastered on the side of it with two Latina actresses on it. Neither of which was me. At that point I just started laughing, like, are you kidding me? What a sense of humor you have, God...

or Los Angeles Department of Transportation. I guess I was lucky I wasn't run over by the bus. Now that would be poetic.

Welp, I always had my stand-up. One weekend around this season, I went to DC to headline a Latino heritage comedy show, which included my friend Cristela Alonzo. After the show, all of the comics and the organizers of the show went to dinner, and Cristela, whose career paralleled mine, announced she'd just sold her own sitcom to Fox. "It's really crazy," she said, "because when I first moved here, I worked on the Fox lot as a page. I always dreamed of having my own show on the same lot where I started. And here I am ten years later!" As she literally said the words out of my journal, all of the life, joy, hopes, and dreams left my body. My journals were my prayers, my private conversations with God, and I felt betrayed. It felt like I was sitting at this metaphorical dinner table in a beautiful restaurant, and God was whispering all these sweet nothings in my ear. Then I looked over to the table across the way and there He was giving her the diamond ring. I wanted to suck it up and be happy for her, but I sobbed myself to sleep that night.

That incident took my inspiration and mojo and dimmed my dreams for a few years. I wasn't the dreamer girl anymore, the one who had exuded the powerful attitude of "I can do it!" for a decade. I got jaded. Now if I had an audition, I was more, "Sure, I'll go, but if they pick me, I'll be surprised." Back in the day, if I saw a new movie come out and it took place in Mexico, I could visualize it and see myself doing it, even though I had no credits/fake credits on my resume. My attitude was "I would love to film a movie in Mexico and be able to live there for a few months! I can immerse myself in the culture and finally learn Spanish! I bet I'll get to do an action scene and I'll get to chase down a bad guy and cock my shotgun while riding a motorcycle!"

After you experience some nos and rejection and disappointment, it's less "I can definitely do that!" and more "I hope I can do that one day, but we'll see." I was in the phase of "we'll see" for a few years before the color returned to my dreams. There wasn't an on/off switch; it was a gradual shift in me that knew once again it was possible to be successful. It was reminding myself often that I was enough and that I had heard yes before and I would hear yes again. It could happen for me again; it was possible, if I just didn't give up.

The problem with not giving up was that I had to keep putting myself out there and that meant being vulnerable. Being an actress is an exercise and lesson in humility a high percentage of the time.

Early in my career I auditioned for one of the *Bring It On* movies and didn't book it. I'd been a cheerleader since I was eight years old—I mean, we're talking top of the pyramid skills—and I couldn't even book a cheerleading movie? That was embarrassing. Another time I got cast in a show—I didn't even have to audition for it; they just hired me. I had two lines in the pilot, and they had me come to the Sony lot and do a table read with the rest of the cast in front of all of the studio executives. I said my two lines…and then they cut my part out of the show.

"She didn't really do anything with it," they told my manager. "It wasn't that special, so we didn't need it."

Did they expect me to win an Oscar with their two lines? Maybe their lines were the problem and not me.

Being humbled left and right, the constant rejection and failure, is not easy, and it's not for everybody. If you don't want it to destroy your soul, you cannot let it fester inside your heart and mind. I've figured out my own ways to deal with it. First, and always, I turn to God. Romans 8:28 says, "And we know that all things work together for good to those who love God, to those who are the called according to His purpose." Which basically means that God can turn anything into good.

I'm constantly realigning my outlook and turning a negative into a positive. I am very well versed in switching my perspective so that it's a win. And that's how you stay positive and stay at a higher vibration. You could say I am the queen of changing my perspective. I am the queen of "You don't *have* to go on the road; you *get* to go on the road." Or "I got recast off the show? Maybe it was because I was so much younger than the rest of the cast, not because I sucked."

You have to change your perspective to survive and succeed in the entertainment world for sure, but this advice really goes for any career path. You have to remind yourself constantly that life has highs and lows and everything in between. Nobody is at the top of their game 100 percent of the time. Life is a roller coaster: There are peaks and dips, and sometimes the ride breaks down and you get stuck hanging upside down after you ate a funnel cake and a gigantic spicy pickle, and the fire department has to come save you.

I've had so many projects almost happen, including a project produced by *The Office* star Ed Helms that took place in an immigration office in downtown LA. We called it *We the People* and came up with some amazing characters that were hilarious. We pitched it at NBC, and they bought it "in the room" right away. They were like, "We want it; don't take it anywhere else!" We got the script written, we loved it, we turned it in, but then they passed on it and didn't even film the pilot.

The high was being chosen to develop with Ed and his partner Mike Falbo, and meeting and brainstorming and having so much fun and pitching it to NBC and them saying on the spot, "Yes, we want it!" and walking out head held high going, "Oh my God, we're doing it." The low was the same people saying, "Actually we don't want it, just kidding!" You never know why decisions are made and what God has in store for you elsewhere. At least after meeting Ed, he ended up casting me in a role in another project for Comedy Central, so that was fun. Negative to a positive.

Relationships matter, and I learned early not to burn bridges because it's a small industry and everybody knows each other. I met

America Ferrera when we starred in *Our Family Wedding*, and eight years later, my now friends America and Kevin Hart, who I had worked with before, teamed up as executive producers to develop a show based on my life called *All Fancy* for NBC. I'd play a young painter who blew up on social media, got rich and famous, and moved her whole Mexican family from the 'hood to the Hollywood Hills. It was about balancing life with the way we grew up and the way we live now. Blend in, but never forget where we came from. Like my godson Austin's birthday party, when we strung a piñata from the roof of our house to my brother-in-law's pickup truck in the front yard. Our rich Jewish neighbors had never seen anything like it, but they loved it. It was sort of like *The Beverly Hellabillies*.

It meant the world to me that both America and Kevin co-signed me. The vibe was, "We believe in Anjelah so much, we're developing a show around her. You need to believe in her too." People have said no to me before, but who would say no to America and Kevin teamed up together? Turns out NBC would. We wrote the script, but the same thing happened. They didn't even make a pilot for it.

Sometimes my near misses were beyond my control, but I admit I made some questionable decisions that might have changed the trajectory of my career. These choices were often related to my devout religiosity at the time. For example, I turned down a role in the Anna Faris movie *What's Your Number?* because the R-rated rom-com was about a girl who'd slept with nineteen men and was trying to find number 20 to marry. The movie didn't really go with the super Chrish brand I had created for myself.

You're going to be mad about the other movie I turned down, but probably not as mad as I still am at myself. I was sent a script for a movie about a bunch of young girls who sang a cappella competitively. I met with the director, who really wanted me to be in the film. "What characters did you respond to?" he asked me.

Every role! It had singing! It had dancing! It was funny! It had you-go-girl power! But it also had a couple of raunchy jokes and a scene where a character took a shower with her boyfriend. I didn't want to be part of a project that was doing nasty jokes. I was so conservative, I passed.

The movie was *Pitch Perfect*.

When it came out, it wasn't even raunchy.

I was being holier-than-thou, trying to do the right thing, and missed a golden opportunity. I would have loved to work with Anna Kendrick. Are you kidding me? I love her so much. And Elizabeth Banks, too, ugh, she's so good. The movie ended up being something so positive, but I was trying to be who I thought I was supposed to be and honor God. The truth is, I don't think God cared one way or another if I did that movie or the Anna Faris movie or any movie. I do, however, think Christians would care, and I would hear about it on social media or in person or wherever. That's one thing that happens often—my fellow Christians like to "hold me accountable" to what they think is right and wrong. Forget the fact that they don't know me personally and don't have a relationship with me or know my heart or motives or what God is doing in my life personally. They will let me know what their interpretation of the Bible says, and they will always include that they are "so disappointed" when I don't live up to that.

That movie, *Pitch Perfect*, is definitely one that Manny and I shake our heads about, still to this day. Mistakes happen. Rejection happens. Over and over again. It's the nature of the beast. I was recently up for a big movie musical remake and was championed by the two A+ list stars and the director, only to be told after a torturous months-long audition process that the studio "decided to go in another direction."

The whole ordeal knocked me down for the count. It made me insecure and sad. It cut deep on multiple levels. It wasn't just this one amazing opportunity project that I didn't get. It dug up disappointment from every other project that I didn't get. I tried to do my special spin, like, *Sure, I didn't book this movie, but now the director knows about me and he wants to work with me in the future! At least I'm in these conversations about really big projects!*

But I also had this moment where I was sick of flipping it and making it a good thing. I get sick of learning lessons the hard way. I get tired of always being the positive one who has to change my perspective. I can do it. I know how and I do it all the time. I've been doing it my whole career. Yes, I've had wins, but I've had a lot of losses.

After the studio passed on me, I told my friends, "I want a win. It's been a long time since I've had the kind of win that's a win from all angles. From front, back, left, and right. One I don't have to manipulate or shift to be a win. I want that kind of win again."

Having experienced all of the rejection, sometimes I miss the days of being an extra and dreaming about being on top one day. In Christianity they talk about having a childlike faith. Children believe in the Tooth Fairy and the Easter Bunny. We're instructed to have childlike faith like that. And I'm like, yeah, it's easy to have childlike faith when you don't know better. But when you know better, it's hard when you've felt that rejection, when you've felt the sting, when you've heard the no, when you've been overlooked for a promotion in your job, when you've been recast.

When you know better, it's hard to have that childlike faith. You're so close to being the princess, but then they pick someone else instead. Or you get chosen to be the princess, then they're like, "Just kidding, you weren't as good at being a princess as we thought. So, we just got rid of the monarchy altogether." When you've heard that over and over and over again, it's really hard to be confident and certain and go, *I can be the princess.*

I've built up a thick skin because I have no other choice if I want to be in this creative field. And I want to be in it. I know the disclaimers and warnings. I know there's potential for deep hurt. But it's the whole "Would you rather have loved and lost or never loved at all?" argument again. Would you rather go for your dreams and be vulnerable and possibly be rejected? Or not go for your dreams and sit in a blah job that doesn't inspire you and feed your soul?

I have coping mechanisms beyond changing my perspective. I try to get the hurt and pain and anxiety out of my system physically. After the movie fiasco, I went into a room and locked the doors. I rolled out my yoga mat and meditated and prayed. I did some Non-Linear movement, which is a way of moving trauma and emotions through your body. And I laughed and wept, and tears poured out of me. It was loud and snotty and probably a little alarming for our neighbors. It wasn't just about this project. It was all the built-up disappointment from my entire career, all the way back to Pop Warner cheerleading competitions when my team should have placed first instead of second. Do I still think about Jenny's toes, which weren't pointed enough? Maybe.

After I let it all out, I did the work to pick myself back up. I did it through music. First, I played a sad song, "Say Something" by A Great Big World and Christina Aguilera, to help me move the sadness. Then I put on an empowering song, Andra Day's "Rise Up," so I could picture myself rising up in victory and winning again. I started affirming myself and reminding myself that I am married to the most amazing guy, who loves me and puts me first and rubs my feet every single time I ask him to. He literally never says no, even if it's right after a workout, when they shouldn't be in close proximity to another human. He does so much for me and considers me and my thoughts and my feelings. And then my dog is just the best dog. And he loves all people, and everybody loves him. And I have the best siblings. Like, we just make each other laugh and we support each other and encourage each other. And I won the parent lottery. My mom is amazing. And my dad, he's the perfect dad for me because I am who I am because of him. His personality, even the trauma, has made me who I am today. So I won, and I remind myself of that, and it's helpful.

And then it was that ebb and flow, like, I'm coming back up. I'm good. I'm healthy. I make great salsa, I'm alive, and my family's alive and healthy, and I always have chips. Then a couple of days went by and I resorted back to *Man, that would have been a great opportunity. I could have been singing and dancing in that movie with these big stars and, God, I am a good dancer. I am a good singer. And I'm funny! That was mine.* Then I correct myself. *No, it wasn't. If it was yours, it would be yours. It's not yours. It was never yours. Alright. Okay. It wasn't mine. Mine's out there.*

Keep going. Don't give up.

When you make yourself vulnerable to hope for certain things, then you don't get them, you have to remind yourself to push forward. Because you never know when yours is around the corner. One of my favorite memes is a cartoon of two guys digging under the ground, toward a goal. One guy finds a big diamond and he's holding it, and he's like, "Whoa!" The other guy has already dug past him, but he's looking over his shoulder at the guy, like, "Man, he got the diamond, that sucks." But you can see in the cartoon that if he did two more digs, his diamond is even bigger. It's waiting for him on *his* path.

Everyone can get their diamond. Just because someone else got a role doesn't mean I won't get another role in something else. After I got rejected from *Brooklyn Nine-Nine*, I ended up becoming friends with Melissa Fumero and Stephanie Beatriz, the two actresses who were cast as the two roles that I tested for. I championed them. I rooted for them. They're both perfect in the roles that they play. I love watching them, and I'm a big fan of the show.

Back when I got crushed by my friend Cristela's good news, I didn't understand something so crucial: There's room for everybody to succeed. Yes, I can audition for Detective Rodriguez, and I guarantee there's gonna be fifteen other brown-haired Latina girls wearing a leather jacket, jeans, and boots. You can easily think, *They're probably going to pick her because she's taller, she's been on way more TV shows than I have, and she's way prettier.*

I remind myself, what makes me special is they don't have my childhood, my marriage, my faith, my victories, my evolution, and my seasoning on it. None of them have my dad spanking me when I was young. None of them have me taking second place and not first place in a cheerleading competition. None of them have the story of my sister and me going cruising and pretending to get in fights in the street. Maybe they do speak Spanish, so they don't have the angst of wishing that they spoke Spanish. They didn't grow up wishing that they were more Mexican because they already were Mexican enough. None of them have the myriad of stories from the previous chapters of my life that make me *me*. They don't have my history and my point of view.

Nobody is you, and nobody can ever be you. In that audition, I look just like them, wearing the same outfit, saying the same exact words that they're saying. But I'm saying it with *me* behind it, which already makes it unique and makes it special. Now when I go to an audition, I don't compare myself to anyone. I come in bold and brave, and say to myself, "There's only one you. Just do you and do you well." Show up for yourself by being the best version of yourself. Leave it all in the room.

A friend of mine who works for one of the biggest pop stars in the world told me that every time a competing pop star puts something out and shoots to number one, the other pop star gets really down and doubts themself. But then it inspires this person to pull up their bootstraps and create something equally as great. So the cycle never ends, no matter how successful you get.

I have my times when I'm skyrocketing and times when I'm coasting while someone else is skyrocketing. I can now cheer them on while they soar because I trust that my journey is my own journey; there are special blessings and jewels along the road waiting for me. There will always be another Detective Rodriguez to audition for, another show idea to pitch to a network, and who knows, maybe my dream role is waiting for me in *Pitch Perfect 15*.

CHAPTER 14

The Evolution of Funjelah

For most of my career I was sort of the go-to girl for the church comedy crowd. I was a VIP in the church club world. Before the service, I got to hang in the back greenroom with all the special guests. When worship started, and the band began to play and everybody started clapping and singing, I got to walk out with the pastor and his wife and take my seat in the front row. This is big-time VIP stuff, you guys.

The energy is electric, similar to when an MMA fighter is announced and walks to the ring and the crowd goes wild—but instead of shouting "You're gonna die!" the audience sings to the Lord, thanking Him for dying for us. I remember when I was young sitting in the audience in church, and I'd finally spot the pastor and his special guests parading by, my heart would get all fluttery and I would crane my neck to see who was who and what was what. I grew up and got to be a part of that from the inside for a long time.

I'm still pretty big in the church world, because I do a clean show and I speak the language. But lately, I haven't done many of those appearances. I feel like I offend some people with who I am and the things that I talk about on my social media. That's fine. Perhaps that's even the path my fan base is supposed to take. Everyone's not for everyone. (That's something I remind myself when I'm feeling insecure about losing fans.)

About five years ago, the evolution of Anjelah into Funjelah began. Funjelah is the not-so-square, not-so-rigid version of myself, a more evolved, more relaxed, and more in touch woman of the world. Anjelah was very conservative and did not drink alcohol at all. She thought it was devil juice. Now, not only does Funjelah think it's not devil juice, but she will find any excuse to make a fancy craft cocktail with beautiful garnishes. Not in an "Okay, girl, slow down" kinda way, but in a great appreciation for the gift it is. After all, God and Martha Stewart wouldn't have invented cocktails if they weren't meant to be enjoyed. Within the last couple of years, Funjelah has spread her wings and learned that tequila is the nectar of the gods. Old Anjelah would never have joked about there being more than one God, but look at me now. Funjelah! Manny still doesn't drink much, though. He'll take a sip of alcohol now and again and be like, "Ugh, it tastes like feet." That's his response to almost every glass of wine.

The transformation from Anjelah to Funjelah is partly about surface stuff like drinking and jokes, but it also goes deep. I guess you could say I've been "deconstructing," a term that's very popular right now but also is almost like a cuss word in the Christian world. I am deconstructing my beliefs and reconstructing what my belief system is.

Maybe some people in the church would say "deconstruction" means I've backslidden or fallen away from the Lord. But that's definitely not what it means to me. It means I'm reexamining what my relationship with the Lord looks like. To other people, it means different things. When I say I'm deconstructing, I am breaking apart my whole system of belief, unsubscribing to some things (I have yet to receive a "You've successfully unsubscribed" notification, but I have faith it's been done), and subscribing to other things. I am reconstructing with God at the center and not church culture or traditions at the center.

My deconstruction definitely hasn't been an impulsive, overnight thing. It's been a journey and a process. Like, at the beginning of my process, Manny and I bumped heads, because he didn't understand. In all fairness, we got married believing the exact same things, and then I dropped a bomb on him that I wasn't sure what I believed and I had lots of questions. That must have been hard for him to process, but during that time I definitely wasn't seeing it from his point of view. My husband is a Bible school graduate. Like, I'm sure every Christian wants to be good at reading the Bible, but my husband has to be the best at everything he does, which is why he graduated summa cum laude. He's a debater. He's very smart and knows the Good Book backward and forward. He's intuitive. He hears from God. I am also smart, but in a different way. He can read a chapter in a book and then tell you exactly what he just read. I read a chapter and I understand it while I'm reading it, but then I'm at a loss for words to explain it.

When I changed my views on certain things, Manny wanted me to explain myself fully, and I couldn't do that. I got twisted up and said a lot of *likes* and *ums*. I couldn't articulate my thoughts and explain myself. So we argued a lot.

"The Bible is clear on what it says," he'd say.

"I don't agree," I pushed back.

"So then you don't believe in the Bible?" he'd counter, frustrated.

That wasn't the case. I just didn't see the Bible as black and white as I had before. Now I noticed there was a lot of gray. Like I mentioned earlier, there is a lot of beauty and mystery in the gray. I started to say to myself, "Man, who do I think I am to believe that I have the God of the universe figured out because the ink on this page told me so." I started wrestling with God and asking more questions.

This wasn't a sign of me falling away from God; this was a sign of me getting closer to God. If you think about it, when you wrestle with someone, you are close to them—face-to-face, tangled up. It is actually very intimate. As I asked more questions, Manny and I bumped heads more often, but then something miraculous happened. I started overhearing Manny in conversation with other people and noticed words come out of his mouth that sounded deconstructed and open-minded, such as, "Who am I to say who's going to heaven or hell?"

Something as simple as that was actually a big deal. It was very different from the Manny from before, who'd fiercely debate me on every point. For a time, there were definitely things that I was processing on my own because we were not on the same page. Suddenly I felt comfortable bringing up new ideas I wanted to discuss. My husband and I started to be on the same page again. And he started deconstructing, too.

Something as simple as cussing was a big deal for us. I would only say *shoot* and *darn*, and sometimes I would be extra risky and say *damn*, depending on who was around. If I was real mad I would yell "*F!*" Those were my stand-in cuss words of choice. I actually still say *shoot*, *darn*, and *F*, but I also say the real words too. I started to think, *Ya know what, I'm pretty sure God will still love me if I cuss. I don't think I will go to hell if I switch out the* oot *for an* it. This wasn't about me just wanting to cuss. I never really had a desire to. This was about me understanding the why of my reason for not cussing. Manny used to say *fudge* all the time, but after some in-depth study, he realized that language was subjective based on the culture you're a part of.

He explained what he learned to me, but as I said previously, I'm not really good at recounting information so I asked him to tell me again how he said it so I could include it in this book. "As I traveled, I found out that our cussing isn't everybody's cussing," he yelled from the bathroom.

"No, don't yell it to me. Come here and tell me in regular voice," I yelled back.

"In London, the word *fanny* is a vulgar euphemism, whereas in America it's a cute way to describe a baby's booty," he said when he finally came into the room. "We'll say it all day, like it's nothing, man." Same with the Spanish language. Manny is Puerto Rican, and I'm Mexican American. "There are a lot of words that we say that you would be like, 'Oh no, you can't say that.' And vice versa."

He concluded that when it comes to cussing, it's never about the word; it's about the culture, context, intent, and emotion behind it. That's what makes a cuss word a cuss word or not. "If a guy cuts me off on the freeway and I say, 'Fudge you,' how is that different than the F-word? I'm genuinely angry with this person, and I want bad things for him. But people wouldn't even question my heart because I said 'fudge.' It doesn't matter if I say fudge or the F-word. What matters is that I exploded.

"I will then go to God and say, 'That was pure anger. Sorry, Jesus. I shouldn't let this thing get me that angry.' It has nothing to do with the word because it wasn't even a word that was used in biblical times. The Bible talks about 'out of the abundance of the heart the mouth speaks.' What it's saying is, 'When you speak, usually what's in your heart will come out.' Get to the root of what it is. If somebody cuts me off, my sin is not the bad word. It's 'Why do I have such little patience? Why am I so angry and want bad things for this person? All somebody had to do was just cut me off and all of a sudden, I'm enraged.' That's the real issue. Not that I said the F-word. Who cares?"

Ladies and gentlemen, and everyone in between, a round of applause for that cameo by my husband. Who just said that monologue standing completely naked in front of me because he just got out of the shower. Thank you, Manny. And thank you *LORDT* for this hunk of a man I get to call my husband. Phew.

I totally agree with what he is saying; just don't ask me to explain it again because he already left the room. If some random person called me a bitch, I would be totally offended and mad. But if one of my friends said, "Where my bitches at?!" I would raise my hand and we would probably go grab a drink. It for sure comes down to your intent and culture.

There was a time when I wouldn't even joke out loud about Manny standing in front of me in all his God-given glory. I mean, as we all know now, I turned down a role in *Pitch Perfect* because there was a PG-13 shower scene in the script. Cue Manny and me shaking our heads in disbelief yet again and forever.

Currently, Funjelah is much more open around the topic of sex. Anjelah was proud to be a virgin until marriage. Funjelah is still proud but also sometimes questions her decision to abstain from premarital sex. Maybe it's the trauma from purity culture talking. Anjelah judged that Latina actress who urged her to sleep around. Fifteen years later, Funjelah gets it. For real, I have conversations about this with my husband. Sometimes I tell him, "You know what, I wish I would have ho'd out a little bit before you, but no, I saved myself for you. I hope you appreciate it!" He just laughs and says thank you. These are my questions and thoughts right now as I learn to embrace Funjelah, but a year from now I may decide again, "Actually, I'm glad I did wait."

I kind of wish I experimented and explored and made mistakes. Not the kind of mistakes that get you an STD or a kid, but like a medium mistake. You can watch a romantic comedy where they all go away on a trip, and they have one-night stands and make it look so fun, but they rarely show you the heartbreak and danger aspect of the one-night stand. The reality is, I know someone who threw caution to the wind, had her first one-night stand, and got herpes. She now has that for the rest of her life. I'm not trying to want that.

One time Manny and I were in this little town in Spain with cute cobblestone streets, and our waitress told us she traveled the world working in different places, like Thailand and Costa Rica. She was in her twenties living her best life and it gave me iFOMO (international fear of missing out). It's not like I'd never kissed a boy before Manny—Taranjelah had her fair share of dates—but I told him in that moment, "Part of me wishes I'd gone on an adventure to Costa Rica or Thailand and sowed my wild oats." Or somewhere even more romantic like Greece or Italy, where I could have been temporarily swept off my feet by the dreamiest man with rock-hard abs and a tan, which he got by doing some sort of sexy manual labor outdoors for a living, who barely spoke English but didn't even need to because he knew all the best gelato spots to visit, as well as all the spots on my body to visit. I didn't tell Manny that part.

He didn't get mad or jealous. It's funny, because Manny, who was not a virgin when he met me, said the opposite: "I wish I *wouldn't* have experienced things, because I brought that into our marriage." We both experienced feelings of shame for different reasons. I wished I'd done more freaky stuff before him, and he wished he hadn't done as much freaky stuff before me. Neither one of us knew we were going to have to deal with a lot of emotions around it all. Once we got married, our past sexual history didn't just magically vanish. It came right into our bedroom and wreaked a little havoc. Add Banzo sleeping between us, and that's an instant obstacle. I move him to his kennel for a bit, and I'm like, "Banzo, you don't need to see how you were made." (He is my child, and no one can tell me otherwise.) Manny and I have worked through a lot and will probably continue to work through, over, and under it until we're old. Banzo sleeping in our bed is nonnegotiable, though.

And just a little side note to give you a visual you didn't ask for: I have a friend who walked in on her eighty-year-old parents having sex, but not what you think eighty-year-old sex would be. This was the full-on legs-in-the-air, flexibility-on-point kind of sex. I aspire to be them.

I've relaxed a lot of self-imposed rules I once lived by. Religiously post-Raiderette Anjelah was kind of a buttoned-up tomboy, but Funjelah likes looking and feeling hot when she wants to. One recent night, Manny and I went out in New York City, and I wore super-short shorts and a blazer with just a bra underneath and a fair amount of cleav—the way blazers are meant to be worn in NYC, I think. I posted a picture of us where I was standing behind Manny, sort of groping him. It got a couple of finger-wagging comments from people, including, "That should just be for you and your husband!" That was definitely big for me, to be dressed sexy and not care what people thought.

Back in the day, I was kind of a prude about the types of conversations I was willing to have and also hear. Everyone watched their mouths around me, and I was very aware of it. I gave off a vibe that people knew not to talk about certain things in front of me because I was very conservative. I definitely wasn't comfortable when anyone talked about sex, and some friends actually apologized to me if they cussed while telling a story. It's like they were earmuffs-ing me. Now that I have relaxed a bit, I feel like I can have real, honest conversations. It's liberating because now nobody feels like they have to hold anything back. I do wonder what juicy gossip I missed.

I like that my friends feel freer around me, saying whatever they want to say, knowing that I'm not going to judge them. The other night, I had a heart-to-heart with one of my close friends about his struggle with drugs. It was a lighthearted conversation where we joked and laughed and just understood each other. He knew I was there with no judgment or even opinion. That wouldn't have happened before. I'm learning different things about my friends that they probably would not have been comfortable telling me before. I can participate in more conversations now that I'm not so reserved.

Candid conversations like this have taught me to be more open to all types of lifestyles. I have even been learning more about plant medicine and Mother Earth. Women's bodies have cycles just like her. I meditate regularly, and every month during my menstrual cycle I use it as an opportunity to thank my body instead of cursing it for giving me cramps and making me hormonal and sweaty at weird times. I release not just buildup from my uterus but buildup of my emotions and energy. I release it all to God and I imagine all that I've released flowing into Mother Earth. It's really a beautiful practice and has changed my experience with my body.

I'm not sure how to transition from periods to ghosts, so I'll just jump right in. I now host a podcast called *Ghost Stories with Anjelah* due to my love of all things paranormal. When I first started doing the show, I got a lot of negative comments, squawking, "I thought you were a Christian!" because it's frowned upon in the church to play with this stuff. You could open the door to the demonic. That's witchcraft, so don't even mess with it. Don't talk about white light or meditation or even astrology. All bad.

But I'm fascinated with ghost stories, plus I'm just hoping to say hi to my grandma and other loved ones who passed away. Many Christians believe if I say, "Oh, my grandmother came to visit me last night," that's not actually my grandma, it was a demon disguised as my grandma. They believe my grandma is either in heaven or hell, and there's no way she's here on earth in any form. She's not floating around in my podcast studio like Casper or embodied in the butterfly that just flew past my head.

So, the fact that I'm doing my ghost stories podcast and really loving it is an evolved Funjelah development. I'm starting to get so comfortable with Funjelah, this more loose, open-minded version of myself. I've really pushed my own boundaries to places I couldn't have imagined, especially when it comes to my former strict religious habits, customs, and routines.

But wait…there's more!

Keep reading if I haven't lost you forever yet.

This is a big one. Manny and I don't go to church eeeevery Sunday.

At first there was a lot of guilt around this decision, because that's just what you do every Sunday. You go to church, not even a question. With our changing views, we looked for the right place for us. We started bouncing around, trying different churches for various reasons, like because our friend was on the worship team or we knew the pastor. We ultimately landed on the Potters House at One LA with pastors Touré Roberts and Sarah Jakes Roberts. We love them and their church, but the truth is, we don't go eeeevery Sunday.

The point of church is to meet together as believers and to encourage one another. To hear the Word of God and break bread with each other and be a community. In the Bible, the church was never a building, brick and mortar; it was people. So, we are still having church, just in different ways. We'll have people over to our house and we'll have a beautiful party and a feast. Sometimes we'll go until four a.m. and put on our favorite music so loud on the house speakers. From '90s R&B to old-school gospel classics like "Stomp" by Kirk Franklin to newer worship songs like my friend William Matthews's "We'll All Be Free."

We all dance and sing along. Our hearts are involved, and we're worshipping God and praying for each other. And we're doing this in our living room, with pizza. And that is church, with our people. We've done communion at the house where we all go around the table and share something. There are always tears, and we pray for that person. Then we drink, eat the bread (with butter, because we fancy), and take communion.

We've taken communion at a bar with our friends Abner and Amanda from the band Johnnyswim. It was a beautiful moment praying for each other at a bar while hearing the sound of cocktails being made, glasses being bussed by the barback, and music by Prince playing on the jukebox. We ordered some appetizers, and we all had drinks, then each person said something that they were praying for and believing God for. Then we came in agreement with all the things that they said, we had our wine and our pizza, and we took our communion. (Side note: Is it take communion or do communion? Whatever, the people who care are probably already mad that I did it/took it in a bar.) I think that may be considered blasphemous to some people, but it was so beautiful and so special and so powerful to me. I mean, when the pandemic happened and we legally weren't allowed to attend church in person, we all found ways to worship. We did communion on Zoom for Easter. I feel like that's what Manny and I were already doing before quarantine, we were figuring out different ways to do church. Please don't hear me say that I think going to church is wrong or pointless. I love church. I still attend, just not regularly. I have so many great memories from going to church and have learned so many great qualities in serving, leadership, and community. Not to mention, I wouldn't be a stand-up comedian if it wasn't for that class I took on creative arts night at the Oasis church.

I'm not trying to ruffle feathers on purpose, but that is something I've noticed that happens more now with Funjelah steering the ship. Anytime I post anything even slightly political, I get some grief, especially one particular post I did about love and acceptance for LGBTQ+ pride.

One of my best friends, Jill, and her wife, Becky, have two beautiful children, who are my godkids—although Jill likes to joke around and say, "No, they're not your godkids, because I'm Jewish, and we don't do that."

"But what if you did do that?" I asked.

"Well, then we'd ask our siblings."

I know what she really means—I'm 100 percent their godmother, and to that I say I'm honored.

I have a gay brother, Kennie; an aunt who is a lesbian gym teacher and brings her whole softball team to my shows; gay uncles; gay cousins; and a million other gay family members. We must have a dominant gay gene in our DNA. Before anyone starts DMing me about that, I know there's no scientific proof that being gay is genetic, but my family is all the proof I need. I was raised by a very loving and accepting mother, and I went to churches that were very diverse, with people from all different backgrounds. We were religious and conservative but never ultraconservative.

In the post, I wrote, "I stand with you, I love you, and Jesus loves you," because for me, that's what I feel the heart of God is. I knew people were gonna react in different ways. Some were going to be very upset and tell me that they were going to unfollow me, and others were going to feel seen, supported, and loved.

The truth is, I lost thousands of followers that day. I wasn't surprised, but I was sad—not necessarily that I lost followers, but because that was the reason they chose to unfollow me. I was sad for humanity. It's okay. I lean on my relationship with Jesus more so than religion now.

This is everything I currently believe, and yet I know some people won't be comfortable with me being so direct with my thoughts on the page. I'm still getting comfortable with the idea of being so honest myself. Some may want to debate me on it, but imma go ahead and pass on that. I'm not here to say that the way I live my life is right and the way anyone else lives their life is wrong. I'm just telling you where I'm currently at in my journey. I'm evolving. I'm growing and learning and opening my mind and my heart space to all sorts of different things that are bringing me closer to God.

Like my podcast, *Nights at the Roundtable*, which came out of one of our home church nights. After lots of food and drinks and deep conversations about God, life, love, sex, trauma, and healing, we found ourselves saying, "Man, there are so many people that I wish could hear this conversation." Manny was like, "Let's do this as a podcast." We had no idea how to start a podcast, but he did all the work and research to make it happen, and at this moment we are at about a hundred episodes in. It's been amazing. We have had so many people message us to say they listen to our podcast and feel reconnected with God, when before, they felt hurt, angry, or abandoned by the church and therefore disconnected from God. That they have found a safe place to ask their own questions and know that they are not alone in their questioning.

A lot of people have told us that we are like their church. A place where they have community and can connect with God. Our benediction after every episode is "We pray that you find a seat at the table, but if you don't, you're always welcome at ours." And we mean that. Christian, non-Christian, liberal, conservative, gay, straight, transgender. We may not always agree, but we allow ourselves the room to express our feelings and thoughts that are evolving and changing. You will never hear us say, "We are 100 percent right on everything we are saying," but you will hear us challenge ourselves and each other to grow in love in all areas of life.

There is a difference between conviction and cultural shame. As I learn to embrace Funjelah, I have many opportunities to decipher between the two, like when I say a cuss word or have mimosas (plural) at brunch. There are times when I feel shame over things that, turns out, aren't shameful, and I have a subconscious battle over my old ways of doing things.

But I love Funjelah, and I'm so grateful for her. I'm so grateful that she's finally getting to express herself little by little. I'm also so grateful for reserved Anjelah. The conservative me got me to where I am today, too. She did her best to try to protect me from STDs, unwanted pregnancies, and more heartbreak than a Taylor Swift album. Anjelah always tried to do what was right. She protected me from things that could have hurt me. But then she also protected me from things that would've been so fun, like *Pitch Perfect*.

Who do I think I am? I'm not like the version of myself from ten years ago. Maybe that mold was more digestible to some people; I might give you some acid reflux now because I'm not as easy to swallow. But I'm still me. I still love Jesus. He still loves me. I'm just a little more fun...jelah.

CHAPTER 15

How Do You Spell *Sabbatical?*

I have said that word so many times, and every time I write it, I still can't spell it. I had to google it just now.

After thirteen years touring the world, my world began to fall apart.

First, one of my closest friends told me she wanted to date my ex. Not just any ex—it was one of the guys who was the worst to me. I couldn't believe that she would do that. The audacity—how could she be okay with that? She knew how he was to me. Why would she even want to date him?

The more I thought about it, it was like unraveling a spool of thread. It was the beginning of me realizing that I wasn't doing friendship well. At first I thought, *How dare you!* But then, after further thought and therapy, I realized I hadn't even been in her life lately. I rarely reached out to her to stay connected. Why should she feel indebted to me? Just because of longevity? Then it turned into the epiphany that she, and probably a lot of my friends, didn't feel much of a connection to me anymore. I have a lot of best friends, but I hadn't been the best friend to any of them. I'd been hyper-focused on work. I'd been busy, and distant. My friendships had become "If you can come over while I'm packing and watching *Law & Order: SVU*, we can be friends."

That was the beginning of what turned into a bunch of different things crumbling. I wasn't doing friendship well. Next, I looked at my marriage and realized, *Wow, I operate the same way. Maybe I'm too selfish.* My husband had voiced things to me he felt were lacking. Like, I'd come home from tour, and Manny would ask sweetly, "Do you want to go on a date?" I'd be like, "The audacity you have to ask me that today! You know I just flew back from doing eight shows and meet-and-greets and press, but if you want to bring me back something, that'd be great." I did not have the energy to get dressed up, put makeup on, read a menu, any of those things, because I was exhausted from the hustle.

I wasn't balancing my marriage correctly. I wasn't doing friendship right. Then, in my career, for the first time since "Nail Salon" blew up, my phone stopped ringing incessantly. Like, people were calling me, but they were calling me to say "No, thank you" to whatever I was pitching. Basically, my inbox was empty. Figuratively, because I still got plenty of emails from Nigerian princes needing my bank account info.

As I wrote in an earlier chapter, when you're in the entertainment industry, rejection is a daily part of life. Most stuff rolls off your back; it has to if you're gonna survive. But after more than a decade of touring and hustling 24/7, the fire in me was more like a dimly lit flame. At this point, I had to wonder if there was something bigger at play here. I asked God for answers, but He was all, "I don't know, girl, ask your managers." Touché, God.

My team told me none of the networks wanted to buy my next hour-long comedy special. And that what I had done with my stand-up had worked to get me to where I am today, but maybe it was time to switch it up a little bit, because entertainment executives wanted to know how I was *new and fresh*…as if I were an iPhone that was supposed to have all these new features every year that kept you coming back to me instead of buying an Android. Or something.

I was shook—the *new and fresh* word for *shocked* at the time—and sad, but I can't say I was surprised. I was exhausted and running on fumes, and I knew it, but I kept going, convinced I could fix it if I just tried harder. In a writing session, when I was only able to come up with new material that was just good enough, not what I know I'm capable of, I broke down crying. It was clear that everything that I was creating was being created out of survival mode, not out of abundance and joy, not out of overflow of creativity and connection with my Creator. I wasn't producing excellence.

My priorities were totally messed up and off balance. I'd put my career first, which in an unexpected turn of events was keeping my career stagnant. All my hustling and striving was no longer pushing me forward. I'd been chasing, chasing, chasing, and now I questioned what I was chasing and why. Stand-up comic Ron Funches, known as the icon of self-care, said to me once, so profoundly, "If you're chasing something, you're always behind it."

After some long and hard thinking and processing, I had a come-to-Jesus moment with myself and a breakthrough: I was burned out and hanging by a thread. I didn't need new and fresh material. I needed a break. A real one.

At that moment, I knew I needed to rethink my life and get my ducks in a row. It was time for a pause. I felt in my heart and my gut and my spirit that God was telling me that I was supposed to go on a sabbatical (sabattical?). My husband and I talked about it, and we agreed that the next year, in 2020, I'd come off the road and stop touring for six months. That was scary because I was the bread-winner of our family. It was a big risk and a big decision that we made together. But as soon as we made it, a huge weight lifted off my soul.

I knew I needed a year, but I only felt comfortable asking my husband, agents, and managers for six months off. I was contributing to too many people's livelihoods. When I approached my team, to my surprise, they said, "The fall may not be the best time to tour because of the election, so you should just take off the whole year." It was music to my ears. I really felt like God had answered my prayers.

I scratched all of 2020 off my calendar—no tour dates, nothing scheduled. I'd let go of the hustle and grind and get off the comparison roulette. The goal was to figure out the things that made me truly happy, like spending a lot of one-on-one time with my couch. It was as if my career was a garden, and certain things were flourishing in the garden, and other things were not. But a lot of those things were never meant to be in my garden. I just planted them there because I thought it was what I was supposed to do.

Oh, everyone who's hot right now has a YouTube channel. I should do a YouTube channel! My peers are directing episodes of TV. I should aspire to be a director! The people everyone talks about are creating content every day. I should create content every day! I was pouring myself out into this garden, watering everything, when really I was wasting parts of my energy on things that were not for me. It was time to stop pouring out all of me and let wither away what was meant to wither away. I would be able to see what was flourishing in my garden more clearly without all the weeds and distractions. I'd use the year off to get closer and reconnected to my Creator; reconnect to myself, my creativity, my husband, my friends, and my family; and refocus my priorities and energy.

The year 2020 was going to be epic, phenomenal, my *Eat Pray Love* year. I'd be like Julia Roberts in the movie, but without all the divorce. I was going to rest, get lost in a bamboo forest in Thailand (not for real lost—romantic lost), finally learn real Spanish! All the things I always dreamed I wanted to do but didn't have the time, money, or energy to do.

Right after the holidays, I started off on the right foot with dry January. No alcohol for the entire month. But then I actually watched *Eat Pray Love* and there was a montage where Julia Roberts was in Italy and she ate a giant plate of pasta and poured a glass of wine and another one and another one. And it made me so happy, and I was all, *I want wine, too.* But I said I wasn't going to drink for January. So now I was in this place of debating myself. There were two lessons I could learn in this moment. The first would be learning to stick to the course, stay with the challenge, don't give up. Press on! The second lesson was the complete opposite. It was about learning to let go, relax, enjoy the life that you've worked so hard for. I had already learned and practiced lesson one for the past thirteen years. This season was about lesson two. It was a moment of freedom, where I decided, *Yes, I'm going to have a glass of wine, and I won't even feel bad about it.*

"Hey, babe," I shouted out to Manny. "Can you bring me a glass of wine?"

"Okay!" he said, excited to participate in my lesson.

I sat on the couch, watching the movie, having the glass of wine, and I let go of any guilt for not following through on the "no drinking in January" goal. I celebrated the fact that I was able to relax in that moment and just enjoy my life. That happened within the first few days of my sabbatical, and it was contagious.

I always set aside one day in January to clean my office, because by the end of the year, it looks like a storage room. I usually go from morning until late at night, because I only have the one day before life gets busy and I have to hit the road again. This time, I got about halfway through the day and got tired. Instead of pushing through, I was like, *Hey, self, you don't actually have to finish your office today. You can go sit in the living room and watch Netflix.* And I was like, *Oh yeah, I'm going to go sit in the living room and watch Netflix.*

I had to make myself relax. I kept checking my phone, like, *What am I supposed to be doing? I know I'm forgetting something, because I'm not used to relaxing and not thinking or worrying about anything.* I sat there for a few minutes, then picked up my phone again. *Wait, let me look at my calendar again. Just to make sure I don't have a conference call. Was I supposed to reply to an email? No. Okay.* After doing that a few times, I had to tell myself, *Anjelah, you're addicted to your phone, stop checking. You don't have any responsibilities that you need to tend to. Relax and put your phone down. Don't worry about it.* So I put my phone down. For the rest of the month.

Social media had gotten to the point where, for me, it felt heavy and triggered anxiety. It was not a healthy tool for me or my mental health. That's why I did a social media detox for all of January. I deleted every social app—Twitter, Facebook, Instagram, Timehop. I felt anxious about it because I didn't want to miss out on anything, but then I remembered a fun little thing a commenter once asked: "What happened to your face? You look old AF." I was like, *Oh, mm-hmm, byyyye.*

My social media vacay was so liberating. It was really hard, but really good. It took a while to break the subconscious robotic habit of looking at my phone. I still kept picking it up and going to tap where the Instagram app used to be, even though I deleted it. *Oh wait. I forgot. I don't have Instagram anymore.*

During my hiatus, I was more present in the moment and free from comparison. It's really easy to not compare yourself to your peers when you have no idea what they're doing. It was a whole month of not measuring myself up to anyone else and their career and their journey, not being jealous of anyone else, and not feeling sorry for myself. Because I had no idea what anyone was doing.

I'd wasted so much time looking at what others had created. Now, instead of watching everyone else's hilarious videos, I freed up brain space so I could create things myself. And the less I mindlessly scrolled, the more intentional I was able to be with my time and my relationships, from talking through a painful breakup with a friend, to simple small talk with a stranger sitting next to me in my doctor's waiting room, to smothering Banzo with more cuddles than usual until he'd get up and leave the room to be alone.

My social media break was so cathartic and healing that when it was time to get back on social media in February, I believe I wept. I didn't want to go back and get stuck again. I didn't want to be glued to my phone. But within a few months of redownloading all my favorite apps, I found myself breaking all of my new boundary rules I had given myself, like, no phone after eight p.m., only scroll for fifteen minutes after I've intentionally posted something, and no Instagram first thing in the morning. Every time I tried to get out, they pulled me back in. The addiction was, is, and remains real, my friends.

I'd learned a valuable lesson, though, and continued to make my free time as meaningful and enjoyable as humanly possible. I watched shows, I read a little bit, and I journaled a lot. Penelope and I joined a women's circle led by my friend Christa Gifford. We learned about our chakra energy, our femininity, and Mother Earth, and did meditations on special topics, like healing mother or father wounds, sacred sexuality, a bunch of stuff that helped us get to know ourselves better.

I really love taking self-improvement classes that open my eyes, mind, and heart. Sometimes I make Manny go, too. Years ago, we did a marriage retreat in Nashville over one weekend. At first, he was like, "Is there something wrong with our relationship that you feel like we need this?" When I assured him it was just for fun and for the fact that we could always use more intimacy tips, he was game and got into it.

It was such a beautiful course. They taught us so many things. The men learned how to be "safe containers" for their wives, and the women focused on lessons that helped them move their bodies in order to connect with their femininity and sexuality and work through any shame about their bodies. At one point we basically gave a lap dance to our husbands without laughing. I'm 100 percent sure he'd give the retreat (and my moves) a five-star rating.

I wouldn't say that Manny and I are constantly working on our relationship. I would say that we're constantly in a relationship that works beautifully. We do extra work on it when we feel there's a need for it or an opportunity arises like that retreat. When we're awakened to an issue, then we do the work on our marriage. During my sabbatical (sabbaticle?), it was time to work on prioritizing our relationship again.

I'd been in my hustle routine to the point I was neglecting my marriage and not recognizing where I needed to change. I felt if I did eight shows in a row to help us financially, he should understand that I was tired and didn't want to go on a date. I didn't take into account that I needed to conserve some energy for Manny. And if that meant that I couldn't do eight shows, I should do only seven shows, then that's what that meant. I had always been about the opportunity and money, like I gotta strike while the iron's hot. *I'm already here and more people want to see me, might as well do another show!*

Well, I was paying for it either way. If I added more shows, I paid for it with my energy. Sure, I got money in my bank account, but I depleted my physical account and had no gas left for my husband.

During my time off, I made a huge effort to be connected to Manny. We made dinner and ate together. We went on walks in our neighborhood. We held hands and cuddled on the couch. And enjoyed our sex life, which may or may not have included in-home lap dances. This is a family book.

At the end of February 2020, I had to attend one previously scheduled gig planned way in advance, hosting the HA comedy festival for HBO. HA is a big comedy festival that features hilarious Latino comedians from all over the country. The big finale of the festival was a taped live performance that I was hosting. When I got home from that event, I had a meeting with my managers, because they wanted to brainstorm about what my career would look like after my sabbatical (sabatikal?). If I wasn't going to be touring, did I want more auditions? More film and TV? A podcast? News of a coronavirus had started spreading like wildfire…or like a virus, but nobody knew exactly what it was.

"Hey, this coronavirus thing," I said. "Are your other clients still touring? Is everything good?"

"Yeah, no, all our clients are still touring," they said. "They all had sold-out shows last weekend. They're doing great."

"Oh, okay, that's good."

Just one HBO hosting gig had put me right back on the comparison paranoia train. A month into my hiatus, I broke down again. I really struggled with my decision to take this sabbatical (sabbbatical?), worried that my career would never bounce back. I was like, *Oh my God, did I just take myself out of the algorithm of life? Everyone's going to forget about me. I just ended my whole career, why did I do this?* I started being really mean to myself. *I'm such a coward,* I thought. *Look at all my friends. They're tired, but they're still on tour. They're still hustling. What the heck have I done!*

To make matters worse, I got really sick with a sinus infection, though in hindsight, I do wonder if I had an early version of COVID-19. When I get sick, I get into my feelings. I started doubting that I was supposed to be on sabbatical (sabbaticall?) and that I'd made the right or smart decision. I sank deeper into a hole of fear and depression. I remember scrolling through the Netflix menu and landing on *Spenser Confidential,* a movie starring my friend Iliza Shlesinger, who taught me how to be the best touring dog mom. It was a major starring role for her, and she got to have a sex scene with Mark Wahlberg, which would be a literal dream come true for a lot of women. (Including this woman right here…me. Hi.) I was genuinely so happy for my friend, but I couldn't help but compare myself and question my decision once again. I mean, she was starring in a major movie with Marky Mark, and here I was lying on the couchy couch in my pajamas for the third day in a row, mainlining Mucinex and sinking deeper into my thoughts.

Okay, if I messed up and I took myself out of the algorithm of life, then I will just own that and make the best of it, I thought, channeling my inner queen of changing perspective. If I'm not working, then I'm just going to exercise and make myself have the most bangin' body I've ever had. Well, I said this to myself with a 102 fever, unable to even walk to the kitchen without running out of energy. I was not going to work out. My body was like, "Sit your butt down, you're not goin' anywhere, and you're not doin' nuthin!"

Resigned to my new life embedded into the couch (a very, very comfortable couch at least), I listened to some of my favorite sermons by TD Jakes and some of Oprah's Super Soul Sunday conversations to climb out of the pit that I just dug myself into. I tried to encourage myself and pray, and feed myself good energy, good information, and hope. But even that didn't feel right. If Oprah can't make you feel better, you've got some serious work to do.

Eventually my sinus infection or possible COVID went away (I could still taste my wine, so maybe it wasn't), and I was able to venture out into the world again. A friend asked me to pick her up from the hospital after an outpatient procedure (not fake boobs, not your bizness, okay, fine, it was fake boobs), and I got there too early. I went to a restaurant down the street, and as I was sitting there by myself having lunch, I scrolled through Instagram. God, grant me the serenity to accept the things I cannot change, courage to change the things I can, and wisdom to know the difference. I saw that all of my peers had announced the cancelation of their tours. This person canceled, that person canceled, everyone

CANCELED

CANCELED

CANCELED

I also never know if canceled is spelled with one *l* or two. Is it *canceled* or *cancelled*? Am I even qualified to write a book? Too late.

I called my manager.

"Looks like everybody's going on sabbatical with you," she said. *Whoa.*

It was in that moment that I knew I'd heard from the Lord. I had felt in my spirit several months earlier that I was to take a break and to come off the road for the whole year of 2020. That was a really big, life-changing decision for me to make. The audacity I'd have to have to make that kind of decision! (I've used the word *audacity* a lot in my book, and I actually wanted to include it in my title, but Barack Obama used it in his book title, and because we probably have a lot of the same fans since we're both so famous, I figured I should just let him have it.) I doubted every piece of that decision, my motives for the decision, the actual decision itself, everything, and was so hard on myself. Now, *all of us* were forced to stop and take a break. I didn't relish the fact that my friends had to cancel their tour dates. That didn't make me happy. What made me happy was knowing that I was right where I was supposed to be. I had heard from God, and I was brave enough to listen. I shouldn't have doubted, but even that doubt was all a part of the bigger lesson for me. I needed to go through that. It seemed like the very definition of the phrase "Let go and let God."

So much about the pandemic was about shifting, adjusting, changing, altering, moving—and it happened on a global scale. Every industry—sports, entertainment, education, travel, medical—was shaken. (The toilet paper industry wasn't mad though.) So that also made me say to myself, *Okay, if God is moving on a global scale and shaking and shifting everything in the world, not just the United States, the whole world, why wouldn't my individual world also be called into a season of shifting?*

Hustle was so ingrained in my brain that it took a global pandemic for me to finally be able to press Pause and fully commit to chillax culture. I had no choice. There was literally nothing else to do for months. It was a call to rest for those who could—obviously medical professionals and essential workers could not; it was not their time to rest—but for everyone else, man, we were told it's time to rest and reset. And I did that.

I made TikTok dance videos with Manny, went swimming in the backyard pool I had rarely used before, and made fruity cocktails in the middle of the day. I really enjoyed my property and Mother Earth. I went outside, put my feet in the grass, and meditated. All the trees in my backyard became characters in my life. Not in the sense of, "Hey, there's Tom and that's Patty"; I just talked to them, like, "Hey guys, it's a beautiful day. Thank you." I had the time to sit and appreciate them.

My brother Kennie took me to the Flower District in downtown LA, and I bought myself some houseplants. I made my balcony a sacred space for myself and decorated it with my new snake plants, monstera, and most precious elephant ear, along with a cushiony couch chair and a water feature. I convinced Manny to let me hire a landscaper to build what became a very expensive garden bed at the top of my backyard and took the Masterclass "Ron Finley Teaches Gardening." The self-proclaimed "Gangster Gardener" comes from the 'hood, and he teaches anyone how to garden anywhere, even in an old boot or a suitcase if that's all you have. He makes growing your own food so easy and getting dirty so fun.

I joined a gardening community on Instagram and made a whole new group of friends. We shared tips and advice, like "Cover your lettuces so they don't wilt" and "Don't kill the worms! They are good for your garden."

I mostly learned through trial and error. For example, I realized I pruned my tomatoes incorrectly after watching a YouTube video.

I wanted my tomatoes to have the best experience, so I apologized to them and promised I would do better next time if they didn't die before I had the chance to eat them. I enjoyed doing those kinds of things, but at the same time, pruning was hard for me because it tapped into my sadness around death. When I had to prune certain parts of my plant, I prayed for it and said, "Thank you so much for your contribution, I appreciate you." I played music for my garden, whatever I was in the mood for. Sometimes I asked my garden, "What do you guys want to hear?" and I'd put on whatever I felt in my spirit as if the plants told me so. I always said bye to my garden as I walked away from it back down the path to go into my house. "You guys are awesome," I called over my shoulder. "You're doing a great job." I turned into a crazy garden lady and loved every second.

Sometimes the fruits (and vegetables) of my labor survived. Sometimes they didn't. Failing was part of the process. I just tried the best I could. I had the most bangin' tomatoes, cucumbers, squash, jalapeños, serrano chiles, bell peppers, kale, red leaf lettuce, and arugula. We did one round of little potatoes that didn't work very well. Sadly, our strawberries and blueberries never gave us any fruit.

Our jalapeños and cucumbers were my favorites because I also learned how to pickle them. I combined a couple of different recipes to make my own little blend, then marinated them in old jars, and gifted them to my brother and his partner, Theo, and a few select friends who I knew would enjoy my pickles and give me my jars back.

Vegetables from your own garden just taste different and better. So I really got into cooking using my plentiful bounty. I made homemade fresh salsa with my ripe juicy tomatoes, jalapeños, and serrano chiles. I tweaked Tia Mary's recipe by roasting my produce in the oven instead of boiling them. I threw 'em in the blender, added a little water or chicken bouillon (per my Instagram followers' suggestions), garlic, sometimes onion and cumin (depending on whether or not I planned on doing any kissing that day), and salt and served it with white (not yellow) corn tortilla chips. Just my preference, don't @ me. It was so delicious. I never knew if the peppers in my salsa were going to be spicy or not, but I'd eat it either way. It was like Mexican roulette.

I expanded my culinary horizons and found fun recipes on Tik-Tok to try out. We paired tacos with tequila, and aglio e olio pasta with wine. I found and made the recipes for the Zuppa Toscana soup from Olive Garden and the shrimp from Giovanni's Shrimp Truck in Hawaii on the North Shore. I found my now signature dishes, spicy cucumber salad and shredded chicken with ancho chili (two separate dishes). We bought a bread machine and made a lot of bread. We drank adult bevvies almost every day and had the best time. I gained the quarantine fifteen, for sure, but it was worth every sip, nibble, and bite.

We had a small group of visitors at our house during the pandemic, in the safest way possible. At the beginning of the pandemic, Penelope, who had already gone through a divorce, moved into our house with her son, Elijah, who happens to be my godson. She was now a successful makeup artist, but with the entertainment industry at a complete standstill, she had zero work. Pen had always been there for me early in my career when I needed a place to live, and now it was my turn to open my doors in return.

Our dinners during quarantine were really meaningful and poignant. We didn't just stuff our faces every night; we created these sublime meals using our garden of delights and talked about what we were grateful for during such a difficult time for so many. As the pandemic raged on, my home became a refuge. Our safe bubble of people came over to swim in our pool, rest, relax, and heal, whether it be from marital issues or anxiety from the pandemic. My home was a place of healing not just for me but for my friends and family. We showered our friends with love, and I felt like it was a reflection of

God and the energy we were cultivating. We started calling our house the Castle Retreat.

My house became such a beautiful place that I would never have imagined that I would be moving out of it. I was watching people leave their own homes and move during this pandemic left and right—never in my wildest dreams did I think I would be as well. But there came a time when I did have to start thinking about getting back to work. I couldn't be on a permanent vacation for eternity. When it came time for that conversation for me and Manny, I realized I didn't want to go back to hustling as much as I used to. Then it was like, well then, should we not live in this house anymore? Because we can afford this house because of my hustling.

Maybe this house was not our dream house. We loved it, but also knew there were some things about it that weren't our favorite. It took a lot of processing, conversations, and tears to finally come to the conclusion that we were going to put our house up for sale and go on an adventure with God. It was time to end this season at the Castle Retreat. And what a glorious way to end our time there.

Manny and I didn't know what was next. We just felt it was time to move on to the next thing and trust that we would end up right where we were supposed to be. In my prayer to God, I remember telling Him, "I'm aware that I am surrendering my sense of security and stability during this season because I'm a creature of comfort. I like my house. I like my driveway. I like my street. I like my routine. I like my space. I feel safe here." Also, my neighbor's dog Madie and Banzo had their own little quarantine pod, so it was just as sad to see that end.

For advice, I reached out to my friend Angela Manuel-Davis, the motivational personal trainer who made me bawl on the beach during Oprah's cruise, because she's so connected to God and I feel like she just gets it. I told her how we put the house up for sale and it sold immediately and now we had nowhere to live. "I really wanted to go from security to security, but now I'm going from security to, I don't know, to limbo."

"You know what?" she said. "There is something in this season for you that you wouldn't be able to gain if you went from security to security. There is an ingredient in this season of unknown, this season of surrendering your security and your comfort, that you need to sustain your next season. You have to earn this ingredient in this season."

So, I shifted my perspective to that. And I was like, *Yeah, you know what? I'm just going to say yes to an adventure with God. And I'm going to surrender all of that for the possibility that there's something in this season that I'm supposed to learn. I'm supposed to grow. I'm supposed to attain. I'm supposed to achieve. I'm supposed to gain…something other than pounds.*

Well, after we moved out of the Castle Retreat, we moved four times. From an Airbnb to a fixer-upper house in LA, then from a studio apartment rental to a house in Nashville. So much moving and bouncing around. It was really stressful, but I reminded myself daily that I'd said yes to this adventure with God. And that I was on this journey side by side and hand in hand with the man I love, who always had my back, and I had his…even if I noticed while living in the tiny studio that he eats alarmingly loud. Like, how much saliva do you need to use to chew that chicken? Are your jaw muscles mad because it sounds like they are screaming for help?

I know so many people who quit their jobs during this period. People who moved out of state, who got divorced, who changed careers or let go of a career to go figure it out. People who adopted dogs who had never had a dog before. This was a time when everyone was given permission to look at the system that they'd built and say, "Okay, what works and what doesn't work? What is actually holding me back and what is healthy and what is not healthy? I've built this machine, and it's gotten me to where I am today, but maybe I actually don't need to be living in XYZ. I don't need to be working for so-and-so."

What I've learned during this time of rest, stillness, and reflection is that my original leap of faith to come off the road was the best decision I'd ever made in my life. I felt like I had gotten an early warning alert from God to get off the road. Like Noah, but with fewer animals. When it was time to get off the ark, so to speak, my year-long sabbatical (sabbatickall?) may not have saved the human race, but it definitely saved me.

The other day, I was sitting in my backyard meditating when I suddenly opened my eyes and looked at my house. And I had this overwhelming feeling rush over me—gratitude for my hustle.

I'd spent most of my sabbatical making "hustle" the enemy. I was so burned out, yet I had to convince myself that it was okay to take a break. At first, I was resting "productively," and I had to tell myself to chill, just rest. Good ol' regular rest. If even God rested on the seventh day, I should be able to do it, too. It was important to refill my cup so I could keep going. So I taught myself how to properly rest. I took up gardening and made fresh spicy salsa every day. I finally had time to learn how to cook, and I whipped up tasty dinners. I even gave myself permission to sit on the couch and watch movies while my husband would fall asleep while pretending to be awake. He doesn't have a problem relaxing.

In that aha moment in my backyard, I realized I'd swung too far in the other direction. In trying to detox, I'd demonized "hustle." I made it the bad guy when hustle was not the bad guy. Hustle is what afforded me to take a year off and not stress.

There had to be a happy medium, a balance between the old and new me. I was ready to move forward and evolve again. But into what? So far there'd been so many wild seasons of my life. I'd been:

A wannabe chola.

An Oakland Raiders cheerleader.

An extra on *Friends*.

The Nail Lady and Bon Qui Qui.

A successful stand-up comedian.

A wife. (Hi, babe.)

A dog mom. (I love you, Banzo!)

Oprah's best friend. (In my mind.)

I tried not to overthink it, because there was no sense in trying to figure it out. I mean, I didn't know I was going to be all of those things before I became them. Every single one of those Angelas, Anjelahs, and Funjelahs were in me. I just trusted in God and my destiny to bring them out at the right time.

I recently watched *The Wizard of Oz* again for the umpteenth time, and it's no wonder it's my favorite movie. Dorothy goes on this incredible, arduous journey to figure out how to get back home. She does all these crazy things like battle the Wicked Witch of the West and meets all of these amazing people, like Tin Man, Scarecrow, and Cowardly Lion. She learns so many profound things along the way, but when she finally meets the Great and Powerful Oz, she finds out she had the key to going home the whole time. It was her ruby slippers. She'd been wearing them on her feet the entire time, and that's all she needed. It really got me thinking, *What are my ruby slippers? What's within me that I've been looking for outside myself?*

That's the million-dollar question.

So, who do I think I am and will be? I'm still not sure yet! I have no idea what the future holds, but I'm enjoying the adventure. I'm grateful for all of my life lessons, because they helped make me who I am today. I'm ready for whatever comes my way. As long as it includes a pair of ruby slippers. But flats, my feet hurt.

Live Life with an *!*

Who do you think *you* are? Maybe reading this book has caused you to question some things in your own life, your own systems and beliefs, and your own way of doing things. And maybe not. Maybe it was just a fun read, and you just enjoyed reading about the good, the bad, the ugly, and the funny parts of my life. Or maybe you didn't enjoy it and you're going to write me an email telling me about all the things you didn't enjoy and you're just reading all the way to the epilogue just so you can make sure you don't miss anything for your email. Whatever you decide—whether you're right where you're supposed to be or I've lit a little fire in you—let's make a deal: From now on, we'll live our lives with an exclamation point!

Let me explain. The other day I was writing in my journal, and I was going to put an exclamation point at the end of a sentence. I had this moment where I stopped myself, and was like, *Don't get too excited, Anjelah. Don't put an exclamation point, because when you get too excited, that's when it doesn't happen and you get hurt. If you get your hopes up, you're setting yourself up to fail. Just put a period.*

But the period just didn't feel right, and I don't want to live my life preparing for hurt. I want to live my life manifesting and co-creating with God the life that I want! Speaking things that aren't as though they are, being hopeful, and believing for the best. I was like, okay, let's process this out for a minute. Why was it so hard to choose the exclamation point? Why don't you think about the times in your life where you chose to put an exclamation point and it paid off? And I started writing out a bunch of memories and moments, like:

- The time I had no business showing up to the Raiderettes audition!
- The time I moved to Hollywood in my mom's green station wagon!
- The time I crashed a national commercial audition and booked it!
- The time I booked *MADtv* having never done sketch comedy!
- The time I filmed my first one-hour comedy special, only four years after I started doing stand-up!

These are all examples of times when I was brave enough to live my life with an exclamation point, and there were so many more peppered throughout my journey. I always have to remind myself that I have won before, and I have heard yes before. I can and will hear it again.

Maybe there are daring things in this book you'd never ever do, like wrestle with God, turn down the chance to dance with a celebrity at a fancy party, or chola eyebrows. But I'm hoping if there's one takeaway, it's that you'll be brave enough to put an exclamation point in your own journal—to live your life with hope and expectation of abundance and not fear.

It's vulnerable and it's risky, but it pays off. Cross my heart and hope to die…okay, maybe not *die*, because ya know.

Acknowledgments

God, you are good. I am so utterly grateful for this life you have blessed me with. Thank you, thank you, thank you.

To every single person I mentioned in this book and all the people I wanted to mention but couldn't due to my book being as long as the encyclopedia, I want to say thank you. Thank you for being a part of my story.

To my husband, lovercito, best friend. You are beyond my wildest dreams. I still don't know how I got so lucky to be able to live this life with you. I love you. And to our dog Banzo, I know you can't read this but I love you immensely.

To my parents: I am so grateful for you. Thank you for loving me and letting me talk about you onstage and in this book. Dad, you were the first comedian I've ever met; thank you for showing me how to be funny. Mom, thank you for being my best Lathee and loving me even when I was bad. I won the parent lotto with you guys. Love youz.

To my stepdad, Luke: Thank you for always supporting me and for helping me make the biggest move of my life to LaLa land. I will never get rid of the huge pillow you got me almost twenty years ago. Love you.

To my siblings: You are my best friends. I can't wait for one of us to win the lotto so we can buy a compound and live our best lives with endless delicious food we find on Instagram and cute puppies running everywhere. I also can't wait for Veronica to get an iPhone so we can name our group chat and it won't be green. Love youz.

To Austin, my nephew, my Godson: You are the coolest, funniest, silliest, bravest, smartest boy ever. Nina loves you.

To all my cousins, aunts, and uncles: I love us! We are the best family ever and I'm so grateful for all of my childhood memories with you all.

To my in-laws, Carmelita y Reyes: Thank you for loving me like your favorite child. I love you back.

To my 2620 girls: Sandra, Lesh, Michelle, and Maya: What I would give to climb those four hundred steps to Sandra's house and sit on the stairs recapping an adventurous night with you all. Love you dearly.

To my FRAMILY—Brandon, Mattie, William, Penelope (and Elijah), and Johnny—I prayed and asked God for a community I could love and count on and he gave me you guys. What a blessing. Life would be dumb without you.

To Dibs and Jill: I miss our text thread. Let's keep it going for the next one and the next one. You guys are my dream team. Thank you for everything.

To my team at Hachette: Daisy Hutton, Beth Adams, India Hunter, Melissa Reagan, Whitney Hicks, Kristen Andrews, Catherine Hoort, Laini Brown, Patsy Jones, Kaitlin Mays, and everyone else who helped me make this dream a reality, thank you!

To my team at UTA: Brandi Bowles and Albert Lee for helping me realize it was time for a book and for getting me here. Heidi and Nick for helping me plan and execute my tours and having my back always. Dean and Steve for helping me make my acting dreams come true and never giving up on me.

To my team at Levity: Judi, thank you for seeing greatness in me, believing in me, and fighting for me. I am so lucky to have you in my corner. Stephen, since day one of you joining my team, I have felt protected, covered, inspired, and empowered—thank you. Chase, you are an inspiration; keep fighting!

To my Ja-Keé: You are a rare jewel. I am beyond lucky to have had you by my side for all these years. I love you and I am so grateful for all of our memories together. Corny Chips and Salsa forever!

To Jillian, Roger, and the entire team at AFM: Thank you for not letting us go broke. We love and appreciate you!

To my dear friend Christa Gifford: Where would I be without you. Thank you for your friendship and guidance on this adventure called life. I am so grateful for you.

To Della, Chuck, and the entire Magnet family: Thank you for your powerful prayers. Especially the ones in the middle of the night when I needed them most.

To Joe, my most favorite therapist, big brother, cousin, father, and friend. I love you, roomie.

To Penelope, my sister from another mister: I thank God for you in my life. Love you, friend.

To my favorite photographer, Robyn Von Swank: Thank you for a beautiful cover and a super fun shoot!

I know there are many names that I will forget to type here and I already feel bad about that, but I have to mention these people who have been a blessing to me along my journey: Nick and Yadira Navarro, Jessie and Pedro Latorre, Erica Greve, Elyse Murphy, OG, Darin Rios, Paul Chiames, Iliza, Cristela, Mal Hall, Rahn Hortman, Eddie Sisneros, Danielle Roach, Mike and Vanessa Lopez, Julie and Fuzz, Mikey and Julie, Theo Lewis, Elaina Laughlin, Diona and Ricky, Josh and Ali, Touré and Sarah Roberts, Shane and Eric, Jill and Becky, Erica and Jay, Dave Rath, TJ Markwalter, Rebeca and Skip, Ryan Handelsman, Maya and Dave, The San Jose Improv family, The

Bay Area and anyone who says "yee," every acting coach I've ever had, all my Godkids, Tiff and Ig, Mama Ang, Teri Weinberg, America Ferrera, Eva Longoria, Diana Marie Riva, Reggie Watkins, Dr. Motley, Christina P, Jo Koy, Kevin Hart, Nate Bargatze, Katie Cazorla, Don Hefty, Collette, Ryder Ray, Jessica O, Brian Bates, Erik Rivera, Fluffy, Amy Schumer, Fortune Feimster, Sheng Wang, Michael Yo, Bejarano family, Leigh Holt, Urbana and Phil Lawrence, Candace Cameron Bure, Angela Manuel Davis, Sarah Bernardo, Hun and Grace, The Hagwells, Giselle Bonetti, Cipha, Kevin Campos, Jonathan Martin, Bianca Mauceri, Brenda Franco, Monica Rios, Jesus Gonzalez, Maria Diaz, Jeannie Mai, Jennette "Lathee," Robert Ramos, Aimee Carerro Rock, Laura and Gabriel Allred, Nayda, Anabelle and Izzy, DJ Angie Vee, Nora Gonzales, D'Le, Piamonte family, Coffey and Criscilla, Paige Bryan, Sinbad, Lastassia "La," JD, Donald Sanchez, Abner and Amanda, Robert Para, Bridgette Depolo, Lauren Miller, Adriana Gonzalez, the old Gish Block crew, and I have to stop saying names at some point so I will end it right here. If you are in my life, you know I love you.

About the Author

Anjelah Johnson-Reyes is currently one of the most successful stand-up comedians touring today, selling out theaters across the country. *Maxim* magazine hailed the comedian, actress, and author as "uproariously funny" (weird they didn't write "unapologetically sexy," but okay), and *Time Out Chicago* described her shows as "filled with almost non-stop laughter."

Anjelah, born and raised in San Jose, California, and of Mexican and Native American descent, has guest starred on shows such as *Superstore*, *The Shield*, *Ugly Betty*, and *Curb Your Enthusiasm*. She has also appeared in such films as *Enough Said*, *Our Family Wedding*, and *Alvin and the Chipmunks: The Squeakquel*. After her massive success with the viral hits "Nail Salon" and "Bon Qui Qui," Anjelah released a full album as Bon Qui Qui on the Warner Music label and performed multiple sold-out tours as that character. Anjelah has filmed and released four one-hour comedy specials, all of which are available for streaming online, including the Netflix Original *Not Fancy*.